"God calls us to a risky and sacrificial faith. [...] fear-mongering and the pitfall of 'playing i[...] say, 'Don't take risks for your faith'? Which of Jesus' disciples avoided danger in witnessing to the risen Christ? *Spiritual Grit* is an excellent exploration of the mettle necessary for following Jesus, who literally loved us to death and who invites us on an often-reckless adventure to change the world for him."

**—Richard Stearns**
President of World Vision U.S. and author of
*The Hole in Our Gospel* and *Unfinished*

"In their 2010 remake of the 1969 John Wayne classic *True Grit*, the Coen brothers chose as the movie's theme song the camp-meeting hymn 'Leaning on the Everlasting Arms.' Rick Lawrence's scintillating study of what it means to live in the grip of 'spiritual grit' is a handbook in 'learning to lean' on those 'everlasting arms.' *Spiritual Grit* is a theological counterpoint to Nassim Nicholas Taleb's excellent *Antifragile* (2014), but is more fun and illuminating to read."

**—Leonard Sweet**
Best-selling author, professor, and founder of
and chief contributor to preachthestory.com

"We've seen an explosion of literature on the importance of character traits like resilience, endurance, and grit. Yet as I've read the books on the topic, something was missing. Actually, *someone*. How does grit relate to God? In *Spiritual Grit*, Rick Lawrence makes this vital connection, demonstrating how a 'desperate dependence on Jesus' helps build this cardinal virtue in our lives. Lawrence is a master storyteller. His powerful anecdotes and insights will equip and inspire you to take the hard, uphill path that ultimately leads to life."

**—Drew Dyck**
Senior editor at *Christianity Today*'s online
magazine CTPastors.com, author of *Generation
Ex-Christian*, *Yawning at Tigers*, and the
forthcoming book *Taming Dragons*

"Like never before, our culture is in desperate need of Christ-followers who will do things that others won't do, love in a way that doesn't seem possible, and live with a courage that is divinely inspired. Our world hungers for people with spiritual grit. Rick has written a book that both encourages and challenges us to become the sort of Christ-followers that we know we're called to be, the sort of Christ-followers that embody true grit. I can promise you that this book will fuel your passion for Jesus as it has mine."

**—Dr. Lina Abujamra**
Host of the Living With Power podcast and the
radio program *Today's Single Christian*, author of
*Thrive*, *Stripped*, and *Resolved*

"When it comes to growing into the mature men and women God is calling us to be, we too often look for the easiest path. We want quick results. We look for low-cost solutions. We look for ease. But what we really need is spiritual grit. That's a core message of Lawrence's book, and he drives it right to the heart with a beautiful combination of grace and honesty. All true growth is by nature uncomfortable, and Lawrence not only does a great job demonstrating how developing spiritual grit is essential to following the real Jesus, but also shows us how to do it, starting today."

—**Michael D. Warden**
Author of *The Transformed*
*Heart*, *Leading Wide Awake*, and
*The Pearlsong Refounding* trilogy

"Our culture sets twin idols on pedestals in our hearts: the gods of Comfort and Convenience. Sometimes it seems we would follow them anywhere: eating things that are no good for us and shortchanging those we love by shirking opportunities to serve. Through deep study of Jesus in the Gospels and lots of examples from his own life and the lives of others, Rick Lawrence shows us how and why it's better to stick with Jesus our shepherd, following him through the valley of the shadow of death, rather than to hang with the god of this age on the shortcut, business-class, direct flight to Easy Street."

—**Conrad Gempf**
Lecturer in New Testament at the
London School of Theology and author of
*Jesus Asked* and *How to Like Paul Again*

"From one over-functioning parent to another, this is the book you wish you'd read before you knocked yourself out on that dinosaur diorama. *Spiritual Grit* is awash in stories of grace and resilience, reminding us that discipleship requires durability—and we're not raising kids who have it. With a journalist's laser-sharp observation and a storyteller's spellbinding charm, Rick Lawrence encourages us to love young people better by protecting them less and challenging them more. If we needed permission to let youth actually grow up, *Spiritual Grit* is the place to start."

—**Kenda Creasy Dean**
Mary D. Synnott professor of youth, church and
culture, Princeton Theological Seminary, and author
of *Almost Christian* and *The Godbearing Life*

"Rick has taken my favorite book (the Bible) and combined it with my favorite movie (*True Grit*). In *Spiritual Grit*, he helps us learn how to shed the religiosity of Christianity and find a deeper understanding of what being yoked with Christ can truly look like. This is not just another Christian book; it's a field guide to a deeper understanding of what abiding in Christ is all about. Rick doesn't write books, he lives them out in his life and then empties his heart and soul into them. This is one of those books you want everyone to read so they can experience the same beauty as you have."

**—Tommy Woodard**
Co-founder of The Skit Guys, filmmaker,
and associate pastor of teaching and creativity
at Newchurch in Oklahoma City

"This book tackles a tough subject—but, blessedly, with a gritty grand mentor, Rick Lawrence. Rick not only teaches that Hard = Good (and is the Jesus way) but he guides and equips you to raise your grit game. Rick shares grit encouragement from many fields—academia, sports, military—but my favorite were examples from his own life journey. If you want to grow your soul, read this practicum on grit. You'll be inspired, encouraged, and nourished."

**—Andrea Syverson**
Author of *Alter Girl* and *Brand About*

"I have known Rick for many years as his pastor and his friend. His case for the necessity and impact of grit comes straight from the life he and I have shared. Rick writes clearly and powerfully of the redemptive and formative power of leaning into our difficulties with the courage Jesus provides. If you are looking for the easy path in our quick-fix society, this book is definitely not for you."

**—Tom Melton**
Executive director of Catalyst Leadership
Forum and founding pastor of Greenwood
Community Church in Denver

"What Rick Lawrence writes, I read. His stories make me smile. His thoughts make me think. And at times he makes me mad enough to mend my ways. This is a welcome and timely look at a surprising ingredient to facing the challenges and chaos of life."

**—Phil Callaway**
Author of *Tricks My Dog Taught Me: About Life,
Love, and God*, and host of Laugh Again Radio

# SPIRITUAL GRIT

## A JOURNEY INTO
## ENDURANCE.
## CHARACTER.
## CONFIDENCE.
## HOPE.

RICK LAWRENCE

**Library of Congress Cataloging-in-Publication Data**
Names: Lawrence, Rick, 1961- author.
Title: Spiritual grit : a journey into endurance, character, confidence,
    hope. / Rick Lawrence.
Description: First American Paperback [edition]. | Loveland, Colorado : Group
    Publishing, Inc., 2018. | Includes bibliographical references. |
    Identifiers: LCCN 2017060605 (print) | LCCN 2018005433 (ebook) | ISBN
    9781470750916 (Audiobook) | ISBN 9781470750909 (ePub) | ISBN 9781470750893
    (pbk.)
Subjects: LCSH: Christian life.
Classification: LCC BV4501.3 (ebook) | LCC BV4501.3 .L39393 2018 (print) |
    DDC 248.4--dc23
LC record available at https://lccn.loc.gov/2017060605

ISBN: 978-1-4707-5089-3 (paperback), 978-1-4707-5091-6 (audiobook),
978-1-4707-5090-9 (ePub)

Printed in the USA.

10 9 8 7 6 5 4 3 2 1          27 26 25 24 23 22 21 20 19 18

# ACKNOWLEDGMENTS

On the long journey that began the day I was first captured by the promise of spiritual grit and ended the day this book was sent to the printer, I've experienced mercy on top of mercy. Thank you to all of those who have had the courage to tell me the truth when a false platitude would have made your lives a lot easier—especially you, Candace McMahan. The rest of you know who you are—Bev and Brad and Stephanie and Andrea and Joani and Mikal and Jobe and Jon and Scotty and Michael and Tom. Thank you. This book wouldn't be what it is without your love for me and for its message.

Thank you to Jeff Storm for your (typically) brilliant design work on the cover and Darrin Stoll for your creative work on the interior of this book. Thank you to Cherie Shifflett for summiting your own mountain of source material as you did the hard work of copy editing this book. Thank you to Melissa Towers for driving this project and Stephanie Hillberry for your creativity and grit in promoting it. And thank you to my partner-in-podcast-crime Becky Hodges, the Becky-nator, for paying ridiculous attention to Jesus with me and for your passionate advocacy of all things Jesus-centered.

Special thanks to Jack Benzel and Charity Aslin for helping me pioneer the *Spiritual Grit* micro-journaling project.

Finally, thanks (as always) to my beloved Bev and Lucy and Emma—yes, the seat of my "writing chair" has a permanent Rick-shaped indentation, but you have all left a permanent indentation on my heart (see what I did there?).

# TABLE OF CONTENTS

# INTRODUCTION

A couple of mornings every week, I walk my middle-school daughter and my cabin-fever dog to the bus stop on the corner before I head off to work. We live in Denver, and during the winter months it's as cold as you think it's supposed to be in the Mountain time zone. When the bus is late, the kids are shivering—especially the boys, who insist on wearing basketball shorts no matter what the weatherman says.

The recipe for misery, if you're a teenager shuffling your feet and pleading for the bus driver to hurry up, is the prospect of a long, marginless day of school preceded by icicles forming at the corners of your mouth. It's a purgatory these kids can't escape. So most of them turn to their screens, hovering over them as if they were tiny campfires. They're doing their best to cope with a hardship they can't escape. But not all of them cope alone...

On one of these frosty mornings I see a mom, then two moms, then three moms drive up in their battleship SUVs and line the curb opposite where I'm standing. All of them are wearing their early-morning uniform: a sweatshirt and a ball cap that shadows their makeup-free faces. At first I don't understand what they're doing there, idling and staring straight ahead like mannequins. But soon I hear the squeal of air brakes as the bus pulls up to the corner, and the back doors of these SUVs burst open in unison, spitting a backpack-toting boy out of each. They hustle their way into line and scramble onto the bus. I watch and wave as it pulls away in a cloud of black smoke, and then the armada of mom-ships pulls away from the curb and drives the block or two back home.

For weeks I witnessed "The Dance of the SUVs" play out until something finally boiled over inside of me. I turned to my daughter as we walked toward the corner and told her that these moms were, of course, well-meaning, but what they were doing was *not* a gift to their sons. She looked at me, incredulous. "What's wrong with it?" she asked. "I wish one of them would invite *me* to sit in their SUV."

Well, I told her, it's obvious that these parents feel bad for their boys, forced to stand on the corner for seven-ish minutes in the frosty air. But protecting them from a minor hardship is like siphoning water from the reservoir of their resolve. I mean, they're unwittingly undermining the strength their sons will need to face and overcome hard things in their lives.

She didn't say it, but her look did: *Dad, you are so...weird.*

Like most parents, these bus-stop moms feel empathy for their kids and are determined to do whatever they can to reduce hardship in their lives. Because I'm a fellow-traveler parent, I know that extracting difficulty from our kids' lives *feels* like love, because we typically treat *hard* things as *bad* things. But, in truth, it's just that *edge of hardship* that hones our kids' ability to persevere through the challenges they're sure to face in life. And when we mistake *rescue* for *love,* we're harming them more than the "threat" we've helped them avoid. Sometimes our rescue strategies deny our kids a great treasure.

It's called *grit.*

## WHAT IS GRIT?

Grit is the nuclear reactor at our core that drives perseverance and profound impact in life. It's the steely determination to keep going when it would be easy to give up. It's the will to keep going when persistence isn't enough. And when I see these boys racing from the warmth of their SUVs to the warmth of the bus, I'm imagining them 20 years from now, when most of them will be in the thick of their careers and marriages, and some will be parents themselves. And I can see what they can't possibly see right now—that they will need a strength and determination beyond their capacity to persevere when their marriages seem impossible, their jobs seem like a marathon, and their kids push their buttons. On these cold mornings at the bus stop, their empathetic parents are just trying to help, but love cares as much about the future as it does the present. And love always adds to our strength; it never saps it from us.

> *Love cares as much about the*
> *future as it does the present.*

## WHEN HELPING HURTS

In "The Lesson of the Butterfly," writer Paulo Coelho offers his own spin on a well-known parable: "A man spent hours watching a butterfly struggling to emerge from its cocoon. It managed to make a small hole, but its body was too large to get through it. After a long struggle, it appeared to be exhausted and remained absolutely still. The man decided to help the butterfly, and with a pair of scissors, he cut open the cocoon, thus releasing the butterfly. However, the butterfly's body was very small and wrinkled, and its wings were all crumpled.

"The man continued to watch, hoping that, at any moment, the butterfly would open its wings and fly away. Nothing happened; in fact, the butterfly spent the rest of its brief life dragging around its shrunken body and shriveled wings, incapable of flight. What the man—out of kindness and his eagerness to help—had failed to understand was that the tight cocoon and the efforts that the butterfly had to make in order to squeeze out of that tiny hole were Nature's way of training the butterfly and of strengthening its wings." [1]

The message of the parable is clear: Sometimes a gift of empathy does more harm than good; it can be a kind of Trojan horse that sneaks past our defenses to rob our strength. And we must have strength to stay the course when things get difficult or when we must seize an opportunity and make the most of it. Empathy stops being a gift when it eats away at our ability to do what the Apostle Paul says we must do: *To stand our ground, and after we've done everything, to stand* (Ephesians 6:13, NIV).

Standing our ground is an everyday necessity. It's very often the difference between...

- faithfulness and betrayal in marriage...

- respect and abuse in the workplace...

- fitness and the status quo in the gym...

- a good report and a bad report in the doctor's office...

- justice and capitulation in a conflict...

- responsibility and entitlement in parenting...

- success and failure in the classroom or on the field...

- beauty and ugliness in the arts, and...

- maturity and immaturity in our relationship with God.

It's not easy to gauge the long-term impact of standing our ground, because it's so challenging to compare what *could have been* to what *is*. How can we account for the "butterfly effect" [2] of our tenacity when a small act of grit sets in motion a chain reaction that leads to something great? Or when a subtle capitulation—a nearly unobservable act of cowardice—steamrolls into disaster?

## THE TIPPING POINTS OF GRIT

When I tried out for my high school football team, I was a gangly, uncoordinated quarterback trying to make it on a squad that was just one year removed from a state championship. The team was stacked with all-state players, and I had no shot. But it was a no-cut sport, so the coach moved me to running back, a functional death sentence for a slow-footed rail of a kid. I came home that day and told my dad it was obvious the coach was trying to cut me without really cutting me. I thought I should take the hint and quit. My dad listened and then did something small that later turned out to be huge in my life. He told me I had every reason to quit, but to consider first how I'd reflect on the decision five years later.

After a restless night, I showed up the next day at practice. And every day after that I came home bruised and battered. Slow, uncoordinated running backs might as well be tackling dummies. During football season, I remember my mom wiping away tears when she saw my bruised forearms. But I stuck it out for four years as a terminal backup who rarely got to play, and in my senior year, I lettered as a football player.

That letter jacket still hangs from a rafter in our basement. I can't bear to pack it away because it reminds me of a gritty choice that's still paying dividends in my life 40 years later. It's not a symbol of success; it's a kind of *cairn* that reminds me I'm the sort of guy who sticks to his commitments even when it's brutally hard.

Twelve years ago my wife was diagnosed with a chronic lung disease. The standard treatment requires lifelong doses of powerful steroids. These drugs would sap her strength and produce cataracts, high blood sugar, psychological instability, weight gain, and an increased risk of infections. The disease can kill you, and the cure can wreck you.

In the wake of her diagnosis, Bev was desperate to find alternatives to what seemed like a hopeless path. So she made a bargain with God to pursue any new option he brought her way, no matter how far-fetched it seemed. At the time, we'd created and were leading a 10-week class called In Pursuit of Jesus for adults in our church. After one session, Bev shared her diagnosis with the group, and a man we didn't know well approached us to recommend a miracle-working immunologist who'd produced incredible results for his son. His story seemed too good to be true, but Bev remembered the deal she'd made with God, so we made an appointment.

After a long conversation with the doctor and a massive regimen of sophisticated bloodwork, Bev was told she'd be a good candidate for a treatment that had rarely, if ever, been tried with someone with her disease. The therapy requires transfusions of human immunoglobulin and has no harmful side effects. We trusted this doctor because he'd poured his energies into research to advance his strategy and he was passionately committed to his patients. But we first had to overcome a huge hurdle. Because the treatment was experimental and expensive, we were warned we'd have to do battle with the insurance company.

I told Bev we were partners in this adventure and I would take on the insurance blowback so she could concentrate on improving her health.

At the time, I had no idea what I was signing up for.

Over the course of this journey, my company has changed insurance providers four times, and in the last year we made the decision to move Bev to private insurance. That's five transitions in a little more than a decade, and every time we start over with a new insurer we face a long and exhausting approval process. It means countless hours on the phone, long slogs into confusing appeals processes, meticulous record-keeping, mountains of paperwork, and many, many blunt conversations. Twice we've faced short gaps in her treatment. The process seems specifically designed to weed out those who lack resolve. It's a calculated and colossal test of grit for those who are already facing daunting health challenges. But today, Bev is healthy and thriving. Her treatments have not only stopped the advance of her disease, but they've also slightly improved her lung condition. Her doctor plans to submit her case to medical journals because it's a breakthrough that could be a game-changer for millions, ultimately reducing its price. And none of this would have happened if Bev hadn't had the grit to pursue other options, and if I hadn't had the grit to stay in the ring and keep punching as one insurance goliath after another climbed through the ropes.

Grit matters.

Sometimes, it's the difference between life and death.

# A GRIT BEYOND OUR OWN

Though we're often desperate for the strength we need to persevere through our challenges, our supply is sorely limited. We can't sustain our gritty determination for very long, or very deeply, on our own. All too often, circumstances push us to the end of ourselves. Like Sisyphus, the mythological Greek king condemned to roll a boulder up a hill for eternity, our everyday boulders test the limits of our endurance…

- Your travel schedule at work heats up, taking you away from home for long stretches just after you get the news that your mom has been diagnosed with terminal cancer.

- You're nine months into an international adoption process when the child's host country changes the rules, requiring adoptive parents to establish 90 days of residency before finalizing the paperwork.

- You've been single well into your 30s when you (finally!) meet "the one," but on a dinner date that looks like it might end with a proposal, he breaks up with you instead.

- You get a phone call at 3 a.m. from your son who's been out drinking with friends and has gotten into an altercation with a transit cop—he's calling from jail, asking if you can bail him out.

Our "impulse grit" will get us past the first few hurdles, but what happens when a hardship spreads like an infection through our soul, sapping the determination we need to push through? Ultimately, we need a source of strength *outside of ourselves* to help us face and overcome the challenges that demand more than we have to give. We need something more than mere grit.

We need *spiritual grit…*

> *Ultimately, we need a source of strength outside of ourselves to help us face and overcome the challenges that demand more than we have to give.*

In the Sinai wilderness, a sheepherder named Moses is minding his own business when an odd sight stops him in his tracks. Flames are engulfing a bush, but the bush doesn't appear to burn (Exodus 3). And he mutters, "This is amazing…Why isn't that bush burning up? I must go see it." As he draws near, a voice tells him to stop and take his sandals off because he's in the holy presence of God. Cowering, Moses buries his face in his hands as Yahweh lays out his massive and improbable plan to free millions of enslaved Israelites from captivity in Egypt. The strategy, Moses discovers, will require *him* to spearhead this boondoggle. The bush-Voice describes the most daunting "special forces" mission in history as if it were a quick trip to the grocery store: "Now go, for I am sending you to Pharaoh. You must lead my people Israel out of Egypt." And Moses, just as you and I would likely do, reacts to this impossible request with despair: "Who am I to appear before Pharaoh? Who am I to lead the people of Israel out of Egypt?"

"Who am I?" is shorthand for *Are you kidding me? I don't have what it takes to do what you're asking me to do. You've got the wrong guy, because this is way over my head.*

And God's pragmatic response to this protest is ridiculously blunt: **"I will be with you."**

No, Moses does not have the grit to persevere and succeed in this impossible mission…alone. But yes, he will succeed anyway, because God will give him what he needs most—his own determined strength to keep pushing, against all odds. My friend Scotty Priest, a pastor and church-planter, reveals what's really going on in this burning-bush encounter, and in our own impossible challenges: "Ever have someone tell you that God will never give you more than you can handle? Well, that's not true. God *will* give you more than you can handle. But not more than you can handle *together*."

God's "I will be with you" means much more than an arm around the shoulder and a pat on the back. It's a promise to infuse his bottomless supply of grit into our best efforts. When God is with us, and we are with God, we get what he has. *That's spiritual grit.*

I have 13 versions of this book sitting in a digital folder on my computer right now. If you're an author who's written dozens of books, that's about 12 versions too many, actually. Writing a book is like an expedition to the summit of Everest. When you're finally standing on the wind-whipped mountaintop, you raise your hands high, take a quick photo, then beat a path back to base camp before you collapse. Then you leave that summit behind you. But a week after I delivered *Spiritual Grit* to my editor, Candace McMahan, she summoned the courage to give me the bad news: The book needed a major rework. Worse, it was quickly apparent I would have to take it "back down to the studs" and start over. The problems she found didn't require tweaks—more like decapitations. Like Moses cowering before the bush that wouldn't burn, the shocking reality overwhelmed me: *I don't have what it takes to do what you're asking me to do.*

It's a hopeless irony when you're forced to admit you don't have the grit to finish your book about grit. Well, contrary to the "take a break first" counsel of my friends and my editor and my wife, I gave myself one night of toss-and-turn sleep, then got up early and tried to climb that mountain again. I felt empty and desperate and alone—propelled toward a dependence on God's strength not as a spiritual practice, but as a down-and-dirty necessity. Some days I thought I might go crazy; other days I inched my way forward. But the same God who promised Moses "I will be with you" pushed and pulled and dragged me up the mountain. Six weeks later, and 12 versions after that rejected first draft, the book you're now holding emerged from the smoke and chaos of my own exodus from Egypt. If I did not have access to God's reinforcing grit, I could not have completed this work. I'm sure that one day he and I will have a good laugh about all of this…but not quite yet. I'm picking my way back down the mountain to base camp, one last time, filled with grateful joy for his mercy and his strength.

The Apostle Paul describes the mechanics of spiritual grit in his letter to the Roman followers of Jesus: "We can rejoice, too, when we run into problems and trials, for we know that they help us develop endurance. And endurance develops strength of character, and character strengthens our confident hope of salvation. And this hope will not lead to disappointment. For we know how dearly God loves us, because he has given us the Holy Spirit to fill our hearts with his love" (Romans 5:3-5).

A heart that is filled up with the "dear" love of God endures when endurance seems humanly impossible. When Jesus advises his disciples that "it is easier for a camel to go through the eye of a needle than for a rich person to enter the Kingdom of God" they respond with despair: "Then who in the world can be saved?" Well, Jesus tells them, "Humanly speaking, it is impossible. But with God everything is possible" (Matthew 19:24-26). With the Holy Spirit "filling our hearts with his love," our impossible problems and trials are the on-ramp to a life marked by endurance, character, confidence, and hope.

We stick with things, no matter what.

We tackle the tough stuff, with no excuses.

And we find ourselves rejoicing in the middle of it all, because nothing is more deeply satisfying than overcoming hard things in the close company of a God whose greatest gift to us is his intimate presence.

*At the beginning of this journey, it might be helpful for you to take the Spiritual Grit Self-Assessment toward the end of this book. This will add to your self-awareness as you interact with the challenges ahead.*

ENDNOTES

1   Paulo Coelho, "The Lesson of the Butterfly,"
    www.paulocoelhoblog.com (December 10, 2007).

2   The "butterfly effect" is a central aspect of chaos theory, and
    describes how a small change in a nonlinear system can result in
    a large difference later on. The term was first used by American
    mathematician Edward Lorenz to explain how a developing
    tornado can result from the tiny alterations in the atmosphere
    caused by the earlier flapping of a butterfly's wings (*MIT
    Technology Review,* technologyreview.com).

# CHAPTER 1

# THE GRIT WE NEED, AND WHERE IT COMES FROM

## THE JOURNEY INTO SPIRITUAL GRIT

When our path in life leads us into tough terrain, we often need more than our own limited supply of determination. In this chapter you'll discover exactly what spiritual grit is—and how a growing passion for Jesus gives you the strength at your core to face and overcome challenges.

# "The future bears down upon each one of us with all the hazards of the Unknown..."

—Plutarch, quoting Solon, Greek statesman and poet

"Never, never, never give up."

These words, first uttered by Britain's wartime leader Winston Churchill, are burned into a piece of barn wood that I've mounted above our kitchen sink. It's a necessary reminder for our whole family because the gravitational force of everyday life continuously drags us back from our resolve. We start things, but we don't always finish things. We vow we won't give up, but we do anyway. We just as easily talk ourselves *out* of our resolve as we talk ourselves *into* it. We know perseverance is the fuel our forward momentum needs, but it often feels like we're running on fumes.

It helps to remember that Churchill delivered his iconic challenge to a roomful of British schoolchildren while the fate of the world, and the survival of England, was in great peril.

After the Blitz, when London was systematically reduced to rubble by wave after wave of German bombers, Churchill showed up at Harrow, his old boarding school, to speak to the students in a special assembly. Pearl Harbor was still more than a month away, and the United States had stayed cautiously on the sidelines of what would soon become World War II. Like a drowning swimmer, the British were caught in the undertow of their despair, and their prime minister understood what was at stake. So in his closing remarks at Harrow, Churchill lowered his bulldog gaze and declared: "Surely from this period of 10 months, this is the lesson: Never give in. Never give in. Never, never, never, never—in nothing, great or small, large or petty—never give in, except to convictions of honor and good sense. Never yield to force. Never yield to the apparently overwhelming might of the enemy." [1]

Churchill's coldblooded resolve gave his beleaguered country a place to stand as the war dragged on. Without it, who knows what our reality would be today? Boris Johnson, the former mayor of London who left that office to become Britain's foreign secretary, says, "We dimly believe that the Second World War was won with Russian blood and American money; and though that is in some ways true, it is also true that, without Winston Churchill, Hitler would almost certainly have won." Johnson points to a tipping point in 1940, when the British parliament was locked in a debate over a proposal to negotiate a "cut our losses" peace with a German state that had already gobbled up the rest of Europe. In a hastily organized gathering of his cabinet ministers, Churchill delivered a Shakespearean speech that brought the divided body to its feet and ensured England would persevere to the bitter end in the fight against a consuming evil. He sealed his case with this: "I am convinced that every one of you would rise up and tear me down from my place if I were for one moment to contemplate parley or surrender. If this long island story of ours is to end at last, let it end only when each one of us lies choking in his own blood upon the ground." [2]

The force of Churchill's grit in the face of monumental pressure persists over the decades, inviting me to recalibrate my own courage while I'm washing the dishes or helping my kids with their homework or packing my computer bag before I head to work. "Never, never, never give up" reminds me to keep moving through my everyday cataclysms, the humdrum "hazards of the unknown," [3] as the Greek poet Solon called them. And sometimes, when I'm dreading failure or negotiating with my own interior enemies to throw in the towel, I'll glance at that barn-wood plaque and repeat Churchill's declaration out loud. The effect is like dipping a bucket into a well, hoping to find the spiritual grit I need somewhere in the depths of my soul.

But how do I know if I'll find water in that well, and what is its source?

> *"Never, never, never give up" reminds me to keep moving through my everyday cataclysms, the humdrum "hazards of the unknown."*

## THE SOURCE OF OUR STRENGTH

Before the Apostle Paul implores us to stand our ground, he tells us what we must do first. We'll find the resolve we need, he says, when we "draw our strength from [Jesus] and are empowered through our union with him" (Ephesians 6:10, amplified rendering from the AMP version). The steely determination strengthening us in the midst of fear and confusion and pain is fed by a deeper well. *And we discover that deeper well in the heart of Jesus.*

It was spiritual grit that drove Jesus to the Cross, and it was spiritual grit that kept him there until he declared, "It is finished." The Cross, Paul says, "is foolishness to those who are perishing...but to us who are being saved it is the power of God" (1 Corinthians 1:18, AMP). Grit on top of grit on top of grit is "the power of God." It is Jesus' resolve in the face of torture and death and—chief of agonies—separation from his Father that has freed us from our captivity to sin and joined us to God's family as adopted sons and daughters. Like a garden hose tapping into an oil pipeline, we gain access to this same resolve when we embrace his imperative: "I am the vine; you are the branches. If you remain in me and I in you, you will bear much fruit; apart from me you can do nothing" (John 15:5, NIV).

When we attach ourselves to Jesus in an intimate relationship, our lives become tributaries fed by the torrent of his spiritual grit. We can do nothing apart from him, but we can endure and overcome anything when we are "in him" and he is "in us."

> *When we attach ourselves to Jesus in an intimate relationship, our lives become tributaries fed by the torrent of his spiritual grit.*

It's helpful to remember that enduring and overcoming are not innate abilities that some are born with and some are not. Spiritual grit is not a birthright; it's a core strength that must be developed in us. King Solomon observes: "The fastest runner doesn't always win the race, and the strongest warrior doesn't always win the battle. The wise sometimes go hungry, and the skillful are not necessarily wealthy. And those who are educated don't always lead successful lives" (Ecclesiastes 9:11).

## RESEARCHING GRIT

After Angela Lee Duckworth left a prestigious Manhattan consulting job to teach math to seventh-graders in a New York public school, she noticed that her best students weren't necessarily the smartest. The kids who excelled were scrappy, determined to succeed. Meanwhile, some of her naturally gifted students under-shot their potential. "What if," Duckworth asked, "doing well in school and in life depends on much more than your ability to learn quickly and easily?" [4]

Fascinated by the dogged determination she observed in some of her students, Duckworth left teaching to earn a graduate degree in psychology. Her goal was to understand why some push through challenging circumstances while others don't. Her research led her to West Point cadets who managed to persevere through the "Beast Barracks" portion of basic training, to contestants in the National

Spelling Bee who advanced the furthest, and to rookie teachers working in tough neighborhoods who stuck it out in the face of overwhelming odds. [5] "One characteristic emerged as a significant predictor of success," says Duckworth, "and it wasn't social intelligence, it wasn't good looks or physical health, and it wasn't IQ. It was grit. Grit is passion and perseverance for very long-term goals. Grit is stamina. Grit is sticking with your future day in and day out, not just for the week, not just for the month, but for years. And working really hard to make that future a reality. Grit is living life like it's a marathon, not a sprint." [6]

People who live with a marathon mentality, Duckworth discovered, have developed a passion for something higher than themselves. "Grit is not just having resilience in the face of failure," she says, "but also having deep commitments that you remain loyal to over many years." [7] The line separating follow-through from failure transcends our limited capacity to persevere in our own strength.

> *People who live with a marathon mentality have developed a passion for something higher than themselves.*

As Paul explains, and Duckworth's research suggests, we need a source of grit that is higher than ourselves. Of course, we rarely give in to our challenges at the first sign of resistance, and many of us know very well how to muscle through hardships and make the most of what we have. But it's only a matter of time before we reach the shallow bottom of our own well—when we recognize "hang in there" and "keep fighting" as the frustrating platitudes they are.

In the week before I graduated from high school, my friends filled my yearbook with the usual clichés, but one attempted to say something deeper and more honoring to me: "Rick, you're the hardest try-er I've ever known." For years I looked back on that scrawl in my yearbook with pride. I secretly believed my capacity for trying harder could overcome anything life threw at me. That is, until I quit my first real job after a year because my conniving, hypocritical boss made my workplace feel like a torture chamber. Or the time I asked my girlfriend to marry me and she accepted but then broke off the engagement after three months. That happened twice, by the way—with the same woman (who's now my wife). Or the time I was a camp counselor responsible for a cabin full of urban teenagers who had gang ties, and I narrowly thwarted their plan to murder me. Or the time…Well, you get the picture.

When we're tested beyond our capacity, we naturally look for help outside of that capacity. This is why it's so important to embrace the implications of Duckworth's research by paying better attention to what Paul is revealing to us—that we are empowered by our union with Jesus when our intimate attachment to him releases his core strength to flow into and through us.

## A POWERFUL WHY

Award-winning *New York Times* columnist David Brooks pounced on this "passion for something higher" dynamic in Duckworth's research, insisting that it deserves more attention: "I don't know about you, but I'm really bad at being self-disciplined about things I don't care about. For me, and I suspect for many, hard work and resilience can only happen when there is a strong desire. Grit is thus downstream from longing. People need a powerful *why* if they are going to be able to endure any *how*." [8]

This vital insight—the call to find and develop our *powerful why* in life—elevates grit from a personality characteristic to an orientation toward the Divine. If a passion for something higher than ourselves is what fuels our ability to persevere through great challenges, then we find it only in a Source that is beyond our human potential. The higher the focus of our passion, the deeper the well of our spiritual grit. And we desperately need a well with deeper resources than our "try harder to get better" determination—an ultimately shallow source of grit that is nevertheless the focus of many sermons, "Christian living" books, and a church culture that is addicted to self-help schemes.

> *The higher the focus of our passion, the deeper the well of our spiritual grit.*

It's not the Christian principles we follow or the Christian character qualities we strive for that fuel our spiritual grit; it's the way we are captured and romanced by the heart of Jesus. Relational intimacy with God generates the powerful passion that spiritual grit requires.

Psychologist and spiritual director David Benner writes, "After decades of Bible reading, I realized that my relationship with God was based more on what I believed than on what I experienced. I had lots of information about God but longed to deepen my personal knowing. Getting to know Jesus better seemed like the right place to start. It was." [9] Benner's journey from mere belief to "personal knowing" highlights a universal truth: Spiritual grit is fed by our *experience* of Jesus' heart, not the *information* we've collected about him.

> *Relational intimacy with God generates the*
> *powerful passion that spiritual grit requires.*

## THE HEART IS THE POINT

I lead a small group for young adults in our home every week, and the focal point of our gathering is this: Pursuing the Heart of Jesus, Not His Recipes. When a guest joins the group, I always ask one of the "lifers" to explain the meaning behind our unusual battle cry. And they never disappoint, because they've experienced firsthand the passion that grows out of a focus on the heart of Jesus, rather than a fixation on how his principles—his "recipes for life"—will improve their lives. When our goal is to pursue the heart of Jesus, rather than morph everything he says and does into life applications, we find the "something higher" that fuels our passion and grows in us a greater capacity for spiritual grit.

Author, C.S. Lewis expert, and Boston College professor Peter Kreeft describes Jesus as a *shocking wonder.* "I think Jesus is the only man in history who never bored anyone," he says. "I think this is an empirical fact, not just a truth of faith…Not everyone who meets Jesus is pleased, and not everyone is happy. But everyone is shocked." [10] This is relational language, not academic data. Kreeft is a respected scholar, but he understands that passion is more about the heart than the head. Paul's great hope, he tells his friends in Ephesus, is that all of us would somehow comprehend "the breadth and length and height and depth" of Jesus' love, "to know the love of Christ which surpasses knowledge" (Ephesians 3:18-19, NASB).

The most damaging outcome of our overly empathetic choices as parents is that we sap our kids' strength, and the most damaging outcome of a "formulas and recipes" approach to our spiritual lives is that we siphon passion away from our relationship with Jesus. When we treat him as if he's a bullet-point vending machine for self-help ideas, or a "try harder to get better" guru à la Tony Robbins, we miss (or consciously avoid) his invitation to abide in him. What does Jesus really want? We know the answer because he made it plain in a public prayer, just before going to the Cross: "As you are in me, Father, and I am in you…may they be in us" (John 17:21). He is describing what happens on a wedding night, not during a wedding ceremony. He wants intimacy.

St. Clare of Assisi says, "We become what we love and who we love shapes what we become. If we love things, we become a thing. If we love nothing, we become nothing. Imitation is not a literal mimicking of Christ; rather, it means becoming the image of the beloved, an image disclosed through transformation." [11] When Paul, who was schooled by the leading rabbi of his time and was himself one of the smartest men in the ancient world, declares, "I determined not to know anything among you, save Jesus Christ, and him crucified" (1 Corinthians 2:2, ASV), he is describing the *relational* force that has transformed his life. He has become what he *loves*, not what he *reasons*.

> *"We become what we love and who we love shapes what we become."*

There is a vast chasm between a heart that has an *affinity* for Christianity and a heart that has been *conquered and captured* by the person of Jesus. The first does not always bridge to the second. And since passions are developed, not inherited, our journey into spiritual grit will require that we "taste and see" Jesus as he really is, in all his shocking wonder. Tepid versions of him naturally produce a tepid relationship. In contrast, our passion for him grows when we slow down and pay ridiculous attention to him. That means…

1. We prioritize "Why?" questions about the things he says and does, not "What?" questions.

2. We open ourselves to *experience* him, not just study him.

## WHY BEFORE WHAT

For more than a decade, I've been helping thousands of people discover and practice a simple, subtle, and powerful habit that cracks open the door to Jesus' heart. To move toward intimacy with him, I emphasize "Why?" questions about the things he says and does, because "Why?" targets his motivations and his value system. Instead of "*What* would Jesus do?" I ask "*Why* did Jesus do it?" And then we consider our initial answers and ask "Why?" one or two more times to drill down into territory we rarely explore: Jesus' core motivations. "Why?" is a heat-seeking-missile sort of question, and the "heat" is the heart of Jesus.

Here's a simple example of how this works. In Matthew 15, an "unclean" Canaanite woman is following Jesus and his disciples as they travel from Galilee to Tyre in the north. As they go, she is groveling and pleading with Jesus to heal her daughter of demon possession. At first Jesus ignores her; then he treats her with apparent scorn: "It isn't right to take food from the children and throw it to the dogs."

In the awkward silence that follows, the woman's spiritual grit rises to the surface: "That's true, Lord, but even dogs are allowed to eat the scraps that fall beneath their masters' table."

Jesus is astonished and thrilled by this response, and replies, "Dear woman, your faith is great. Your request is granted." (We'll explore this story in greater depth in Chapter 2.)

A conventional understanding of this story might focus on *what* Jesus said and did in this encounter: *He told a woman he wouldn't help her, called her a dog, then changed his mind—that's Jesus for you.* Left unresolved is *why* he would behave this way. We don't learn anything about his heart by focusing on *what*. If instead we slow down and focus on *why* Jesus said and did these things, we launch ourselves into the rich mystery of his passionate core.

I asked the young adults in our Pursuing the Heart, Not the Recipes group to come up with all the possible reasons Jesus would interact with this desperate woman in such a disturbing way. They launched into a vigorous conversation fueled by follow-up "Why?" questions intended to drill down past their initial answers. *(Yes, he appears to be purposely making it hard for this woman to get what she wants, but why? Yes, he seems to quickly change his attitude toward her, but why?)* And then, their verdict…

> Jesus takes great risks with people to surface their courage. He's passionate about setting people free from their captivity, so he purposely treats this woman with the scorn everyone (including her) expects, to bait her into the courageous response he's hoping for. When she responds with "great faith," he delights in celebrating her sassy determination and treats her with admiration and respect. The heart of Jesus is motivated by courage. [12]

When we use "Why?" questions as a way to "taste and see" the heart of Jesus in everything he says and does, we discover he is greater and better than we ever imagined. He really is a shocking wonder. And when we encounter Jesus in this way, our passion for him grows organically. The distance that separates us from him, created by our headfirst approach to his story in Scripture, evaporates. Our desire for union with him grows as our longing intensifies.

The key is to continue asking "Why?" questions until we reach the bedrock of Jesus' heart, because we almost always default to "What?" answers that don't really take us there. *(Yes, Jesus is comfortable making people uncomfortable, but why?)* "Why?" requires us to explore the heart, rather than the head. When we persist with "Why?" questions, we lower our pursuit 18 inches—from the brain to our core, the seat of passion. In my experience, especially with adults, that's a challenging 18-inch journey. We're stuck in a head-rut.

# THE MECHANICS OF PASSION

Pursuing "Why?" rather than "What?" is not merely a psychological or emotional exercise, it's a biological imperative. "Why?" questions help us connect with Jesus at a level that changes us from the inside out.

In a TED Talk that's been viewed more than 35 million times, marketing consultant Simon Sinek explains: "People don't buy *what* you do, they buy *why* you do it…It's all grounded in the tenets of biology. Not psychology, biology…The brain's neo-cortex is responsible for all of our rational and analytic thought and language…*(This is the "What?" part of our brains.)* Our limbic brain is responsible for all of our feelings, like trust and loyalty. It's also responsible for all human behavior, all decision-making, and it has no capacity for language…*(This is the "Why?" part of our brains.)* If you don't know *why* you do what you do, then how will you ever get someone to be loyal and want to be a part of what it is you do?" [13]

Sinek is targeting the mechanics of passion, because passion is what motivates us to pursue hard things, commit to epic causes, and endure great difficulty. And understanding the *why* of Jesus is the catalyst for moving us toward a deeper, more intimate relationship with him. His *why* gives us our *why*. Over the course of the last year, our Pursuing the Heart of Jesus group has tackled dozens of these why-based challenges as we learn how to pay better attention to Jesus, and we've uncovered these treasures along the way…

**Question:** Why does a good shepherd leave his whole flock to graze on a hillside to pursue and rescue the one sheep that has lost its way?

**Answer:** *The heart of Jesus is focused on individuals, not crowds.*

**Question:** Why does Jesus instruct Peter to pay his portion of the Temple tax by throwing a fishing line into the sea and finding a valuable coin in the mouth of the first fish he catches?

**Answer:** *The heart of Jesus is playful.*

**Question:** Why does Jesus often speak to religious leaders without a filter—casually offending them instead of treating them with deference and respect?

**Answer:** *The heart of Jesus is disruptive, often "upsetting the apple carts" of others.*

**Question:** Why does Jesus so often overlook people's sordid reputations to celebrate something he loves about them?

**Answer:** *The heart of Jesus is determined to morph ugly things into beautiful things.*

**Question:** Why does Jesus seem to have so little patience for the religious elite?

**Answer:** *The heart of Jesus longs for authenticity, not performance.*

**Question:** Why does Jesus forgive the soldiers who are executing him?

**Answer:** *The heart of Jesus defines true love by how we treat our enemies.*

**Question:** Why does Jesus talk so much about the bad things that will happen to those who ignore the truth?

**Answer:** *The heart of Jesus has a sharp edge.*

**Question:** Why does Jesus delight so much in people who wholeheartedly trust him?

**Answer:** *The heart of Jesus values dependence, not control.*

**Question:** Why doesn't Jesus just tell people what he wants them to do instead of telling them stories that often don't make immediate sense?

**Answer:** *The heart of Jesus loves story and metaphor and parable.*

**Question:** Why is Jesus so impressed by over-the-top expressions of faith and love—the woman who weeps on his feet and dries them with her hair, for example?

**Answer:** *The heart of Jesus values extravagant expressions of genuine worship and love.*

**Question:** Why does Jesus use the ancient equivalent of profanity—"whitewashed tombs" and "snakes" and "hypocrites," for example—in his interactions with powerful people?

**Answer:** *The heart of Jesus speaks truth to power.*

**Question:** Why does Jesus reiterate to his disciples that they're going to suffer and die for him?

**Answer:** *The heart of Jesus spotlights brutal realities.*

**Question:** Why is Jesus so willing to lose fans and followers?

**Answer:** *The heart of Jesus is humble and secure.*

**Question:** Why does Jesus stop on his way to meeting an urgent need to free a marginalized woman who has lived in shame?

**Answer:** *The heart of Jesus is generous and kind to "the least of these."*

**Question:** Why does Jesus tell the parable of the talents?

**Answer:** *The heart of Jesus expects us to take courageous risks.*

**Question:** Why does Jesus insist on praying out loud so his disciples can hear what he says to his Father just before he is arrested, tortured, and crucified?

**Answer:** *The heart of Jesus longs for us.*

**Question:** Why does Jesus cry out on the cross, "My God, my God, why have you forsaken me?"

**Answer:** *The heart of Jesus is fully abandoned to our redemption.*

**Question:** Why does Jesus tell the parable of the prodigal son?

**Answer:** *The heart of Jesus is quick to forgive, quick to restore, and eager to celebrate.*

💬 **Question:** Why does Jesus turn over the tables of the money-changers in the Temple?

**Answer:** *The heart of Jesus is angered by injustice and is not afraid to confront it.*

💬 **Question:** Why does Jesus tell the thief on the cross who sticks up for him that he will be with him in paradise that day?

**Answer:** *The heart of Jesus is determined to invite.*

💬 **Question:** Why is Jesus so excited about leaving his disciples behind, promising them it will be better for them once the Spirit comes in his place?

**Answer:** *The heart of Jesus is not stingy, but shares everything he's been given without reservation.*

# BETTER THAN NICE

Years ago, as part of a research project, I hired camera crews in five major cities around the U.S. to stop young people on the street and record their answers to a simple question: "What one word would you use to describe Jesus?" When I got the raw footage back from all five cities, I was astonished by their singular, universal response: *Jesus is nice.* The truth is, Jesus is always kind but only sporadically nice (you get a taste of that reality from the preceding list). "Nice" is the result of a surface, thumbnail assessment—the expected outcome of a "What?" approach to stories about him, not a "Why?" pursuit of his heart.

> *The truth is, Jesus is always kind but only sporadically nice.*

When we embrace Paul's proclamation as our own—*"I am determined to know nothing but Jesus Christ, and Him crucified"*—we intentionally move from a benign affinity for the Christian life to a consuming passion for something higher than ourselves. And our "whys" lead the way. David Brooks writes: "[Let's] say you were designing a school to elevate and intensify longings. Wouldn't you want to provide examples of people who have intense longings? Wouldn't you want to encourage students to be obsessive about worthy things? Wouldn't you discuss which loves are higher than others and practices that habituate them toward those desires?" [14]

Our own School of Intensified Longing is like a culinary institute, where the students feast on the heart of Jesus. The psalmist urges us to "taste and see that the Lord is good. Oh, the joys of those who take refuge in him!" (Psalm 34:8). "Taste and see" is metaphoric language for "know by experience," and "take refuge" is metaphoric language for "go inside" or "immerse yourself in." Eugene Peterson, in *The Message*, gives this psalm a poetic spin: "Open your mouth and taste, open your eyes and see—how good God is. Blessed are you who run to him."

"Taste and see" is the same invitation Jesus offers the crowds gathered to see him on a hillside near Capernaum (John 6). When they ask him to give them a "miraculous sign" before they will believe in him, he responds by offering himself as the "true bread from heaven." He tells them that if they won't "eat the flesh of the Son of Man and drink his blood" they'll never find the life they're looking for. To eat Jesus and drink Jesus, we open ourselves to him with abandon. *We embed him inside our identity.*

We develop our great passion for Jesus and begin to abide in him when we invite him from the periphery of our lives into the core of our hearts. And we're motivated to do that as our "Why?" questions reveal his essence.

## Bonus: The School of Intensified Longing

As an extended exploration of Jesus' heart and as a companion to your journey into spiritual grit, I've included a bonus resource toward the end of this book. It's called The School of Intensified Longing, and it's designed to unveil the shocking wonder of Jesus' heart using "Why?" questions. From nine vantage points, you can explore what makes Jesus tick, tasting and seeing him as he really is, not as we'd like him to be. The result of this little appetizer, I hope, will be to increase your hunger for him and to help you find your passion for something higher as you encounter his heart. Enter the School of Intensified Longing on page 179.

# EXPERIENCING JESUS, NOT JUST STUDYING HIM

I met Joann Richardson at Simply Jesus, an annual gathering in the Colorado mountains that's like a family reunion for people who are related to each other only by their love for Jesus. She's an occupational therapist in Indianapolis who's done master's-level research on the resilience of stroke patients. When I first met her, I was collecting stories and insights into grit, so I asked if her work with stroke survivors had revealed anything that might help me.

"These people," she told me, "became my heroes and teachers, and I have thought of their stories, their resilience, and their integrity often as I face trials in my own life."

Richardson's research isolates the factors that help some people persevere through the damage caused by their trauma better than others. She and her team conducted in-depth interviews with a small sampling of survivors who agreed to share their stories, and common strengths emerged. Most of the "intrinsic factors contributing to recovery" they discovered were predictable: a good sense of humor, a strong desire to maintain independence, regular and prolonged exercise, and a positive attitude. But one surprising factor surfaced as well: *More than half of the people Richardson's team interviewed pointed to a deepening relationship with Jesus as a bedrock of their recovery.* [15]

These stroke survivors are fighting against the physical and mental incapacities of their trauma. Recovering some semblance of normal life requires grit. But they're also fighting to recover their incapacitated identities. When their bodies lose functional ability, their sense of self disintegrates. The "me" they thought they were is no longer the "me" the stroke has left in its wake. Against this assault, they need more than Christian principles and apply-it-to-life recipes; they need to *experience* the power and presence of Jesus actually strengthening their core identities from the inside out. They need to know Jesus, not just know *about* him.

You and I may not be facing the sort of interior crisis that follows a stroke or other trauma, but all of us are vulnerable to assaults on our identities. We doubt our intrinsic worth, we believe plausible lies about ourselves, and we concoct elaborate façades to prevent others from discovering our real selves. We, too, need more than sound-bite truths about Jesus and the Christian life. We need direct experiences of his power, reshaping and confirming who we really are. The kind of knowing we need requires us to immerse ourselves in Jesus the way two lovers immerse themselves in each other. This immersion—or union—is possible only because we have a Helper who is able to lead us into experiential intimacy with Jesus. That Helper has many names, including Advocate, Counselor, Comforter, Encourager, and Holy Spirit—but I've added a new name to the list that targets the Spirit's primary occupation in our lives: *Invisible Rabbi.*

> *We need to know Jesus,*
> *not just know about him.*

# THE INVISIBLE RABBI

"Don't let anyone call you 'Rabbi,'" Jesus tells his disciples, "for you have only one teacher" (Matthew 23:8). Later, just before he is arrested in the garden of Gethsemane, he promises them a "Friend" he's nicknamed "the Spirit of the Truth" (John 16:13), whose job description is to "take you by the hand and guide you into all the truth there is" (John 16:13, MSG). He is about to go away, he tells them, and his departure will pave the way for this Friend—this "Paraclete," this Invisible Rabbi—to make a home in their souls, teaching them from the inside out. The Spirit will "bring me glory by telling you whatever he receives from me," he says (John 16:14). He reiterates that promise twice, for emphasis. Until now, his influence on their lives has been from the outside in, with marginal results. Soon, the Invisible Rabbi will be teaching them about his heart from a place of intimacy, and they will understand him for the first time.

In the time of Jesus, it was a great honor to be "yoked" to a rabbi— to be under his influence and instruction. Jewish boys started their education in the synagogue at the age of 6, during a season of their childhood called *Bet Sefer* (which means House of the Book). Their teachers were scribes and rabbis, and their challenge was to memorize the first five books of what we now call the Bible. They studied seven days a week, memorizing their way through massive sections of Scripture. The goal was not to think about what they were memorizing or to analyze it in any way.

During the next stage of their education, from the ages of 10 to 14, they entered into a season called *Bet Talmud* (which means House of Learning). Over the course of these five years, they memorized the writings of the prophets. In addition, they were introduced to the art of rhetorical debate and critical thinking, learning to answer questions with even better questions. By each boy's 14th birthday, his academic potential had been tested and revealed. The brilliant ones continued on to *Bet Midrash* (the House of Study), and the less-than-brilliant ones ended their formal education and joined the family business, whatever that was.

At this point, the boys who were pursuing a *Bet Midrash* trajectory had to find a rabbi they respected and lobby to become that great man's *talmid*, or disciple. There were very few rabbis to attach themselves to, so the competition for the best-of-the-best was fierce. A rabbi interviewing a potential talmid would put the boy through a grueling quiz to test both his knowledge of Scripture and his critical-thinking skills. If the boy made it through this *Survivor*-like competition, the rabbi might invite the talmid to "take his yoke upon him." [16]

To hopeful, earnest, young Jewish males, the invitation to take on the yoke of a respected rabbi was their ticket to a bright future. It was also the start of a demolition/reconstruction project that would form their core identity around the *essence* of their teachers. Once the relationship was confirmed, the talmidim were required to leave their parents, synagogues, communities, and family businesses and devote every waking moment to following their rabbis. It was boarding school on steroids. And this was no conventional education; a talmid's goal was to immerse himself in the life of his rabbi—to *experience* the truths embedded in the rabbi's heart, not merely study them in scrolls. The goal was to "taste and see" (or "know by experience") the heart of the rabbi, then live out his essence by modeling the man's "core operating system"—his walk, talk, mannerisms, personal preferences, values, and affectations. The rabbi's job was to infect his talmid's heart experientially, not just by focusing on the law and the prophets.

> *The goal was to taste and see the heart of the rabbi, then live out his essence by modeling the man's "core operating system."*

The epic journey of the talmid—a path from obscurity to significance, from childhood to maturity, from ignorance to mastery— is our journey as well. We are all talmidim who've been invited to take on the yoke of the great Rabbi—to live with him, learn from him, and become just like him. If we embrace this invitation, the Invisible Rabbi will make it possible for us to immerse ourselves in his presence, experiencing him in a way that goes far beyond intellectual pursuit. In essence, this is Jesus' rabbinical invitation to us:

*I have chosen you as my talmidim, and I'm inviting you into all of the secret places of my heart. I want to walk and talk and play and eat and work and banter and scheme with you—to fully open my interior life to you. And in turn, I invite you to do the same with me.*

As we yield ourselves to the forming influence of the Spirit of Jesus who is at home inside us, we slowly adopt the patterns of thought and behavior he has already modeled for us. It's this immersive influence that forms in us a spiritual backbone; we develop spiritual grit because we're yoked to its very Source.

And so, if we hold to the reality that our Invisible Rabbi helps us experience (not just study) Jesus, it's wise to pay attention to the way an ancient talmid related to his rabbi so we can learn to relate more deeply to our own.

**First, we must be willing to submit to the Invisible Rabbi's authority.** A talmid voluntarily submitted to the authority of his rabbi—this is the literal meaning of the word *yoked*. A yoke is a curved piece of wood with leather straps that allows drivers to direct a team of oxen as they drag a plow through rough ground. In the ancient world, it was also a symbol of captivity. So when a rabbi invited a talmid to "take my yoke upon you," he was asking for a kind of willing captivity to his authority.

Likewise, we experience Jesus more intimately by taking his yoke upon us. By submitting ourselves to his guidance and direction, our actions (more than our words) acknowledge his authority in our lives. Easier said than done, of course, because actually submitting to authority runs contrary to our love affair with control.

A friend, posting on a private Facebook page for fans of the podcast I host ("Paying Ridiculous Attention to Jesus"), targets our default resistance to submission: "Why do we run from attachment [to Jesus] and dependence and freedom? For me, it's because I like to feel in control or at least maintain the illusion of it. Because even after all these years in relationship with Jesus, there are still parts of my life (worth, body image, etc.) that I don't trust him with and tend to think I can do better myself."

Submission to Jesus exposes our willingness to trust him. And trust is the key to experiencing him. In a postscript to her own question, my friend goes on to say, "We see control as our safeguard and defense, but really it's our prison. I'm grateful for the patient and gracious Bridegroom who is willing and able to pursue me no matter how many times I run back to my captivity. That's his heart." [17]

> *Submission to Jesus exposes our willingness to trust him. And trust is the key to experiencing him.*

How does submission to Jesus—an embraced captivity—free us from our overshadowing captivity as human beings broken by sin? Well, the same way a formal apprenticeship to a skilled mentor helps us transcend the limits of what we think we can do. Isaac Newton submitted himself to the apprenticing authority of the world's leading scientists, then later wrote, "If I have seen further, it is by standing on the shoulders of Giants." [18] And the incomparable Leonardo da Vinci, born in 1452 to unmarried parents and poverty, would never have escaped the prison of his origins if not for his apprenticeship as a teenager to Andrea del Verrocchio, a master artist in Florence. [19] Submission to a greater presence infects us with that person's catalyzing habits and values, opening up possibilities and pathways we'd never discover otherwise. And when we submit to the authority of Jesus—pledging ourselves to cling to his habits, decisions, plans, and priorities—his influence on our lives expands, deepening our intimacy with him.

Practically, our submission looks like this...

- **We make a public commitment to him.** Baptism is often a primary way we do this, but it's also courageous to post something on social media about your "status" as a follower of Jesus, or to go forward for prayer or confession at a gathering, or to "out yourself" as a follower of Jesus in a public setting such as a class or conference or debate, or even to slap commitment-related stickers on your car or laptop. (I'm not kidding; you should see my laptop.) Public acts of commitment, no matter how small, have a powerful impact on our ability to trust Jesus because they require risk, and risk helps us experience his heart. And when we act on the guidance we receive from Jesus, that is just another form of public commitment.

  After a recent health scare with my wife, I was driving home from work, contending with Jesus about the dire possibilities ahead of us. My conversation with him was fierce. In response, he said, "Rick, it's going to be okay. I'm sorry this news is so upsetting." When I got home, I had to decide whether to share with Bev what I felt Jesus told me. What if it was just my own wishful thinking? Do I really believe in this response, and will I harm Bev if this is all just my manufactured hope? I decided to tell her, because that would be a risky act of trust. And trust builds intimacy. Walking into her next appointment, a test that would tell us if we were facing a hard and scary road ahead or nothing at all, we both felt the relaxed determination that is the fruit of risk-taking in our relationship with Jesus. Whether the news was bad or good, we stood on the foundation of his good heart toward us, embodied by "It's going to be okay." And it was.

  We've heard church leaders urge us to embrace a personal relationship with Jesus, but it's far more important to live out our passion for him in public ways. To his disciples, Jesus says, "Everyone who acknowledges me publicly here on earth, I will also acknowledge before my Father in heaven" (Matthew 10:32). This is why our family holds hands and prays before a meal, no matter how public the venue. It seems like such a small statement of submission, but every small thing matters.

- **We ask Jesus for guidance before saying things, doing things, or praying things.** When his disciples asked Jesus to teach them to pray, he responded with "This is how you should pray..." (Luke 11:2). This rhythm—submitting to his guidance first, then acting on what we receive from him—helps us experience him. The Invisible Rabbi is also called Counselor. A counselor's job is to listen well, then give feedback and guidance. But a listener requires a talker, so we must talk if we want feedback. We don't have because we don't ask (James 4:2), and we don't hear from Jesus because we don't pursue his guidance.

Here's how this works when we pray, for example. Before we pray we stop, quiet our own voice, and take authority over the voice of the enemy of God. Then we ask the Spirit of Jesus to show us how to pray. We wait in silence for direction before we continue. Once we sense a word or a phrase or a picture or a Scripture reference or even a strong feeling, we accept it wholeheartedly and pray using that guidance. We are most often overly concerned about "getting it right" when it comes to seeking guidance from God, but this kind of exacting mentality quashes the kind of playful risks that a relationship with Jesus thrives on. If we don't take ourselves too seriously, "getting it wrong" won't matter so much. This pattern has radically changed the intimacy I experience in my relationship with Jesus, and it has charged my prayers for others with supernatural impact.

Yesterday I prayed with a friend who is facing a life-shattering reality in her marriage. I asked Jesus for guidance, and before I opened my mouth to pray, I "saw" a hand pulling a weed from the ground, with clods of earth falling off the roots. And then I "saw" that hand take a trowel and dig up the ground where the weed had been, in preparation for planting new seeds. I asked Jesus what all this meant and then prayed this way: "Jesus wants you to know that he is replacing something ugly in your life with something beautiful—the pulling-up is going to be painful, but right now he's planting flowers where weeds once grew." When we pray this way, our posture is defined by humility, because we give Jesus the "first word," rather than assume we already know what's best to say or do.

- **We submit our treasure to Jesus, to use as he sees fit.** I'm not talking just about money. Time, talents, and expertise are also treasures. Jesus already has all the resources he needs, but what he doesn't have is our whole heart. "Wherever your treasure is," he reminds us, "there the desires of your heart will also be" (Matthew 6:21). Simply, our treasure is tethered to our heart. When he reveals to his disciples that "it is very hard for a rich person to enter the Kingdom of Heaven" (Matthew 19:23), he's making the point that the rich have more to submit, and therefore have more of their heart on the line. So when we loosen our grip on the riches of our finances, our time, our talents, and our unique abilities, offering them to strengthen and encourage others, here is the trade-off: We get to experience the heart of Jesus when we consider him more valuable than what we're giving up.

What do you love to do, and what are you good at? If you love making money and you're good at it, then give money. If you love cooking and baking and you're good at it, volunteer to make and serve a meal for people who need it. My daughter Lucy invited her friends to do this as an alternative to a birthday party. They gave a home-cooked Italian meal to the stressed and exhausted parents of seriously ill children living at a Ronald McDonald House. We all know that when we give from our good treasure, we always gain more than we give. That's because the gift of our treasure wins us an even greater treasure: a taste of the heart of Jesus and a feeling of congruence with his purposes in our lives.

**Second, we develop a passion for wrestling with God's Word in a conversational community.** As the talmid immerses himself in his rabbi's revelation of truth, he learns to flesh out that truth in a *Yeshiva*, a closely knit community of fellow talmidim. Marked by intense dialogue and deep, enjoyable conversation, the Yeshiva is an incubator for living out the stories of Scripture in everyday life. In this gathering of talmidim, the focus is not so much on what Scripture says (they've already been memorizing that since they were small children), but on how it's influencing the way they live. The primary focus in a Yeshiva is the heart behind the truths the talmidim are learning, and how that might inform the decisions they make about every aspect of their lives. In our lives, this might mean...

- **We join a formal Bible study, book club, discussion group, or recovery ministry that gives us a window into how others live out their relationships with Jesus in everyday ways.** Of course, most churches offer something like this, but they're not always built on a foundation of conversation. We need interaction-rich environments that focus on our relationship with Jesus, not lectures on Scripture or biblical principles. To sniff out this sort of "seeking community," look for one that has a conversational structure and a leader who values many voices, not just one. If this proves too difficult to find, it may be time to start your own Yeshiva. (You could use the "Questions for Small-Group Discussion or Individual Contemplation" at the end of each chapter as your launching pad.)

- **In the context of informal conversation, we ask questions that help us understand the habits, values, and everyday choices of those who are maturing in their relationship with Jesus.** I'm suggesting that we treat the stories of others with the curiosity they deserve. These sorts of questions will help:

"What do you do every day to stay connected to Jesus?"
"How did you discern between those two choices?"
"What do you do when you're tempted by something?"
"How have you managed to maintain that habit in your life?"

"When Jesus said/did _____, what do you think he meant?"

"What are you doing to show others 'the real you'?"

Of course, these are just sample questions; the goal is to ask more questions whenever we're talking to another Jesus-follower, to immerse ourselves in the unique expressions of the Spirit within them.

**Third, we commit to asking our Invisible Rabbi real questions, in real circumstances, about real issues, all the time.** Rabbis encouraged their talmidim to ask them lots of questions. Questions are like backhoes—their purpose is to dig and dig and dig until we uncover buried treasure. So for example, all talmidim knew that God had commanded his people to observe a Sabbath day, a rest from work that reminded everyone that God, not their own efforts, was the ultimate source of sustenance and life. But they pursued their rabbi to understand better what a "rest from work" really implied. Jesus did this very thing with his disciples when he responded to some religious leaders who were upset that he'd healed a man on the Sabbath: "If you had a sheep that fell into a well on the Sabbath, wouldn't you work to pull it out? Of course you would. And how much more valuable is a person than a sheep! Yes, the law permits a person to do good on the Sabbath" (Matthew 12:11-12).

Our Invisible Rabbi expects us to ask real questions about real challenges we're facing—to reason together as we face situations that aren't directly addressed in the Bible. We face dilemmas that have little to do with sheep falling into wells on the Sabbath. But we do need help discerning how much social media is too much, whether to buy a conventional carbon-emitting car or a hybrid, or how to confront a friend who is headed down a destructive path. We experience Jesus more deeply when we view no situation as too small or insignificant or "unspiritual" to exclude from the dialogue. For example:

- A friend seems suddenly distant and cold. *Ask the Spirit what to do; then "keep knocking" until you sense a way forward.*

- A man with a cardboard sign is asking for money at a busy intersection. *Ask the Spirit what to do; then keep knocking until you sense a way forward.*

- A distant relative is facing a medical struggle. *Ask the Spirit what to do; then keep knocking until you sense a way forward.*

- You're forced to choose between a family commitment and a work commitment. *Ask the Spirit what to do; then keep knocking until you sense a way forward.*

- You wonder if you should pay for something your kids want or tell them they'll need to earn the money themselves. *Ask the Spirit what to do; then keep knocking until you sense a way forward.*

When we embrace a spirit of dependence, we make it a habit to ask the Spirit of Jesus more questions, attaching ourselves to him again and again. The more questions we ask, the more deeply and normally we experience him. And the more we get used to his influence in the everyday rhythms of our lives. Yes, this is not an exact science—it's not even an *inexact* science. It's playful in the way art is playful. Ask like a child, receive like a child, and don't let silence or confusion discourage you from continuing to ask.

**Fourth, we desire to emulate every aspect of the Rabbi's life.** Talmidim were not *required* to mirror their rabbis' personal mannerisms, habits, and eccentricities, but this immersive way of living inevitably led to it.

I co-authored my first book with Ben Freudenburg, a pioneering pastor who innovated an approach to church ministry that prioritizes the family as the primary faith incubator. The book is called *The Family-Friendly Church*, and I was first approached by the publisher to help Ben, who was not an experienced writer, produce a sort of manifesto for the church. I had no desire to write a book with someone and no practical experience in Ben's area of expertise. I should've said no. But I knew that I deeply respected how Ben lived his life, and I decided that writing a book with him would saturate me in his presence so much that it might change me. And I was right. Working closely with Ben over the course of a year—living in each other's homes for weeks at a time—*infected* me with his innate likes and dislikes. I learned to think the way he thinks and value the things he values. The experience helped form who I am today. We can experience Jesus this way when we…

- **Pay close attention to the things Jesus does and doesn't like.** Whenever we experience something Jesus says or does—in the Bible or spotlighted in a book or a film or a conversation—we slow down to focus on both his preferences and the things that drive him crazy. What does Jesus like and not like?

  We do the same with the people we love. For example, I know my wife loves to have coffee waiting for her when she wakes up, she's addicted to cute puppy videos, she processes her thoughts by journaling, and for some reason it drives her crazy when I forget to fold the top of our sheet over our comforter when we get into bed. When we bring this same level of *behavioral saturation* to our pursuit of Jesus, his heart infects us. We pay attention to the nuances in his behavior the way we do when we first fall in love with someone—every little detail matters. In his message to the church at

Ephesus, recorded in Revelation 2, Jesus honors his friends for their perseverance and their dogged adherence to the truth, but laments that they have "lost their first love." A first-love relationship with Jesus pays ridiculous attention to every little distinction in his words and deeds.

- **Pay close attention to the passions of others in the body of Christ.** Whenever we're in the company of other friends of Jesus, we notice what they appreciate and what they don't. We're called the body of Christ because, together, others get a taste of him when they get a taste of us. Consider our passions as the fruits of our Invisible Rabbi's presence in us.

  For example, I have several friends who are committed to CrossFit, the grueling approach to fitness that has rapidly spread across the U.S. My friends know it's important to stay fit, but what they really love about CrossFit is its emphasis on community. And they're passionate about community because the Spirit in them is passionate about it. If we slow down and explore the passions of other believers, we get infected with the passions of Jesus. Our collective passions loosely describe the passions at the heart of Jesus, so paying better attention to the individual passions of other Christ-followers helps us broaden our experience of Jesus.

- **Ask, "What *did* Jesus do?" not "What *would* Jesus do?"** The path to becoming more like Jesus is less about WWJD and more about WDJD. The first approach is hampered by false beliefs about Jesus and a surface understanding of his heart; the second is focused on the hard facts of what he actually said and did. When we fix our attention on the shocking ways Jesus interacted with people, we experience the height and breadth and depth of his heart. Our guesses about what we think he might do in any given situation are wholly dependent on our assumptions, which are tied to how well we actually know him. So WDJD rivets our focus on what is knowable about him, not what we assume about him. Because Jesus is the Truth, not just a prophet pointing to the truth, assume everything he says and does is deeply good; then dig until you discover *why* it's good.

  Instead of defining what we think is good first, then attempting to understand how the sometimes-baffling behavior of Jesus fits our definitions, we let *him* define good for us. The Victorian journalist and Christian apologist G.K. Chesterton says it best: "If you meet the Jesus of the Gospels, you must redefine what love is, or you won't be able to stand him." [20]

**Finally, we are determined to live out our personal beliefs rather than just talk about them.** To a talmid living in the first century, the word *believe* was an action, not a mental assent. The true standard for belief was the way you lived your life, not the way you espoused your convictions. If you believed something, that meant you were living that belief in everyday circumstances. Actions fuel our experience of Jesus far more than our words do. For example:

- **If we say we believe Jesus has a special place in his heart for the poor and marginalized but ignore their needs, we don't really believe.** Actually helping and serving the poor helps us experience the depth of Jesus' heart because we learn to appreciate what drives him when we do the things he loves. My wife has a passion for people who have been marginalized, people who have been counted out by others. Why? Because she grew up feeling unseen and unappreciated, and she feels driven to help those who are experiencing the pain she knows all too well. When I enter into her passion with her, I see her heart from the inside out.

- **If we say we believe that Jesus lives sacrificially but serve ourselves before we serve others, we don't really believe.** Over the years, my wife's trust in me has grown because of what I do, not what I talk about. It's my lifestyle of sacrifice for her and my family that reveals my heart—a heart that reflects my experience of Jesus' values and priorities.

- **If we say we believe Jesus loves his enemies but hold on to our hatred for our own enemies and dream about our revenge, we don't really believe.** On an episode of the show *What Would You Do?* a hidden camera records the reactions of unsuspecting bystanders when they encounter an actor playing the role of a thief stealing gas from another person's pump. Most respond by confronting the thief and "outing" her to the victim (another actor), but one person does something extraordinary: He approaches the enemy thief and boldly asks if she needs money for gas, then gives her some cash. [21] After watching this, my daughter Emma pointed out that this man's surprising act of selfless generosity reflected the heart of Jesus toward an enemy, and she was right.

Our response to our enemies reveals the level of our belief in Jesus' standard for love.

## RESISTANCE TRAINING

Because the Invisible Rabbi helps us experience Jesus from the inside out, we not only have fuel for the spiritual grit we need to live a life of perseverance and impact, but we also have an ongoing way to develop that spiritual grit. What we often lack is a bucket of possibilities, or real-world modeling, for living in a grit-growing way. To do that, we need to see the value of hardship when it comes our way—and maybe even seek it out when it doesn't come our way—with a determination that comes from a passion for something higher than ourselves. And we also need to help others grow in their spiritual grit because it's the most loving thing we can do. We don't get in the way of a hardship that promises to produce good fruit in them, and sometimes, when love requires it, we *introduce* hardship into their lives. We do these things because we're immersed in the heart of Jesus, trusting the Invisible Rabbi to lead us into an abiding relationship with him that feeds our growth and the growth of others.

> *We need to see the value of hardship when it comes our way, with a determination that comes from a passion for something higher than ourselves.*

Researchers' interest in the importance of grit and perseverance has mostly focused on *what it is* and *how it works*. They generally admit they don't have much direction to give on how people actually grow it in themselves and in others. Angela Duckworth says, "To me, the most shocking thing about grit is how little we know about building it. Every day parents and teachers ask me, 'How do I build grit in kids?' The honest answer is, I don't know." [22]

To go further than the researchers can take us means we do things that invite transformation in ourselves and others. And this is holy ground. Risky stuff. We'd better take off our shoes if we're going to cross this border, because redemption stories are always sacred.

No wonder the research community is mute on this aspect of grit—it's not their job to lead us into transformation.

And while we may struggle to understand how to help ourselves and others grow in our capacity for spiritual grit, Jesus does not. In fact, he's intentionally testing the limits of perseverance in every single person he interacts with, even those who come to him with great needs...

- In the John 9 story of the man born blind, Jesus smears a mixture of dirt and spit on the man's eyes, then tells him to go to the pool of Siloam outside of town to find his sight. Would you force this marginalized, needy man to undergo such a seemingly unnecessary gauntlet of shame and uncertainty?

- In the John 5 story of the crippled man who has languished by the pool of Bethesda for 38 years, waiting night and day for an angel to touch the pool and restore him, Jesus asks a question that seems either silly or lacking in compassion: "Would you like to get well?" When the man ignores the offense of the question and says yes, Jesus tells him, "Stand up, pick up your mat, and walk!"

Jesus is a master grit-grower, and he's inviting us to learn from him.

I go to a class at our health club called CXWORX, where the trainer's job is to build our core strength through resistance exercises. Most of them involve some form of "planking," forcing the muscles in our torsos to stay in tension until they collapse. Resistance builds core strength by taking us to the end of our capacity so we can stretch its boundaries. Likewise, Jesus uses resistance to strengthen our core identity so that the challenges we face produce hope in us, not resignation or despair.

In the pages that follow, we'll slow down and pay ridiculous attention to the ways he grows spiritual grit in people, embrace the beauty of what he's trying to do, then explore everyday ways to live into what we're learning. This is resistance training with a highly engaged Personal Trainer; it's not about following formulas or principles to produce an expected outcome.

And we need Jesus' resistance training because we so often crave more strength than we have—every day we face tough challenges that push us to give up or give in. We must develop ways of thinking and living that strengthen our determination, not undermine it. And as parents and friends and spouses and leaders, we need better ways to help the people we care about grow in their core strength.

As we pay better attention to the heart of Jesus and open ourselves to experience—not just study—him, we discover a consuming passion for something higher than ourselves. And we find a source of strength that supersedes our "just try harder" mentality. It's the living water Jesus promised the Samaritan woman at the well—a life-water that quenches our deepest thirst and produces four precious fruits: endurance, character, confidence, and hope (Romans 5:3-5).

Because Jesus is a resistance trainer, his love language is spiritual grit. He will do whatever it takes to help us grow because he loves us and wants us to experience "abundant joy" (John 16:24). When we draw our strength from the well of his passionate heart and learn to rely on the Helper—the Invisible Rabbi—to empower us, we are reminded again of one of his blunt and beautiful truths: "What is impossible for people is possible with God."

# QUESTIONS FOR SMALL-GROUP
# DISCUSSION OR INDIVIDUAL CONTEMPLATION

1. Do you consider yourself to be a gritty person? Why or why not?

2. In general, do you face challenges with a sense of confident strength, or do you face them well-aware of how weak you feel? Explain.

3. When in your life have you felt the need for a source of strength that's beyond your own capacity, and why?

4. What are the benefits of pursuing the heart of Jesus more than focusing on the "life principles" embedded in his teaching?

5. In what ways do you resonate with the idea that simply believing in Jesus is different from experiencing him?

_____

_____

_____

_____

6. Tell a story about your relationship with Jesus that relates to one of the five ways a talmid is influenced by his rabbi: (1) submitting to his authority, (2) wrestling with Scripture, (3) asking him real questions, (4) imitating him, and (5) living—not just talking about—your beliefs.

_____

_____

_____

_____

1   Winston Churchill, Harrow School, October 29, 1941
    (www.school-for-champions.com).

2   Boris Johnson, "The Day Churchill Saved Britain from the Nazis,"
    *The Telegraph* (October 13, 2014).

3   I. Scott-Kilvert, *The Rise and Fall of Athens. Nine Greek Lives by
    Plutarch* (New York: Penguin Books, 1960), 43-76.

4   Angela Duckworth, "Grit: The Power of Passion and
    Perseverance," TED Talk (April 2013).

5   Angela Duckworth, Christopher Peterson, Michael D. Matthews,
    and Dennis R. Kelly, "Grit: Perseverance and Passion for Long-
    Term Goals," *Journal of Personality and Social Psychology* (Volume
    92, Number 6, 2007), 1087-1101.

6   Angela Duckworth, "Grit: The Power of Passion and
    Perseverance," TED Talk (April 2013).

7   Deborah Perkins-Gough, "The Significance of Grit: A
    Conversation With Angela Lee Duckworth," *Educational
    Leadership* (Volume 71, Number 1, September 2013), 14-20.

8   David Brooks, "Putting Grit in Its Place," *The New York Times*
    (May 10, 2016).

9   David Benner, *The Gift of Being Yourself* (Westmont, Illinois: IVP
    Press, 2015), 39.

10  Peter Kreeft, "The Shocking Life of Jesus" (Saddleback Church's
    Ahmanson Lecture series, December 18, 2010).

11  St. Clare of Assisi (1194–1253, born Chiara Offreduccio), quoted
    by Timothy Johnson in *Franciscans at Prayer* (Brill Publishers,
    2007), 54.

12  Condensed from responses from members of the Pursuing the
    Heart of Jesus, Not His Recipes group on June 8, 2016, when they
    were asked to explore how Jesus redefines love in his encounters
    with needy people in Matthew 15 and elsewhere.

13  From the author's transcription of Simon Sinek's September, 2009
    TED Puget Sound talk.

14  David Brooks, "Putting Grit in Its Place," *The New York Times* (May 10, 2016).

15  Annie Colavincenzo, Krista Evans, Marc Holderead, Joann Richardson, Allison Spenner, and Kathryn Wilcox, "Understanding the Experience of Stroke and the Client Identified Factors of a Successful Recovery," a research project submitted to the School of Occupational Therapy at the University of Indianapolis, December 5, 2013.

16  Dan Stolebarger, "Discipleship vs. Talmidim" (www.khouse.org), with additional material from blogger Steve Corn on his "Faith, Family, Leadership, etc." site, from a post titled "Jewish Educational System."

17  Posted on the private Facebook page for listeners to the "Paying Ridiculous Attention to Jesus" podcast, www.mylifetree.com/paying-ridiculous-attention-to-jesus.

18  Isaac Newton, "Letter from Sir Isaac Newton to Robert Hooke," Historical Society of Pennsylvania (February 5, 1675).

19  Claudia Kalb, "What Makes a Genius?" *National Geographic* magazine (May 2017).

20  G.K. Chesterton, quoted in *The Everyman Chesterton* (Everyman's Library, 2001), xviii.

21  "Then and Now," *What Would You Do?* (September 22, 2017).

22  Angela Duckworth, "Grit: The Power of Passion of Perseverance," TED Talk (April 2013).

# CHAPTER 2

# CHASING RISK IN A CULTURE OF SAFETY

When we take risks as a result of our deepening relationship with Jesus, we develop the courage to endure what life throws at us. In this chapter you'll get a taste of why the writer of Hebrews said, "It is impossible to please God without faith," and you'll learn what it looks like to ratchet up your risk-taking in everyday ways.

*"To dare is to lose one's footing momentarily. Not to dare is to lose oneself."* —Soren Kierkegaard

### The Faith of a Gentile Woman

Then Jesus left Galilee and went north to the region of Tyre and Sidon. A Gentile woman who lived there came to him, pleading, "Have mercy on me, O Lord, Son of David! For my daughter is possessed by a demon that torments her severely."

But Jesus gave her no reply, not even a word. Then his disciples urged him to send her away. "Tell her to go away," they said. "She is bothering us with all her begging."

Then Jesus said to the woman, "I was sent only to help God's lost sheep—the people of Israel."

But she came and worshiped him, pleading again, "Lord, help me!"

Jesus responded, "It isn't right to take food from the children and throw it to the dogs."

She replied, "That's true, Lord, but even dogs are allowed to eat the scraps that fall beneath their masters' table."

"Dear woman," Jesus said to her, "your faith is great. Your request is granted." And her daughter was instantly healed" (Matthew 15:21-28).

Which is a greater threat to your life: death by suffocation or death by terrorist attack? If we gauged these threats by the level and tenor of our fear, terrorism wins, hands-down. But we're *75 times* more likely to die from suffocating than we are at the hands of a terrorist. We are, of course, immersed in threats and fears and warnings in our media-saturated culture. They're the wallpaper of our lives, a constant drumbeat of anxiety that has made "Be safe!" our common replacement for "Have a nice day!" Our caution is fed by a steady stream of risk-averse stories and threat alerts. For example:

- The nationwide scare among parents that was sparked after Eden Hoelscher, a 6-year-old girl in California who loves gymnastics, did a backbend at home and ended up paralyzed. [1]

- The 43 active traveler warnings issued by the U.S. government at the time I'm writing these words, with the ominous imperative to

"consider very carefully whether you should go to a country at all."
These warnings reference "unstable governments, civil wars, ongoing
intense crime or violence, or frequent terrorist attacks," and target
countries on every continent except Australia and Antarctica.

- The almost-weekly revelation that our privacy and digital security
  have been compromised. Already, nearly two-thirds of Americans say
  they've experienced a major data breach. [2] And not long ago, a secure
  website for the Bilderberg Group, host of an uber-secretive annual
  gathering of global leaders, was breached by hackers working for the
  digital guerrilla group Anonymous. The hackers warned the leaders,
  "From now, each one of you has one year to truly work in favor of
  humans and not your private interests." [3] If one of the most protective
  groups in the world can be hacked, we're told, then our privacy and
  digital security are a joke.

In the midst of this barrage, our brains are ill-equipped to
differentiate between reasonable and unreasonable concerns. Should
parents be more concerned about the guy driving the windowless van
slowly through their neighborhood or by the airline ticket they just
bought for their child? Well, a child is twice as likely to die in a plane
crash than to be abducted by a stranger.

We don't calibrate these risks well because threatening experiences
condition us to fear. Our fears grow, for example, from an encounter
with a *specific* dog into a fear of *all* dogs. Fear is part of our souls'
immune systems, and most of us have an immune-system disorder
when it comes to legitimate threats to our safety.

Rather than spend our time, attention, and energies trying to
neutralize the mostly unreasonable risks we fear, we're much better
off growing our core strength so we can persevere through the *actual*
hardships we face. We're far more likely to need strength and spiritual
grit to overcome our everyday challenges than protection from
epic threats we're unlikely to face in our lifetimes. This is not just a
pragmatic issue; it's a kingdom of God issue. Healthy risk-taking fuels
a healthy trajectory in life, for both ourselves and those we care about.

> *Rather than trying to neutralize the mostly*
> *unreasonable risks we fear, we're much better*
> *off growing our core strength so we can*
> *persevere through the actual hardships we face.*

To love someone well requires courage, because vulnerability is risky. That's why a risk-averse mentality doesn't mesh well with a life committed to following Jesus—we have a foundational calling to partner with him in his missional purpose in the world. This necessarily involves risk-taking, because "setting captives free" is courageous work.

## THE MECHANICS OF RISK

In Jesus' encounter with the Gentile woman, risk-taking is the key to her freedom from captivity. She's an outcast well-acquainted with systemic bias, but her daughter's desperate need overwhelms her caution as she pleads with Jesus for help. Because she's socially forbidden to approach Jesus, his disciples are quick to condemn her when she persists. Jesus responds with icy silence, apparently confirming their bias: "Tell her to go away. She is bothering us with all her begging." In an act of startling vulnerability, the woman kneels before Jesus and worships him. But instead of responding with empathy, Jesus pours fuel on his disciples' fire, telling the woman he won't give her what she wants because he's reserved healing for the privileged few, not "dogs" like her.

And then this impossible woman does the impossible—she responds to this denigration with risk-taking chutzpah: "That's true, Lord, but even dogs are allowed to eat the scraps that fall beneath their masters' table." She's respectful but determined, appropriate but disruptive, humble but fierce. Moved by her courage, Jesus stuns his disciples by honoring her with tender respect: "Dear woman, your faith is great. Your request is granted."

Jesus *takes* great risks to *surface* great risk in this woman—a common practice of the Invisible Rabbi, who leverages our circumstances to goad us into chutzpah. The Spirit is always prompting us, even *provoking* us, to risk on our behalf and on behalf of others. That's because courage, not caution, grows our core strength.

In a seminar for parents I lead called Fighting the Entitlement Dragon, I directly address our ubiquitous acceptance of "Be safe!" as a guiding value. I ask parents to throw out the names of leaders who have changed the world for the better. I always hear Martin Luther King, Mother Teresa, Nelson Mandela, Billy Graham, Harriet Tubman, and other usual suspects. Then I ask the crowd how many of the people they've named likely lived their lives by the motto "Be safe!" There's always a lot of self-conscious laughter at this point, because everyone in the room knows no one can have an impact on the world by playing it safe. I leave them with this challenge: *Do you want your kids to grow up into adults who have a good impact on the world? A fixation on safety won't help them on that journey.*

We need a lifestyle of risk, guided and empowered by our Invisible Rabbi. Using the Gentile woman's example as a helpful template, let's explore what this might look like.

# REINTRODUCING RISK INTO OUR LIVES

In each of the risk vectors that follow, we'll reference something the Gentile woman does in response to the challenge she's facing. We'll pay closer attention to her context and the threats that nearly derail her quest. And we'll make direct connections between the types of risks she takes and equivalents in our everyday lives.

**1. Take the risk to go where you don't belong, ask what you shouldn't ask, invest what you can't afford to lose, and give what you're not supposed to give.** I'm at a large worship gathering, held in an enclosure that's open on the sides, looking out onto a beautiful mountain landscape. A band is playing on a stage about 75 feet from where I'm standing, and outside the enclosure, wandering up and down the concrete deck that surrounds it, is a woman playing her flute as if she's up there with the band. She is clearly a talented player, lost in the music and harmonizing her instrument to complement what's happening on stage.

Once I understand what she's doing, I can't stop staring at this woman. She's offering her gifts from the sidelines, as an outsider. What could've been an annoying distraction instead reminds me of the Gentile woman's magnetic act of courage. Rejected, she ignores the boundaries imposed on her and draws near to Jesus, kneeling before him in worship. She disrupts the status quo of discrimination when she asserts her identity as an insider, not an outsider. Because she's determined to get what she came for, she humbly insists on her place at the table. Likewise, the lone flutist, playing her instrument out there on the deck, finds a way to "add to the beauty." [4] She's a passionate interloper who ignores convention to give what she has to give.

After the worship time is over, I stop this woman as she passes by to tell her how profoundly she's affected me. She's quick to explain that she's asked the worship leader for permission to play her flute as long as she remains outside. She's not forcing herself on the band; she's simply breaking down the barrier between insider and outsider. She risks being misunderstood, she risks rejection from the official worship band, she risks drawing attention to herself and away from the band, she risks the possibility that others will be annoyed by her playing, and she risks being asked to leave altogether. And because she's willing to risk, she adds a dimension to the worship experience that leads me into the heart of Jesus. She gives me a taste of beauty I wasn't expecting, and her passion moves me.

That's a big payoff for a little investment of risk.

And a risk-taking posture, with a specific focus on multiplying whatever gifts we've been given, is what Jesus is trying to encourage in us. In the parable of the talents (Matthew 25:14-30, AMP), a master is about to leave on a long trip and gives three servants a portion of his savings to invest while he's gone. One gets five bags of silver, another gets two, and the last gets one. Two of the three men risk what they've been given and double their master's money. But the third is afraid he'll lose what he's been given, wary of his master's harsh reputation, so he buries it. When the master returns, he praises the two who risk to gain more, giving them even more to invest. But he condemns the one who plays it safe, and takes back what he'd already given. The third servant has misunderstood the heart of his master, holding back because he was afraid to make a mistake. He is risk-averse because he does not trust his master, allowing fear to dominate his interior narrative.

Jesus is telling us that risk, calculated to bring exponential growth, is one dialect of his spiritual grit love language—that's because risk grows our core strength. When we take chances with what he's given us, we're trusting his heart, multiplying our impact, and opening the door to even more opportunity in our lives. The Gentile woman, like all women in her position, has learned to guard the status quo in a culture that negates her. She knows that if she plays by the rules, no one will get hurt. Safety dictates caution, even though her daughter is tormented by a demon and Jesus has already demonstrated his authority over demonic forces. Push too hard, and she risks abuse, rejection, or worse. But she risks anyway, because the magnet for her courage is the heart of Jesus. She's betting on his heart and is willing to ignore the conventions of her culture to do it.

Do you have gifts to give that you withhold because you're not on the "approved list," an outsider?

Do you have resources or talents that you've held back, simply because you're afraid of what might happen if you gave them?

Recognize that this is an issue of trust. On the surface, you might acknowledge that you distrust yourself, but the truth is, self-doubt is the fruit of God-doubt. It's been 25 years since I was first asked to speak in front of groups. In the beginning I was a ball of insecurity, self-conscious and gripped by anxiety. I didn't trust myself because I didn't trust Jesus (or the people who paid to listen to me) to put up with my failure while I learned how to grow in the gifts he'd given me. In those early years, an older man who'd been speaking for years pulled me aside and advised me to stick to writing. "Leave the speaking to the speakers," he said with a condescending smile. And of course, he had plenty of evidence to say such a thing to me. I was a terrible speaker.

But a funny thing happened on my way to a life of "giving what I have to give" as a speaker: I've discovered that the more I understand and trust the heart of Jesus, the more space I give myself to fail, learn, and invest again. I've learned to trust myself to influence others because I've learned to trust the God who gave me these gifts in the first place. Slowly, my focus has shifted from my deficits to his assets, and he has redirected my passion from self-preservation to the needs of others.

> *Slowly, my focus has shifted from my deficits to his assets.*

Will you give your gifts in the face of potential rejection—from yourself and others?

Risk the treasures Jesus has given you—your skills, abilities, resources, and knowledge—even when it feels awkward. If you do, you'll learn to trust his heart, and you'll grow your core strength. My friend Greg Stier, founder of the Dare 2 Share evangelism training organization, says it best: "Awkward is awesome."

**2. Take the risk to be boldly specific about what you want and why you want it.** On the risk scale, the general requests we spray at God are a hedge against disappointment and require little faith. It's much safer to pray for world peace than it is to pray for reconciliation between a son and daughter who say they hate each other, for example. The more specific we get with Jesus, the bolder our conversations with him, the more spiritual grit we develop. The Gentile woman doesn't merely ask Jesus to help her; she asks for specific help: *Cast out the tormenting demon from my daughter.* When that request is challenged, she doubles-down by pointing out that even dogs get to eat the crumbs from the table. The more specific we are with Jesus, the greater the risk. And the more we risk in our relationship with him, the more our trust and intimacy develop.

Specificity in our conversations with Jesus immerses our relationship in risk. We put on the table aspects of our lives that we've kept from him because they seem too small or insignificant for him to bother with. My standard for this is simple: If I'm driving around looking for a parking space in a crowded area, I ask him to find me one. If it matters to me, why wouldn't it matter to him? I don't mean that I expect him to grant my every whim—he is the Lion of the Tribe of Judah, not the three-wishes genie in a bottle. I mean that we expand the boundaries of our relationship with him to include the specifics of our lives, not just our epic needs.

Yes, it's true that the more specific we are in our relationship with Jesus, the more we expose ourselves to disappointment. He will say no as well as yes. But it's also true that we create many, many more opportunities to experience the miraculous—to encounter his heart in the everyday rhythms of our lives, not just during a worship time at church. A "lifer" in our Pursuing the Heart, Not the Recipes group told me this story:

> I was on a date with my boyfriend, downtown at an underground arcade. We were playing pinball, and he beat me by five million points—that was sad. So then he suggested that we play Skee-Ball together. I didn't tell him, but before we played, I prayed, "Hey, God, I know this is kind of silly, but I'd really like to win this. I know it doesn't matter, but it would be pretty cool." We both put in two quarters and got a round of balls. Of course, he beat me by a couple hundred points. But then my machine automatically spit out a whole new round of balls, even though I didn't pay for them. I knew it was Jesus, because it was so playful. So I played again, added the score to my first round, and beat him by a lot.

CLOSER LOOK From her place at the bottom of the cultural food chain, the Gentile woman asks God himself for mercy, then tells him what she wants. She responds to Jesus' common and expected bias with an extraordinary act of vulnerability: She moves toward him, not away, and kneels to acknowledge his beauty. To worship means to open ourselves to taste and see goodness, then risk to express our awe. Fueled by this act of emotional courage, she pushes back in the face of cold dismissal and social convention. She asks, again, for help.

When we de-compartmentalize big requests from small requests, we invite Jesus into our nooks and crannies, sharing our everyday minutiae with him, just as lovers do. It's a risky way to live, because specific requests—*Jesus, I need _____, and here's why I need it*—require courage. But courage grows spiritual grit, even when the only thing on the line is bragging rights with your boyfriend.

**3. Take the risk to welcome trouble rather than avoid it.** Jesus offers us comfort, yes, but it's always in the context of a vigorous focus on our growth. After all, he is life itself, and growth is intrinsic to life. When he's on his way with his disciples to Jerusalem and the Cross, he approaches a fig tree that's leafy but has no fruit. Usually, a leafy fig tree has figs growing on it, but it's out of season, so the tree is barren. Earlier, when the religious leaders question Jesus' rule-breaking attitude toward the Sabbath, he bluntly explains how things work: "The Son of Man is Lord of the Sabbath" (Matthew 12:8, NASB). In the same way, in the presence of a fig tree that will not bow to his authority, he reminds everyone that he is also Lord of the Seasons. If hurricane winds and towering waves and the fish of the sea and even death itself must give way to the authority of Jesus, then so must the barren fig tree. Growth and fruit are the result of every encounter with Jesus, and so he curses the "disobedient" tree, withering it.

Jesus is looking for opportunities to produce growth in us because growth is life. That means, from his perspective, *anything* that has the power to leverage growth in us is just another assignment in the Invisible Rabbi's syllabus. This is why James, one of the four original apostles, writes: "Dear brothers and sisters, when troubles of any kind come your way, consider it an opportunity for great joy. For you know that when your faith is tested, your endurance has a chance to grow. So let it grow, for when your endurance is fully developed, you will be perfect and complete, needing nothing" (James 1:2-4). Troubles, as much as we hate the truth of it, deliver the growth opportunities Jesus is looking for.

CLOSER LOOK

The Gentile woman is well acquainted with the "silent treatment" the Jews employ when they run across someone they see as "untouchable." Nothing about Jesus' initial reaction to her is surprising to onlookers, brutal as it is. If you are reckless or stupid enough to approach a Jewish religious leader in this way, you should expect a brutal, dismissive retort. But this woman refuses to slink away, even when the disciples take Jesus' bait and ignore her dire situation, demanding that he get rid of her. In the face of all of this, she stands, determined to plunge into the challenge, not retreat from it.

Every year my daughters have to decide whether to take regular classes at school or the advanced-placement versions of them. Their risky calculation is simply *How much trouble do I want to take on?* An advanced-placement course is going to be more demanding, but the payoff for that risk is greater growth.

> *Troubles, as much as we hate the truth of it, deliver the growth opportunities Jesus is looking for.*

Jesus understands that we naturally recoil from life's advanced-placement classes, so as our Rabbi, he has chosen to let us "audit" every one of the challenges we must face or that we choose to pursue. That means he's not grading our performance on an A to F scale; he's only paying attention to whether we show up for class and participate. Are we running from hardship or leaning into it? This frees us to consider our challenges as "opportunities for great joy." We say to ourselves, *I'm going to show up for this class and learn what my Rabbi is trying to teach. I'll pay attention. I'm going to finish this thing, even if I feel like a mess.* Here are some examples:

- *Did you handle yourself poorly in a hard conversation with your spouse?* We show up for class when we face our insecurities and vulnerably own our responsibilities, asking for forgiveness without the subtle qualifiers we like to add to make sure our spouses know there are two sides to every argument. That's embracing, not running from, tough things, and it's risky.

- *Did you get laid off six months ago, and are you now in danger of losing your home?* Of course, you have moments of profound fear and frustration, and your identity seems to be perpetually on trial. But we "audit" this class by doing the work we *can* do, every day, and opening ourselves to an entirely new career trajectory when we would normally lack the courage to take such a chance.

- *Because you had the courage to see a counselor, you've now embraced a hard truth about your childhood: You were sexually abused by a family member. And now that you have shared this truth with your family, your sister refuses to speak to you.* When we're auditing our tough relationships, we resist the temptation to write off those who reject us. Instead, we maintain whatever connection is possible for us. And sometimes we embrace the reality that years may pass before others soften enough to open themselves to us again.

- *Have you disappointed someone whose opinion means a lot to you?* Taking the advanced-placement course from Jesus means we embrace a hard truth he shared with Paul: "My grace is all you need. My power works best in weakness" (2 Corinthians 12:9). The weakness we feel when others are disillusioned with us can be a door into strength, if we trust the power of grace instead of the wispy promise of our own reputations. That's taking the risk to embrace tough things, not run from them.

Here's the beauty of living this way: Every class has an end to it, when the teacher has decided the goals of the course have been met. Audit your challenges, persevering through them until you've learned the coursework and are ready to graduate into what's next. (And don't forget to show up for the end-of-year pool party and bring your yearbook for others to sign…)

**4. Take the risk to embrace your God-given identity in the face of threats and lies.** Not long ago I was washing up in the shower, thinking about a problem that had cropped up in my soul. A few days before, my wife and daughter were angry with me for something I'd done, and I responded like a little boy having a tantrum. After the emotion of the moment had died down and I'd reconciled with both of them, I "showed up for class" and asked the Invisible Rabbi what he wanted me to learn from this meltdown. I "heard" Jesus respond, with what seemed like a smile in his tone, *When are you going to leave behind all your other lovers and cling only to me?*

I shot back, "What the heck are you talking about?"

And Jesus replied, *You have attached yourself to others and let them define who you really are. You've given them permission to mold your identity in the warped image of their mirrors. When will you stop allowing anyone other than me to define who you really are?*

Wow. Jesus was asking me questions that weren't really questions; they were shots across my bow. He was exposing the subtle ways I'd allowed others to define my worth and given permission to forces other than him to "grade" my heart.

In the original Hebrew, the word *dogs* actually means something like "the little dogs that play with children," and the Gentile woman understands the nuance right away. If she's a dog, sitting at the feet of the messy-eating children of Israel, wouldn't it be okay for that dog to gobble up the scraps that fall to the floor? Hers is a brilliant, creative, and savvy answer that delights Jesus but shocks those who are standing nearby. She's saying, effectively, *Come on, Jesus, you have inexhaustible healing resources, and the Jews are messy eaters. Isn't it right for others to feed on the stuff that drops off the table?*

Jesus leaves a trail of redemption and transformation in his wake because he refuses to be leveraged by forces that are contrary to his mission and heart. At the core of his good impact is a determination to maintain his core identity, his "self-differentiated" presence. Self-differentiated people keep deep attachments to others while guarding the boundaries of their own identities, refusing to allow outside forces to fundamentally determine their course. Jesus' calm, determined, mission-focused presence is a catalyst that transforms environments dominated by conflict, criticism, and fear. He's like a healthy cell with a clearly defined nucleus and strong walls, fending off assault from the cancerous cells that threaten to invade and destroy.

The Gentile woman can gain what she wants from Jesus only if she differentiates herself from the defining messages that are thrown at her. She has to maintain her "cell walls," not allowing the lies she's been told about herself to enter into her soul and do damage.

A healthy cell has what you might call a little door that opens to friends and closes to foes. If the cell is approached by another healthy cell for the purpose of a healthy connection, it opens the door to it. But if a damaging, unhealthy cell approaches, the differentiated cell keeps that door shut and locked. In the face of all the distorted mirrors in our lives—the voices that demand to define our identities in twisted ways—we keep our doors closed. We open them only for Jesus.

And this is what his reference to other lovers meant to me. I'd unconsciously allowed others to determine the truth about who I am, and my tantrum was the little boy in me refusing to accept that verdict because it scared me. I'd let the distorted reflections of others define my identity, like a cell that fails to guard its boundary walls against an invader. Now, my response had nothing to do with the legitimacy of my wife's and daughter's beef with me—I was wrong in the first place. But my "lover's attachment" to their complaint meant that I let it define me.

Here's what I did to reassert my true identity and reengage my wife and daughter in a more self-differentiated way. I simply stopped and asked Jesus this simple question: *Who do you say I am?* Then I waited in silence for a response. I've done this many, many times in my life. Sometimes he gives me a descriptive word, sometimes a picture, sometimes a Scripture reference from the psalms, and sometimes a full-blown sentence. I ask with the attitude of a child and receive with the openness of a child. And then I am recalibrated, because I have his perspective on who I am to stand on now.

Only Jesus can define us in truth. And that means we take the risk to stay connected to others, open to their feedback and even their criticism, but we don't allow their verdict about who we are to be the last word. Like the Gentile woman, we're aware of how others are trying to define us, but we take the bold risk to hold fast to the truth about our identities, moving with conviction toward what we've been called to do.

> *We take the risk to stay connected to others, but we don't allow their verdict about who we are to be the last word.*

**5. Take the risk to move toward Jesus when he doesn't seem to care.**
By 1992 the beautiful cosmopolitan city of Sarajevo had morphed into a killing field, imprisoned by the longest siege of a major city in the history of modern warfare. More than 10,000 Serbian troops encircled the city, raining shells down on soldiers and civilians alike, night and day. At 4 p.m. on May 27, a long line of starving and desperate people snaked down the block from a bakery that had somehow retained a supply of flour. The owners of the bakery were making bread and distributing loaves to the people waiting in line. That's when a Serbian shell landed in the middle of the line, killing 22 people instantly, splattering the streets with blood.

Just down the block from this carnage lived Vedran Smajlović, who had been principal cellist of the Sarajevo Opera Company before the war. An eyewitness to this horror, Smajlović decided he'd seen enough. He could no longer allow fear to control his life and bully him into submission. So the next day at 4 p.m., and every day afterward until the war ended, Vedran dressed up in his performance tuxedo, hauled his cello to the crater where the shell had landed, sat on a little campstool, and played. Bullets tore through the air around him, mortars landed near him, but he played. Over the months and years he kept this vigil, he was never hurt—though once, when he left his cello to stretch his legs, his beloved instrument suffered a direct hit from an exploding shell and was destroyed. [5] Some called his act of defiance a "protest of beauty." [6]

In Jesus' celebratory response, the Gentile woman gets what she came for: Her daughter is instantly delivered from the tormenting demon. But because Jesus is perpetually extravagant, she also gets a treasure she never asks for: She is released from the shame of her second-class status in the culture and elevated by the Master as a person all people (including the Jews) can emulate. The chosen ones learning from the hopeless dregs of society? It wasn't the first time and won't be the last. A woman so desperate she had nothing to lose risks everything to ask Jesus to give her what she wants, and he frees her from captivity as a bonus.

And this, in essence, is what the Gentile woman does after Jesus responds to her pleas with silence and the disciples respond to her vulnerability with disdain. Instead of retreating into her fear, away from this emotional violence, her act of defiance is to move in even closer to Jesus and worship him. It's a protest of beauty, focused on Beauty itself.

So many of our hopes and dreams and desperate needs seem to be met with God's inexplicable silence. Like the disciples on a swamped boat in the middle of a terrible storm who wake Jesus, apparently unconcerned, from his nap, we ask, "Teacher, don't you care that we're going to drown?" (Mark 4:38). *Don't you care?*

Under the pressure of despair, we're tempted to retreat into spiritual cynicism, fatalism, and bitterness. But a protest of beauty defies the darkness that threatens us, because we draw near to Jesus in the face of his silence, or even what seems to be his opposition. We're determined to "touch the hem of his garment," just as the desperate woman suffering from a hemorrhage does (Matthew 9, KJV). We move close enough to taste and see what is true and good about him, leaning into him when circumstances are pressuring us to move away.

> *Under the pressure of despair, we're tempted to retreat into spiritual cynicism, fatalism, and bitterness.*

I was speaking at a big ministry conference in Maryland, and Rob Benson, a former street cop in Baltimore who volunteered to help at the event, was assigned to drive me around to my commitments. He'd left behind a grim life in law enforcement to plant a ministry outreach to the poor in the inner city. He was well acquainted with the sort of people who intimidate normal adults—the people we do our best to avoid. Rob, instead, moved toward them. For example, sitting just behind me in Rob's van, *always,* was a young man who was born in one of the former Soviet-bloc countries. He'd been adopted by an American family in Rob's church. Whenever there was a lull in the conversation, I asked this young guy about his life. The stories started out slightly over-the-top and quickly progressed to unbelievable and bizarre: midnight escapes from the Russian Mafia, cross-border treks to freedom, and so on. It dawned on me that this guy was either delusional or the lost son of James Bond.

Early on, Rob could see my mental gears grinding and pulled me aside. He told me that this guy had serious mental-health issues. His outbursts, delusional ramblings, and sometimes scary behavior had forced his adoptive family to find a special group home for him. Meanwhile, Rob had latched on to him, picking him up for every ministry gathering and taking him to conferences like the one we were attending. Rob was living his own protest of beauty, leaning into fearful situations and hopeless people instead of away from them, worshipping Jesus at the bottom of a shell crater. In the face of a lost cause, Rob was determined to move *toward* Jesus, not recoil from him.

When we're convinced in the moment that Jesus simply doesn't care about what we're going through, or our circumstances seem hopeless, we take a risk by launching our own protests of beauty. We defy the darkness, and what *appears* to be true, by drawing near to Truth itself. We don't recoil from Jesus; we lean into him…

- **We open one of the Gospels (Matthew, Mark, Luke, or John) to a random page and read for five or 10 minutes, simply paying ridiculous attention to what Jesus says and does.** Then we ask the Invisible Rabbi to show us the heart of Jesus in what we read. Then we worship him—we tell him (or sing it with a favorite worship song) who we believe him to be, describing the beauty we taste in him from what we've read. We do this out loud whenever we can, making it a courageous proclamation, not a safe and silent assent.

- **In the midst of our darkness (whatever form it takes) we reject inertia and "do the next thing we know to do."** I learned this truth from George MacDonald, the 19th-century Scottish author, poet, and pastor whose gospel-infused fantasy novels were the magnet that drew C.S. Lewis to Jesus. Of him, Lewis wrote: "I know hardly any other writer who seems to be closer, or more continually close, to the Spirit of Christ Himself." [7] In the years after I graduated from college, I read every one of MacDonald's more than 50 books, immersing myself in his prophetic value system. "Do the next thing you know to do" is one of his core convictions, and he threads it into every one of his books, including his novel *The Seaboard Parish.*

  In the story, a father tries to help his teenage daughter discern her calling in life by offering this advice: "What God may hereafter require of you, you must not give yourself the least trouble about. Everything He gives you to do, you must do as well as ever you can. That is the best possible preparation for what He may want you to do next. If people would but do what they have to do, they would always find themselves ready for what came next." [8]

  After his wife died in the mid-1980s, leaving him alone with two young sons to parent and a church to pastor, Timothy Smith was heartbroken, confused, and uncertain of what to do next. In the midst of his darkness, Smith recalled his father's favorite advice: "You do what comes next, and do the best you can." Soon after, he rammed into this same advice while reading MacDonald's novel. And so, he says, "After Melodee died, I decided I'd do the next thing. Getting breakfast ready. Getting the boys off to school. Heading off to work. Not worrying about tomorrow, but doing the next thing. I left the rest to God."[9] This was an act of defiance in the face of his fears, a protest of beauty from his own bomb crater.

- **We open our needs to a community of warriors, rather than muscling through on our own.** As the Gentile woman well knew, exposing our needs to others requires risky vulnerability, especially when others don't seem inclined to respond tenderly. To ask for help is an act of courage. Leaning into Jesus instead of away from him when we're plunged into darkness means we haul that darkness into the light.

> *To ask for help is an act of courage.*

When my wife called me at work to tell me her latest mammogram detected an oval mass that required immediate attention, the first thing I did after hanging up was ask a large online community of friends and warriors to intercede on her behalf. I did this in spite of my subtle reluctance to appear needy, a protective reflex that grows like a weed deep in my soul. Inviting others to fight with us is a protest of beauty, because it propels us into a dependence on Jesus (through his body) at the very time our trust in him is threatened.

Leaning into Jesus instead of away from him when we face great fear is risky because it feels unsafe to open ourselves to a God who has already disappointed us. But this is the kind of courage that "kicks at the darkness until it bleeds daylight,"[10] an iconic phrase from a Bruce Cockburn song that would make Winston Churchill smile.

**6. Take the risk to face your fears, refusing to back down when the going gets tough.** As the Gentile woman knew, it takes courage to stand our ground when the whole world seems arrayed against us. When movement feels impossible, standing is an act of war against retreat.

Never was this truth more evident than when America was in the throes of the Great Depression. In great need of a leader who understood how to help it stand "when the day of evil comes," the country elected Franklin D. Roosevelt. In his famous 1933 inaugural address, FDR began by saying, "First of all, let me assert my firm belief that the only thing we have to fear is fear itself—nameless, unreasoning, unjustified terror which paralyzes needed efforts to convert retreat into advance."[11]

By the end of World War II, FDR's determination to stand against fear had laid a foundation for victory over evil and launched the world into a long season of growth and prosperity. A year after the end of the war, the classic holiday film *It's a Wonderful Life* was released. In the story, a villainous robber baron named Henry F. Potter tries to expand his small-town financial empire. Fear sparks a run on the banks on the eve of the Depression, so Potter seizes the opportunity to take over all of the financial institutions in town. Only the owner of the town's Building and Loan, George Bailey (a subtle archetype for FDR), refuses to cave in to the pressure to sell out. When Potter promises all of Bailey's customers 50 cents on the dollar for their investment shares, the desperate crowd panics. But Bailey physically blocks the door to his business to plead with them to stand...

> Now wait...now listen...now listen to me. I beg of you not to do this thing. If Potter gets hold of this Building and Loan, there'll never be another decent house built in this town. He's already got charge of the bank. He's got the bus line. He's got the department stores. And now he's after us. Why? Well, it's very simple. Because we're cutting in on his business, that's why. And because he wants to keep you living in his slums and paying the kind of rent he decides.
>
> *(The people are still trying to get out, but some of them are standing still, listening to him. George has begun to make an impression on them.)*
>
> Joe, you lived in one of his houses, didn't you? Well, have you forgotten? Have you forgotten what he charged you for that broken-down shack?
>
> *(To Ed)* Here, Ed. You know, you remember last year when things weren't going so well, and you couldn't make your payments? You didn't lose your house, did you? Do you think Potter would have let you keep it?
>
> *(Turns to address the room again)* Can't you understand what's happening here? Don't you see what's happening? Potter isn't selling. Potter's buying! And why? Because we're panicky and he's not. That's why. He's picking up some bargains. Now we can get through this thing all right. We've got to stick together, though. We've got to have faith in each other. [12]

To stand when the going gets tough, we *slow down* in the face of fear so we can find our footing. Panic produces behavior that's inconsistent with our true character. The drowning person who attempts to drag his rescuer down is not a murderer, but panic produces murderous behavior. So we slow down, take a deep breath, and remember what we're standing on—the "foundation stone" prophesied in the Old Testament book of Isaiah and realized in the person of Jesus. Jesus is the granite surface under our feet. And we stand on that foundation when we acknowledge our fears but refuse to obey them. "Even dogs are allowed to eat the scraps that fall beneath their masters' table" are the words of a woman standing on granite. And like her, we stand in the face of fear when…

- **We remind ourselves of the more than 200 promises Jesus has spoken over us,** including: "You will do greater things than these" and "The very hairs on your head are all numbered" and "If you give up your life for me, you will find it" and "I will give you the right words at the right time" and "Those who want to kill your body…cannot touch your soul" and "If you sinful people know how to give good gifts to your children, how much more will your heavenly Father give good gifts to those who ask him" and "People who hear God's word and cling to it" will "produce a huge harvest" and "Forgive others, and you will be forgiven."

  Here's an everyday way to soak in these truths: Copy "The Promises of Jesus" on page 218 and post the list on your refrigerator. Each morning, choose a promise to focus on. Then, as you go through your day, every time you drive through a green light, simply thank Jesus for "the promise of the day." Every time you're waiting at a red light, simply talk to Jesus about a roadblock in your life (a lie you believe about yourself or a fear you're holding onto). If you use public transportation, do something similar at every subway or bus stop, alternating what you do at each stop.

- **We trust in the teachings of Jesus, not our circumstances.** Jesus says, "Anyone who listens to my teaching and follows it is wise, like a person who builds a house on solid rock. Though the rain comes in torrents and the floodwaters rise and the winds beat against that house, it won't collapse because it is built on bedrock" (Matthew 7:24-25). The bricks of the foundation beneath our feet are fashioned from Jesus' teachings, and the mortar that holds them together is our determination to follow those teachings. For example, when circumstances press us to worry, we trust Jesus' teaching instead: "Do not worry about your life…Look at the birds of the air; they do not sow or reap or store away in barns, and yet your heavenly Father feeds them. Are you not much more valuable than they?" (Matthew 6:25-26, NIV). He will be a bulwark against the anxieties that press in on us if we will embrace his prerequisite: to listen to and follow his teachings.

- **We fight back against the spiritual forces of fear that Paul calls the "mighty powers in this dark world."** To do this, we'll need what Paul calls the "armor of God" so that we can "resist the enemy in the time of evil" (Ephesians 6:10-17). Paul is urging us to wear what Jesus has modeled for us—the *truths* he's revealed, the *righteousness* he conveys to us, the *peace* that comes from knowing he was sent to rescue us, the confidence we have in *his heart,* the protection we're given by the *salvation* he's won for us, and the weapon he's given us in *his words.* Armor implies warfare, plain and simple. We don't like to think about everyday life as a battleground, but it undeniably is—and no good king sends warriors into the fray unprotected and unarmed. For more on what this looks like on a practical level, check out John Eldredge's *Waking the Dead* or *Spurgeon on Prayer & Spiritual Warfare* by Charles Spurgeon. Paul adds an important imperative to his battle instructions: "Pray in the Spirit at all times and on every occasion" (Ephesians 6:18). We do not fight or stand alone. When I'm battling to stand my ground, I'm whispering this to the Invisible Rabbi all day long: *Jesus, have mercy on me. Jesus, have mercy on me. Jesus, have mercy on me.*

## BEYOND ADAM AND EVE

It is in God's nature to risk, because intimate relationships require it. Vulnerability, by definition, exposes our tender core to betrayal and abuse and disappointment. In the face of these exorbitant costs, trust is a miracle. But intimacy is God's end game—not merely the restoration of the kind of relationship he had with Adam and Eve "in the cool of the garden," but a trusting friendship that's deeper than was possible for the first human beings. They had no concrete reason to distrust the heart of God; we often do. So when we trust Jesus, even though we have reason to cave in to the challenges we face in everyday life, we're speaking the lover's language of risk.

> *It is in God's nature to risk, because intimate relationships require it.*

# QUESTIONS FOR SMALL-GROUP DISCUSSION OR INDIVIDUAL CONTEMPLATION

1. This chapter opens with a quotation from Søren Kierkegaard: "To dare is to lose one's footing momentarily. Not to dare is to lose oneself." When have you taken an important risk and momentarily lost your footing? And when have you failed to take a risk and "lost yourself" as a result?

_____

_____

_____

_____

2. In what ways has the "Be safe" message of our culture influenced your life?

_____

_____

_____

3. What's one way you've experienced Jesus taking a great risk with you, and what was the outcome?

_____

_____

_____

_____

4. What's one way you've risked to give what you have to give in your life, and what was the outcome?

_____

_____

_____

5. When have you welcomed trouble into your life instead of avoiding it? Why did you do it, and how did you grow because of it?

_____

_____

_____

6. When you're in the midst of a challenge or threat, do you tend to draw near to Jesus or keep him at a distance, and why?

_____

_____

_____

7. Tell a story about a time you refused to back down from a fear.

_____

_____

_____

_____

1   Erin Hill, "6-Year-Old Girl Paralyzed After Backbend Takes First Steps Since Injury," *People* magazine (January 12, 2017).

2   Kenneth Olmstead and Aaron Smith, "Americans and Cybersecurity," Pew Research Center website (January 26, 2017).

3   Jon Austin, "Anonymous Hacks 'Illuminati' Placing Warning on Mysterious Bilderberg Group Website," *Express* digital magazine (January 5, 2017).

4   Sara Groves, *Add to the Beauty* (New York: Sony BMG, October 4, 2005).

5   "Cellist of Sarajevo Story," (SoundFaith.com).

6   Musician Sara Groves used Vedran Smajlovic's story as the basis of her song "Why It Matters," and called what he did a "protest of beauty."

7   C.S. Lewis, from the preface to *George Macdonald: An Anthology* (New York: Macmillan Publishing Company, 1947), xxx-xxxi.

8   George MacDonald, *The Seaboard Parish* (Wheaton, Illinois: Victor Books, a division of SP Publications, Inc., 1983), 9-10.

9   Dr. Timothy Smith, "Doe the Next Thynge" (www.waterfromrock.org, January 19, 2015).

10   Bruce Cockburn, "Lovers in a Dangerous Time" (A&M Records, 1984).

11   Franklin Delano Roosevelt, 1933 Inaugural Address (www.historymatters.gmu.edu).

12   Philip Van Doren Stern, Frances Goodrich, Albert Hackett, Frank Capra, Jo Swerling, and Michael Wilson, *It's a Wonderful Life* (Liberty Films (II), 1946).

# CHAPTER 3

# FINDING THE GOOD IN THE HARD

## THE JOURNEY INTO SPIRITUAL GRIT

The source of our character, and of our good impact on the world, is always tied to the strength we gain when we walk through hard things in life. We naturally shy away from tough stuff, but in this chapter you'll discover the good hiding behind every hardship and learn how to gain a treasure that can never be taken away.

"It is easy to hate, and it is difficult to love. This is how the whole scheme of things works. All good things are difficult to achieve; and bad things are very easy to get." —*Confucius*

"The way is hard that leads to life."
—*Jesus (Matthew 7:14, ESV)*

### The Rich Man

As Jesus was starting out on his way to Jerusalem, a man came running up to him, knelt down, and asked, "Good Teacher, what must I do to inherit eternal life?"

"Why do you call me good?" Jesus asked. "Only God is truly good. But to answer your question, you know the commandments: 'You must not murder. You must not commit adultery. You must not steal. You must not testify falsely. You must not cheat anyone. Honor your father and mother.'"

"Teacher," the man replied, "I've obeyed all these commandments since I was young."

Looking at the man, Jesus felt genuine love for him. "There is still one thing you haven't done," he told him. "Go and sell all your possessions and give the money to the poor, and you will have treasure in heaven. Then come, follow me."

At this the man's face fell, and he went away sad, for he had many possessions.

Jesus looked around and said to his disciples, "How hard it is for the rich to enter the Kingdom of God!" This amazed them. But Jesus said again, "Dear children, it is very hard to enter the Kingdom of God. In fact, it is easier for a camel to go through the eye of a needle than for a rich person to enter the Kingdom of God!"

The disciples were astounded. "Then who in the world can be saved?" they asked.

Jesus looked at them intently and said, "Humanly speaking, it is impossible. But not with God. Everything is possible with God" (Mark 10:17-27).

Western culture has an obesity problem, the result of a sedentary lifestyle and undisciplined eating habits. To address it, many of us maintain our physical health by going to the gym, furiously pedaling our bikes (never getting anywhere) because we know the grueling work will ultimately be worth it. And likewise, we need a fitness regimen to combat our obesity of the soul. I mean, we learn to embrace and even appreciate soul hardships because they help us stay spiritually fit. Gritty fit.

> *To combat our obesity of the soul, we learn to embrace and even appreciate soul hardships because they help us stay spiritually fit.*

This is the point Paul is making when he celebrates his own hardships in his second letter to the Christians in Corinth:

> In everything we do, we show that we are true ministers of God. We patiently endure troubles and hardships and calamities of every kind. We have been beaten, been put in prison, faced angry mobs, worked to exhaustion, endured sleepless nights, and gone without food. We prove ourselves by our purity, our understanding, our patience, our kindness, by the Holy Spirit within us, and by our sincere love. We faithfully preach the truth. God's power is working in us. We use the weapons of righteousness in the right hand for attack and the left hand for defense. We serve God whether people honor us or despise us, whether they slander us or praise us. We are honest, but they call us impostors. We are ignored, even though we are well known. We live close to death, but we are still alive. We have been beaten, but we have not been killed. Our hearts ache, but we always have joy. We are poor, but we give spiritual riches to others. We own nothing, and yet we have everything (2 Corinthians 6:4-10).

Paul doesn't *enjoy* angry mobs, beatings, imprisonment, sleepless nights and hunger, but he *values* the endurance they're producing in him (maybe this is why the French word *blesser* means "to wound or hurt"). Later, Paul tells the Jesus-followers in Colossae: "Now I rejoice in my sufferings for your sake, and in my flesh I do my share on behalf of His body, which is the church, in filling up what is lacking in Christ's afflictions" (Colossians 1:24, NASB). The grit that is growing in Paul, born out of a determination "to know nothing but Jesus Christ," is a source of strength, encouragement, and growth to those he serves.

Hard is bad, if your standard for bad is anything that threatens your comfort. Hard is good, if your standard for good is anything that gives you the strength to participate with Jesus in setting captives free. This is not work for the faint-hearted. It requires courage to face and overcome the captivity that we experience ourselves and that we see in others. And there's only one way to grow our courage: a fitness regimen designed to increase spiritual grit.

> *Hard is bad, if your standard for bad is anything that threatens your comfort. Hard is good, if your standard for good is anything that gives you the strength to participate with Jesus in setting captives free.*

In Jesus' encounter with the rich young man, we get a tour of the Cornerstone Gym—owned, operated, and managed by a guy nicknamed "the Rock of Offense" (Romans 9:33, NASB). Jesus is moving through Judea on his way to Jerusalem, when a wealthy young man races to stop him, then kneels before him to ask what seems like an honest and even desperate question: "What must I do to inherit eternal life?" Because the man first calls him "good teacher," Jesus (perhaps with a wry smile) first toys with him, asking if he realizes that it's only appropriate to describe God as good. The subtle message, from the beginning of their conversation, is that this unsuspecting man is about to tangle with the ultimate Personal Trainer, so strap it on. Jesus genuinely loves the man, so he invites him into a challenge that is hard to comprehend. Jesus sets the bar so high—*sell everything, give to the poor, and follow me*—that even those who have seen him do the inexplicable are amazed and astounded.

To understand what's really going on here, we must embrace a fundamental truth that Jesus lives out with every needy person he meets: **Hard = Good.** Some hardships crack open the door of our soul to something beautiful. Of course, it's entirely human to gravitate to our default setting, which is Hard = Bad. But in the kingdom of God, where redemption is the air we breathe, good things are often disguised as hard things, and tough stuff is like a crowbar in the hands of a Jesus who is bent on renovating our fixer-upper souls. Because he loves us, he often introduces hardship into our lives. It's counterintuitive, unless we pay better attention to what we actually need to live a life of joy, purpose, and impact. At the heart of spiritual grit: **Hard = Good.**

> *Tough stuff is like a crowbar in the hands of a Jesus who is bent on renovating our fixer-upper souls.*

# THE HERO'S JOURNEY

The stories we love the most share a classic narrative: The hero must transcend a great struggle or challenge, pushing through fear to emerge the victor. That hero's greatest asset is always a catalyzing *presence*, not a catalyzing *idea*. Think Frodo, Katniss, Hawkeye, Darcy, Jack Bauer, Hermione, Han Solo, Dorothy from *The Wizard of Oz*, and any protagonist you've ever loved in any book, film, or story. The hero's heart produces a powerful *presence*, the same way the sun's mass produces a gravitational pull on everything in our solar system.

Mythologist Joseph Campbell has mapped out the 12 steps that define what he calls "The Hero's Journey." In his version of the common plot devices shared by every heroic narrative, the journey begins with an ordinary person who at first resists the call to a challenging adventure. A guiding figure—the mentor—shows up to give the hero what he needs to start the journey, and he's immediately confronted by dangers and difficulties. He meets new friends and foes along the way and must discern between the two as his strength and courage are tested again and again. Soon he's confronted by a fear he must overcome; Campbell calls it the "approach to the inmost cave." Here the hero's greatest anxieties, tied to a "supreme ordeal," will either reveal his strength or force him back from the precipice of risk. And when he moves into and through his anxiety, he is "transformed into a new state, emerging from battle as a stronger person, and often with a prize." [1]

The hero's journey is all about transcending the anxiety produced by the dangers and difficulties of life, revealing an essence in us that's magnetic and trustworthy and inspiring. Screenwriter Dan Bronzite says, "In the final stage of the Hero's Journey, he returns home to his Ordinary World a changed man. He will have grown as a person, learned many things, faced many terrible dangers and even death, but now looks forward to the start of a new life. His return may bring fresh hope to those he left behind, a direct solution to their problems, or perhaps a new perspective for everyone to consider...Ultimately the Hero will return to where he started, but things will clearly never be the same again." [2]

As human beings, we're drawn to this narrative arc, again and again, because we are enticed by this truth embedded in it: *The growth of our good impact in the world has little to do with greater mastery of tips and techniques, and everything to do with the revelation of our life-changing presence.*

It's our presence—the unseen power that radiates from our renovated heart—that seeds transformation and redemption and mission-mindedness. The hero's journey is really our journey in this crucial way:

We are all called by Jesus to discover and harness our core strength in the crucible of our fear. If we're his followers, then we're following him into dangers and difficulties that will surface our deepest anxieties. We'll approach our inmost cave and face our supreme ordeal, as he helps us find our heart's capacity for spiritual grit in him. Jesus uses hard things to first surface, then deconstruct, then reveal our essence. We become who we really are, distinct from those who surround us, when we move through hard things into wonder and then worship.

> *Jesus uses hard things to first surface, then deconstruct, then reveal our essence.*

## THE REVELATION OF THE TRUE YOU

After a long season of struggle in our marriage, punctuated by a three-month separation and twice-weekly counseling sessions, my wife and I had managed to reach a kind of stable cease-fire. I didn't fully understand it at the time, but the primary source of the conflicts that led us to separate was my inability to maintain my independent identity in the context of an intimate relationship. Growing up, I'd been immersed in an environment infected by narcissism, where my formative influences were perpetually self-focused and my heart seemed invisible. Because children treat the authority figures in their lives like mirrors, I developed a deep belief that I had a *hollow nothing* where my core should have been, and that belief was undermining my ability to connect intimately with my wife. I didn't know how to maintain my emotional boundaries, so I lived in a near-constant state of *purple*. I mean, if I was red and she was blue, I was perpetually mixing the two colors into a coagulated mess.

After months of conflicts fueled by my desperate need for my wife to prop me up and breathe life into my empty core, she asked me to move out of the house while we sorted through our next steps. A formal separation represented my deepest fear; because of my Velcro approach to intimate relationships, I didn't know how to separate my identity from hers. A break in our relationship meant a loss of *me*.

While we were separated, we met often with Carl, our counselor, sometimes alone and sometimes together. Two months into my "dark night of the soul," in the middle of an appointment with Carl, the pain I was experiencing in my relationship with my wife forced my deep wounding to the surface. The insidious lie about my core identity—the lie that I had nothing where my heart was supposed to be—rose in my soul like vomit. I couldn't stop the cascading, explosive sobs that began shaking my body, so I told Carl and my wife that I had to leave. I got in my car and drove a few blocks then parked by an empty field until the shaking subsided.

In the weeks that followed, I experienced breakthroughs in my dysfunctional patterns of relating to my wife. What had been hidden in my soul was now out in the light, and it didn't have the power over me it once did. I was able to move back home because my wife could sense something deep within me was changing. But even as a new hope took hold in our relationship, I knew it was a tenuous momentum. I needed something like a boot camp for recovering purple people—people who have lost all sense of their souls' boundaries.

> *What had been hidden in my soul was now out in the light, and it didn't have the power over me it once did.*

Because Jesus is kind to us when we don't understand what will help us the most, he gave me a gift that I didn't want, so hard to receive that I could barely tolerate it.

Our pastor, a man I deeply respected, announced he was starting a 12-week men's group led by one of his close friends, a counselor and chaplain for several professional sports teams. The group was unusual because it was fee-based and counselor-led. Even so, most men in the church decided to give it a shot. At our first meeting in my home, the counselor asked us to each take a few minutes to tell our stories. So we went around the circle until we got to an older man who'd been a lifelong missionary. As he told his story, he focused again and again on the recent betrayal of one of his primary supporters who had inexplicably pulled his financial backing. The missionary told this story with only a hint of bitterness and said all the things Christians are supposed to say when something hard has happened. When the man finished his story, the leader looked around at us and asked, "What did you think of this story?" Most of us expressed compassion, support, and encouragement, exactly what you'd expect a group of good Christian men to say when one of their own experiences hardship. But the leader looked more and more angry as he heard these responses, finally declaring, "Well, I can't tell you how disappointed I am in all of you." Pointing to the missionary, he said, "I experienced this man as full of unexpressed rage, demanding sympathy from all of you, and hiding his outrage under a passive-aggressive façade."

The room was dead quiet. In a heartbeat we'd moved from the expected, predictable, and safe environment of male collusion to the dangerous environment of raw honesty. By "collusion," I mean that we all sensed, under the surface, that this man was venting his rage in the guise of acceptable Christian complaint, and our responses helped enable that subterfuge. In that moment every one of us in that room felt unsafe, in the best sense of that word.

Jesus told his disciples, "The time is coming when everything that is covered up will be revealed, and all that is secret will be made known to all. Whatever you have said in the dark will be heard in the light, and what you have whispered behind closed doors will be shouted from the housetops for all to hear!" (Luke 12:2-3). Well, our time had come. Everything we were hiding in the dark, we knew, was about to be hauled into the light, and it was terrifying. Some of the men in that room left the group, a few stayed but rarely opened their mouths, and a few more stepped off the cliff and showed themselves. I was among that last group, and the process of showing everyone the "nothing" at my core was one of the scariest things I've ever done.

But something happened in this "valley of the shadow of death." The baseline anxiety I'd learned to live with all my life began to dissipate. I hated every minute of my time in that group because it was so hard. But I knew what was happening was setting me free from the captivity of my fluid boundaries and my compromised core. When everything in the dark was dragged into the light, something solid and strong emerged in my soul. I no longer had to expend massive amounts of energy to tamp down my interior reality and maintain my elaborate façade. I found an emerging congruence in my heart, where my true identity began to surface and my resolve to maintain my "cell walls" was growing. My ability to be emotionally intimate with my wife grew right alongside this emerging reality. She sensed a growing non-anxious presence in me. And that makes perfect sense, because the revelation of our gritty core gives us the ability to attach to others without consuming them or being consumed by them.

"Hard" rescued me from destruction.

## STATIONS OF SPIRITUAL GRIT

A typical health club has two or three dozen different types of fitness machines designed to strengthen a diversity of body parts. No matter what muscle group it targets, every machine uses resistance to build strength. If we do not experience resistance when we're working out, we're not going to get stronger. **Hard = Good.**

So imagine we're about to try out an array of resistance exercises that will strengthen our core. Some of these exercises have an overlapping focus on a certain soul-muscle group, and not all will fit your particular soul-fitness needs. But all will help you grow in your spiritual grit, and some will show you how to help others grow. So decide which fitness options work for you, then do something that makes your soul sweat a little.

**1. Throw surprise parties for *hard* things.** Hard = Good is a simple truth and is easy to remember, so I've managed to infect my family with it. When a hard thing comes up, sometimes I hear them reference Hard = Good before I have a chance to. And because it's repeated and embraced and referred to often in our home, we are slowly morphing our challenges from monsters we fear and grumble about to trainers we respect and honor. The key to this is finding simple ways to *celebrate* the hard stuff in our lives. Here are two brief examples that can fuel your own creativity:

• Grit researcher Angela Duckworth told an interviewer that in her family, every member is encouraged to work on something difficult as an everyday practice. They each have freedom to choose whatever appeals to them, but Duckworth says whatever they target, it must include "deliberate practice almost daily." They set a beginning and an end point for each activity, and quitting isn't allowed. [3]

 This sparked an idea in me. I bought a small, magnetic whiteboard with a dry-erase marker and mounted it on our refrigerator door. I wrote "Do Hard Things" at the top and each of our names down the left side, with a large space to the right of each name. Then I asked my wife and daughters to simply write, every week, one hard thing they're facing. Every Sunday we wipe the board clean and start over. At first my daughters had to get over the weirdness of this idea (they are, after all, easily embarrassed teenagers), but after a few weeks it became a habit. The effect of this little addition to our household rhythms has been a subtle shift toward celebrating the hard things we're facing. And because the whiteboard is in a prominent place, it helps us support one another in prayer and captures the attention of friends when they come to visit. Hard = Good is now part of our family value system.

• In our suburban neighborhood, many parents know that child-development experts extol the virtues of learning to play a musical instrument. We drank that Kool-Aid, too, and want live music to be part of the soundtrack of our home. So we bought a keyboard at a garage sale and started both girls on piano lessons when they were very young. Eventually, we managed to buy a real piano for them. Meanwhile, many of their friends were also taking piano lessons— almost all of them grumbling about it, just as our girls sometimes did. Most parents are willing to tolerate grumbling for a season, and none of these kids quit piano lessons in the first year. But we noticed a startling trend as they were all approaching their 12<sup>th</sup> birthdays (including our own Emma). As if an internal switch was flipped, a lot of them ramped up their dislike of piano-playing, and their exasperated parents finally pulled the plug on lessons. The result: There are a lot of dormant pianos and keyboards stored in basements in our neighborhood.

We responded to similar ramped-up pressure from Emma by celebrating the beauty of the music she was producing and openly reiterating the high value we place on mastering an instrument. We were determined to face and overcome the "12-year itch," so we simply told Emma that no, she wouldn't be allowed to quit. (We tried to say that with a smile.) She's 15 now, still playing piano, and still grumbling about it some weeks. But sometimes we're surprised to hear her playing when she doesn't have to, smiling when she doesn't think we're watching. Celebrating hard things means modeling the importance of a long-term payoff in spite of the short-term grind.

Sometimes spiritual grit requires a determination to honor the beauty of a flower *before* it blooms. Jesus, it turns out, is the chief practitioner of this discipline—Jesus, "who for the joy set before him endured the cross" (Hebrews 12:2, NIV).

**2. Embrace brutal realities, and avoid the temptation to spin.**
After a painful divorce, writer Glennon Doyle Melton was speaking at a conference when a woman in the audience stood up to confess she felt like an utter failure because she was unable to hold her family together, and her little boy was hurting as a result. Melton noticed many women in the crowd nodding their heads, and she realized they were all thinking, *None of us can keep our children out of harm's way.* So she asked the woman to offer three words to describe the kind of man she hoped her boy would grow into, and the woman listed "kind, wise, and resilient." Melton responded with a question: "What does a human have to confront in life in order to earn those characteristics?" After an awkward silence, she answered her own question: "Pain! Struggle. It's not about having *nothing* to overcome. It's overcoming and overcoming and overcoming yet again…Is it possible that we're trying to protect our kids from the one thing that will allow them to become the people we dream they'll be?" [4]

We subtly and unconsciously plant seeds of weakness in the people we care about when we habitually shy away from brutal realities. We spin the truth about things because it seems more compassionate and hopeful to do that, but avoiding brutal realities undermines hope and makes compassion a sham. Our family learned this lesson the hard way.

*We subtly and unconsciously plant seeds of weakness in the people we care about when we habitually shy away from brutal realities.*

For years we'd been protecting our girls from a hard, extended-family reality, making decisions that made no sense to them because we were afraid to tell them the real reasons behind them. One day we brought up our dilemma with a family counselor, and she was adamant: "In the absence of the truth, your girls are filling in the gap with their own truth, because they have to resolve the dissonance they feel. Sit them down and tell them what's really going on. You'll be surprised how well they handle it, and you'll help them to do the hard things they need to do as members of your family."

And so we did just what the counselor advised. The impact was profound. At the time, our youngest daughter needed only a Cliffs Notes version, but our older daughter got a more detailed explanation. Then she said, "Now it all makes sense. I know what you're doing has to be done. I'll help."

Whenever we're in the midst of something hard, and it's important to describe or explain it to others, assume it's best to lean toward brutal reality rather than the spin cycle. First try out how you'll say it; then edit yourself until you feel confident enough to take a shot. If you can't conceive of an appropriate, respectful way to convey a brutal reality, then back off until you can. Jesus, by the way, is the king of brutal reality. He's the one who offered these little gems, a sampler I put together by just randomly flipping to two pages in the Gospel of Matthew: "Haven't you read the Scriptures?" "Whoever divorces his wife and marries someone else commits adultery." "Why ask me about what is good?" "That's what my heavenly Father will do to you if you refuse to forgive your brothers and sisters from your heart." "Humanly speaking, it is impossible." "Many who are the greatest now will be least important then."

We can't be with Jesus more than five minutes without hearing a brutal reality come out of his mouth. And this is the more authentic, life-giving way of relating that the Invisible Rabbi is trying to form in us, right now.

> *Whenever we're in the midst of something*
> *hard, and it's important to describe or*
> *explain it to others, assume it's best*
> *to lean toward brutal reality rather*
> *than the spin cycle.*

**3. Start your day with a wake-up call for your soul.** After you get out of bed, and before you enter into the meat of your day, set the tone for your soul by doing something hard—but make it something tiny, something that takes little time and effort.

For example, before I eat breakfast, I go outside to pick up our newspaper on the driveway. While I'm out there, I spend two or three minutes pulling weeds from the landscaping that borders our house. I don't like pulling weeds, so doing it incrementally like this helps me maintain our yard and gives me the satisfaction of completing something hard before I have to face larger challenges throughout the day.

The trick is to make whatever you do a seamless practice, not an annoying interruption. And it's important to make it short, simple to pull off, and within the normal rhythm of your day. A mildly challenging thing at the beginning of your day—and almost anything you do will qualify—reminds your soul that you intend to *lean into* hard. For example:

- Respond to an email you put off yesterday.

- Complete a two-minute chore.

- Repair or maintain something small that you've neglected for more than a few days.

- Serve someone in your household with a kindness that costs less than five minutes (or if you live alone, serve a pet, a neighbor, or your community).

- Write a short note of gratitude and hide it in a lunchbox, a briefcase, or a purse for someone to discover later in the day.

- Complete something—anything—that you stopped midstream.

- Spend 30 seconds talking to Jesus about a challenge or a need someone in your life is facing.

- Take one minute to prioritize, in writing, three things you need to finish during the day.

- Do something that will bless someone in your household but can never be traced back to you.

- Spend exactly one minute straightening up messes in your home—see how much you can do in a minute.

The idea is to prime your grit-pump in some minor way at the start of your day. You have an alarm clock that wakes you physically, so do something a little bit hard soon after you get up to wake up your soul and prepare it for leaning into the difficulties that are sure to come your way.

**4. Follow through on the *easy-hard* things that crop up throughout your day.** The other day I was driving slightly behind a woman in the next lane, and I noticed that one of her back tires was almost flat. How far would I go to warn her? I asked Jesus to give us a red light (that must have sounded strange to him, coming from me) so I could roll down my window and get her attention. Sure enough, the light turned red, and using the universal sign language for "roll down your window," I managed to tell her about her tire. A couple of days later I did the same thing for a driver whose rear windshield wiper was stuck going back and forth on a sunny day. These micro-moments cost me a few seconds and a little bit of awkwardness, but what I did helped these people.

I call opportunities like this Doing Easy-Hard Things; they're so small we soon forget we did them, but they can have a big impact on others. These easy-hard opportunities are also easy to ignore unless we're paying attention to the Invisible Rabbi and living with a lean toward hard.

- You're taking a walk and see landscape rocks or bark that has spilled onto the sidewalk, so you stop to kick it back where it belongs.

- You see a crumpled can lying in the street or on the sidewalk, and you pick it up to recycle it.

- You're in line at the grocery store or Starbucks or the gas station and you notice someone who's in a hurry, so you offer your place in line.

- When someone you don't know rings your doorbell—a salesman, solicitor, or worker—you're the first to volunteer to get the door.

- You walk with your head up so you can look people in the eye as they pass by, a simple act that's harder than it sounds. Most people feel alone in the crowd, so warm eye contact can offer them a micro-blessing.

- You're funny, so you find opportunities to crack a joke when others are struggling with something—in a fitness class, study session, while waiting in a line, in a tough business meeting, or on public transportation.

- You hear someone give the wrong directions or the wrong reference to something or the wrong date or the wrong name, and you politely offer a correction.

- You see someone heading toward the door you've just opened, and they're far enough away that it would not seem impolite to let the door close behind you, but you pause to hold open the door anyway. Most often, when I do this, people feel compelled to hurry because they're embarrassed that I'm waiting to serve them. I'm quick to say, "No need to hurry—I'm having a contemplative moment."

- You're sitting in a public place and notice someone leaving their seat, forgetting to take something they brought with them. So you pick up what they left behind and return it to them.

- And a few ideas just for kids: Put away something you didn't get out, clean something you didn't get dirty, finish a chore someone else started, help someone without being asked, and say thank you to someone who's taken for granted.

Do these examples seem so small and insignificant that you have to suppress your inner cynic right now? I get it. But it's good to remember that Jesus treats small things like big things. Like the mustard seed he uses as a metaphor for how things work in the kingdom of God, the tiniest things can have the biggest impact. Jesus explains, "If you are faithful in little things, you will be faithful in large ones" (Luke 16:10). And if we want to keep our souls in grit-fit shape, the small and insignificant opportunities for resistance training will help do the job. When, prompted by the Invisible Rabbi, you leave your comfort zone to offer help or fix a problem, you've just injected a micro-hardship into your life.

**5. Welcome opportunities to feel unbalanced, and inject healthy unbalance into the lives of those you love.** "If you watch judo," says *Uplifting Service* author Ron Kaufman, "it's the opposite of boxing… In judo, if someone throws a punch, you use the momentum in a way they don't expect so that it causes them, for a moment, to come off balance. And in their moment off balance, you have the opportunity to influence the future of that situation." [5] Whenever you disrupt the status quo or respond in tough situations with unexpected courage, you create the kind of imbalance that builds strength. And whenever you try something new, meet someone new, taste something new, or visit someplace new, you have introduced imbalance into your life. The more you embrace the beauty of imbalance in your life, the more you will grow the core strength that helps you maintain balance.

Years ago, as part of my recommitment to living a healthier lifestyle, I started going to three regular classes at a health club. One of them is called BodyPump; it's a weight training class that involves high numbers of repetitions and a little bit of cardio training. One of the regulars, a man in his 60s, always stands on a half-dome, padded Bosu Ball for a portion of the workout. The half-dome makes it harder for him to complete the exercises because he's always fighting to keep himself from teetering one way or the other. He's intentionally injecting imbalance into his workout and building his core strength as a result.

Daryl Davis is a blues musician whose true legacy is buried under a pile of Ku Klux Klan robes and memorabilia. Davis is a black boogie-woogie piano player who's played backup to Chuck Berry, Jerry Lee Lewis, and B.B. King over the course of a long career. But for decades he's also been doing something that has profoundly disrupted the battle lines of racial hatred. Under the guidance of the Invisible Rabbi, he befriends members of the Ku Klux Klan, sometimes enduring verbal abuse and physical violence, for the purpose of upending their embedded prejudices. His collection of Klan relics is evidence of his impact, a storehouse of clothing once worn with pride but now offered to Davis as the parting declarations of men who've left the hate group for good. "They're done, they're done," he says, "as a result of meeting me and having these conversations, not overnight, but over time."

Not long ago, Davis drove from his Maryland home to Charlottesville, Virginia, to meet one of the Klan's Imperial Wizards in a place considered ground zero for the violent racial clashes of 2017. When the crowds milling around the courthouse square realized that Davis was talking with Billy Snuffer, a notorious Klan leader, the verbal abuse directed at both of them started to rain down. But Davis engaged the hecklers with grace and patience, even defending Snuffer's right to free speech as an American. On the way home from this tense encounter, Davis' phone rang—it was Snuffer calling to make sure he'd made it home safe. A Klansman calling a black man to express his care and concern? That's redemptive disruption, a lifestyle of imbalance that leads to freedom for captives. [6]

In everyday situations, embracing imbalance might look like this:

- Do something your spouse or BFF loves to do but makes you cringe. Bonus points for doing it with a smile and a good attitude.

- Ask someone who's better at a skill than you are to teach you.

- When you travel to a place you've never been, ask a local about a favorite non-tourist place to eat or play or visit.

- If you normally hang back in conversations, ask a question or offer an insight. If you normally dominate conversations, limit your input to asking questions and simply listening to responses.

- When friends or family members or even (hold on there) strangers mention something hard they're facing, offer to pray for them, on the spot. It's safer to say, "I'll be praying for you"; it's more dangerous (and unbalancing) to say, "Can I pray for you *right now?*"

- Ask someone to do something with you—something you know is a little difficult for that person—with the promise of your enthusiastic companionship as incentive.

- When you're traveling, find a local activity you've never done before and try it.

- When you try out a new restaurant, food truck, or street vendor, ask the server what his or her favorite menu item is and order that, whatever it is.

- If you're a husband, ask your wife how she's feeling about your relationship; if you're a wife, ask your husband how he's feeling about your family's finances. Both questions create an imbalance that can lead to a healthy conversation.

- In a conflict, if you typically respond defensively, ask to hear more instead. Or if you typically respond with resignation and withdrawal, share how you're feeling instead. The imbalance might lead to a breakthrough.

An injection of imbalance in *any* area of your life normalizes imbalance in *every* area of your life, including your relationship with the Invisible Rabbi, who is, by the way, defined by a certain unpredictability: "You know well enough how the wind blows this way and that. You hear it rustling through the trees, but you have no idea where it comes from or where it's headed next. That's the way it is with everyone 'born from above' by the wind of God, the Spirit of God" (John 3:8, MSG).

**6. Imagine worst-case scenarios; then chart a path through them.** When facing a challenge, simply ask yourself, "What's the worst that can happen?" Then quickly brainstorm two or three possibilities. Once you have these consequences to chew on, think through what you'd have to do and how you'd cope if they came true. It's like climbing the hill before you have to climb it—when we drag our fears into the light, they lose their power. Once you've determined that you have a reasonable chance of surviving your worst-case scenario, you're free to enter into a hard challenge with conviction and determination.

In John 16 and Luke 21, Jesus invites his disciples to consider their worst-case scenarios as he's headed to the cross. So that they won't abandon their faith when they have to face hard things down the line, he asks them to chew on these future realities:

- "You will be expelled from the synagogues."

- "Those who kill you will think they are doing a holy service for God."

- "You will weep and mourn over what is going to happen to me."

- "You will be scattered, each one going his own way, leaving me alone."

- "You'll be dragged to prison and face trial against kings and governors."

- "The people closest to you will betray you."

- "You'll be hated by everyone because you follow me."

- "There will be wars and earthquakes and famines and plagues."

- "You'll see terrifying things and miraculous signs from heaven."

Jesus is no Debbie Downer—he has a clear purpose for his list of worst-case scenarios: "I'm telling you these things now, so that when they happen, you will remember my warning" (John 16:4). He's giving them a chance to get their minds around the worst that can happen to them so they can enter into the next phase of their lives with a strength calibrated to face brutal reality.

**7. Fill the void left by others who have retreated from *hard*.** If you're living your life with a lean toward spiritual grit, you'll start noticing obvious "grit gaps" at home, work, and in your community. You'll be aware of something that really needs to be said or done but isn't happening because others have shrunk from tackling whatever it is.

For example, I'm in lots of meetings at work, where we're working out tough strategies for thriving in a challenging business climate. The top leaders of my organization have made it clear they want fearless conversation in these meetings, but of course some things seem off-limits to say. We desperately need to confront reality, but it's much easier to paddle with the current. I've known a few people over the three decades I've served as a leader in my company who can be counted on to say and do the hard thing when it really costs them to do it. I've tried to be one of those people, although I've not always done it very well. But those who are able to clear the fog away from a hard reality and offer a way forward build trust within the whole system, breaking up logjams and stirring the pot before the stew burns.

In the beginning of Jesus' public ministry, his own brothers scoffed at his Messianic claims and tried to thwart his mission. Later, they all came to accept and embrace an astounding truth: The brother they'd grown up with was actually the Son of God. One of those brothers, James, became the leader of the church in Jerusalem after the death and resurrection of Jesus. Early on, a major dispute surfaced that pitted one wing of the church, represented by Paul, Barnabas, and Peter, with another wing, represented by converted Pharisees. The three apostles argued that new Gentile believers should not be expected to be circumcised, while the side dominated by Pharisees was adamant that all new converts should be required to follow the law of Moses. Into this worsening quagmire stepped James, who reminded the Pharisees that the conversion of Gentiles was "exactly what the prophets predicted," quoting from the Old Testament book of Amos. Then he said this: "My judgment is that we should not make it difficult for the Gentiles who are turning to God" (Acts 15:19). That's a mic-drop moment in the early church, brought about by James' willingness to step into fearless conversation.

Say what everyone knows needs to be said, and do what everyone knows needs to be done. But say it or do it in consultation with the Invisible Rabbi, who influenced this wise advice in the Old Testament: "[There is] a time to tear and a time to mend. A time to be quiet and a time to speak" (Ecclesiastes 3:7).

**8. Find a community that prioritizes hard challenges in a context of relational depth.** Both of my daughters became cross-country competitors in high school—but not because they loved to run. It was exactly the opposite, actually. They hated the long, arduous training runs, the aching joints, the injuries, the fear that long-distance running produces, and the sight of fellow competitors spending themselves so completely that they vomited at the finish line. Everything about cross-country training and competing is hard. I played football, basketball, and track in high school, but nothing compares to the awe I feel when I'm cheering for my daughters at a cross-country meet.

As she prepared for her first season on the team, my daughter Emma had the example of her older sister's experience, who spent all of the previous four summers in the team's summer running program. Emma was dreading the 4-, 5-, 6-, and 7-mile training runs, and groaned about it every morning when I drove her to the school parking lot at 7:00. But she did it anyway and kept asking me to drop her off. Why? Well, she loved being part of a community of runners who were all doing a hard thing together.

Community fuels spiritual grit.

The Phoenix, a network of nine "recovery gyms" dotted across the U.S., has been praised by the U.S. Secretary of Health and Human Services as an innovative and extraordinarily effective way to combat opioid addiction. The gym's services are free to anyone who has maintained at least 48 hours of sobriety. Clients participate in trainer-led workouts and outside fitness activities. CEO Scott Strode says, "Each sport we choose has this intrinsic strength that helps people see what they're capable of, which helps them heal the self-esteem wounds so often associated with addiction." The key to Phoenix's success, says Strode, is the power of community. "Phoenix is really how people build community in sobriety, and new identity," he says. "It also allows people to dream about who they can be in recovery…When you climb a mountain with somebody, or you do a hard workout, you build a bond. And in that bond, you build friendships. And those friendships are what help pull you back into recovery…As humans, we heal in community, and we have a need for community. We want to find our tribe, and that's what Phoenix becomes for folks." [7]

Once we find a relational connection with a group of encouraging, determined people, we discover a bond that will keep us going when things get rough. In fact, it's almost impossible to persevere through hardships in isolation, outside of community. Online communities can help, but digital devices remove a layer of human connection we desperately need. Face-to-face communities are essential. Common forms of these hard-but-good groups are focused on physical activities (biking, running, climbing, hiking, fitness, and recreational sports). But charitable organizations, service organizations, neighborhood governing organizations, and social/political movements also work. Look for groups that set the stage for deeper connection by requiring participants to do hard things together.

These real/deep groups are everywhere, but you'll have to sniff them out. You're looking for a person or group that can listen to hard things in a relaxed way and can talk about hard things with genuine honesty. Once you get a whiff of the "spice" you're looking for, find a way to connect and stay connected.

**9. When you start something, follow through to the brick-wall end.** Angela Duckworth's research into the mechanics of grit surfaced follow-through as a crucial delineator between those who have grown their resilience muscles and those who haven't. Follow-through, she says, is a "purposeful, continuous commitment to certain types of activities versus sporadic efforts in diverse areas."[8] For example, in one of her studies, the high school students who earned a top five-point rating for follow-through were typically committed to at least two extracurricular activities for several years (for instance, the yearbook staff and the volleyball team). Students at the other end of the scale had no involvement in any activity for more than one year. Duckworth discovered that this follow-through score was the best predictor (better than standardized test scores or academic rank) of which students would gravitate to a leadership role in college. Duckworth's team also discovered that college GPAs had only a minor connection to adult success, while follow-through trumped all other factors in determining a person's eventual impact in life.

> *Follow-through is a crucial delineator between those who have grown their resilience muscles and those who haven't.*

Most of us have half-finished projects and promises we've abandoned midstream. That's human nature. So this week complete something small that's been sitting there in the back of your mind, unfinished and accusing. Then do it again next week. Don't stop until you hit a brick wall. For example:

- Take a quick inventory of the contents of your closet or your dresser drawers; then find five things you can donate to someone who will appreciate them more than you do.

- Find one room in your home that still has an unfinished project waiting for you—decide on a plan to get it done.

- With your spouse or significant other, get out your calendars and set aside one unchangeable date night each month.

- Sometimes important relationships wither because follow-through gets lost in a thicket of responsibility and over-commitment, so reconnect with a friend with whom you've been out of touch too long.

When you're ready to tackle something a little bigger—for me, it's any project that involves the basement or garage, because they're always much bigger than "small"—steel yourself to mark one thing off your list in the next month. Again, growing spiritual grit in *any* area of your life will often spill over into growing spiritual grit in your life with God; every branch of your life is spiritual when you're rooted in Jesus. So if you can finally clean the basement, maybe you can finally contact your church and ask for an opportunity to serve on the worship team, hospitality team, or finance team. Or maybe you can finally stop long enough to have a conversation with that neighbor you barely know, inviting a deeper connection that can lead to something even deeper.

> *Growing spiritual grit in any area of your life will often spill over into growing spiritual grit in your life with God.*

**10. Refuse to let blame, excuses, or unfair circumstances derail you.** In the Frontline documentary *Life on Parole,* filmmakers follow four recently released inmates for 18 months to track the challenges they face as they reenter society and try to abide by the restrictions set forth by their parole rulings. You'd think life outside of prison would make any parole restrictions feel negligible, but the opposite is true. Most parolees must live where they're told to live, maintain steady employment, stay off alcohol and drugs, report regularly to a parole officer who has permission to pry into every aspect of their lives, and refuse to associate with the people who helped influence their crimes or were listed as victims. And they must maintain these disciplines for years.

It's heartbreaking to watch three of the four people in the documentary break under the pressure and return to prison. Only one of them, a 28-year-old woman named Jessica who's spent most of the last decade in prison, manages to persevere through a nursing assistant program, get a decent-paying job, and reunite with a son who's grown up without her. All four people violate conditions of their parole at least once. But I notice a profound difference in Jessica, relative to the others profiled: *She refuses to blame others or make excuses for her situation or complain about the unfairness of her parole restrictions.*

As the challenges and temptations of life on the outside press in, the three parolees who end up back in prison explain why they chose to violate their parole agreement, and their reasons sound plausible and even reasonable. But when I step back from their explanations, the contrast with Jessica is plain to see. Here's a sampling of "derailing" statements made by the three who return to prison:

- "At that point in time, being on parole, they were dictating to me what I could do with my money that I earned. It was totally embarrassing."

- "Needless to say, I was very, very hurt when I saw the neighborhood that the halfway house was in because it was the neighborhood that I bought heroin in."

- "You know, I'm fairly easygoing. I do what's asked of me. You know, I drink. That doesn't even cause any harm to anybody. But [it] basically brings hell upon me...I don't understand that."

Now contrast the *essence* of these statements with something Jessica says to an interviewer after she's reprimanded by her parole officer for a minor violation: "I came home with a plan, and I actually stuck to it. I didn't let little minor setbacks throw me all the way off. They docked me a little bit, and I got right back up and kept moving."[9] Because we get to know these people over the course of 18 months, we see they all have plausible reasons to give up and give in to the hardships they face on the outside. But all of us live inside the narratives we embrace about ourselves, and it's deadly to embrace a blaming/unfair/victim narrative. When we do, we set in motion a downward spiral that's hard to escape.

Steps 4 and 5 in the 12 Steps of Alcoholics Anonymous are "Made a searching and fearless moral inventory of ourselves" and "Admitted to God, to ourselves, and to another human being the exact nature of our wrongs."[10] In a life growing in spiritual grit, we guard well the narrative we choose to live inside. Instead of focusing on the plot devices that propel our story toward helplessness, we take responsibility for what we do and who we've become, depending on Jesus to remake and strengthen us. It's telling that AA's Step 3, the one that *precedes* an honest embrace of personal responsibility, is "Made a decision to turn our will and our lives over to the care of God *as we understood Him.*"[11]

As Jesus and his entourage pass by a blind man begging by the side of the road, his disciples ask if it is the man's sins or the sins of his parents that have caused him to be blind. The victim narrative they assume leads to helplessness. But Jesus turns the tables on them: "It was neither that this man sinned, nor his parents; but it was so that the works of God might be displayed in him" (John 9:3, NASB).

Our true narrative is about the remodeling project Jesus is completing in us, not the victim story we're tempted to embrace.

Today, decide that you will no longer make excuses or blame forces outside yourself for your inability to persevere through challenges. Then start moving again. When we own whatever we need to own, we open ourselves to Jesus' grace and strength. When we need him, we grow to know him, and we access his assets.

**11. Treat failure, setbacks, and disappointments as temporary.**
Martin Seligman, the University of Pennsylvania psychology professor who partnered with Angela Duckworth to research the foundations of grit, says, "People who don't give up have a habit of interpreting setbacks as temporary, local, and changeable. It's going away quickly; it's just this one situation, and I can do something about it."[12] He's describing the way gritty people adopt a flexible approach to processing

their own failures. When we give failure inappropriate permission to mark our identities, we make it hard to persevere through its consequences.

The day after Hillary Clinton lost the 2016 presidential election to Donald Trump, her pastor sent her a note that read, in part: "For the disciples and Christ's followers in the first century, Good Friday represented the day that everything fell apart. All was lost…For us, Friday is the phone call from the doctor that the cancer is back. It's the news that you have lost your job. It's the betrayal of a friend, the loss of someone dear. Friday is the day that it all falls apart and all hope is lost. We all have Fridays…Today, you are experiencing a Friday…But Sunday is coming!... When [Jesus] said, 'It is finished,' it wasn't meant to be a statement of concession. It was a declaration that a new day was on the way…One of my favorite sayings is 'God doesn't close one door without opening another, but it can be hell in the hallway.'" [13]

"Hell in the hallway" is another way to describe the "liminal space," or no man's land, of our journey through darkness. *Liminal* is Latin for "threshold"—the time between *what was* and *what's next*. When we move through our liminal spaces with a Friday-to-Sunday mentality, we treat setbacks and failures as temporary, not permanent. But that's not what failure screams at us, is it?

> *We treat setbacks and failures as temporary, not permanent.*

On a retreat for men in my church several years ago, my friend Bob Krulish kicked off the weekend with an eye-opening question: "What's one lie you are right now believing about yourself?" He asked us to write our answers on slips of paper so he could collect all of them. The next morning he read what this group of 60 Christian men had scrawled on those notes, including these self-assessments:

I don't belong here.
I'm not significant and have nothing to contribute.
I'm not a good person.
I'm not good enough as I am.
I can't do anything well.
I don't have what it takes.
I'm just a big disappointment.
I'm not enough. [14]

If we have any hope of treating our great disappointments as temporary setbacks rather than permanent judgments against our intrinsic value, we'll need to change the way we respond to them. Here are some ways to do that:

- **Guard against using apocalyptic descriptions of your predicaments.** We don't say things like "This is the worst possible thing that could happen" or "I can't imagine recovering from this" or "I guess that's the end of that dream." The brick wall has ends on either side, and we can walk around it.

When the iconic Doobie Brothers frontman Michael McDonald was asked by an interviewer to describe how he learned to navigate his creative and personal challenges over the years, he said, "I don't know that we will ever overcome doubt—we just have to remember that it's more like a poodle in the bush and not a grizzly bear." [15] Exactly. The grizzly bear is the apocalyptic way we magnify our threats. The poodle is permission to laugh in the face of them.

- **Respond with curiosity when you experience failure, discovering what you can learn rather than giving yourself one more reason to quit.** Two years ago I volunteered to help a close friend create a publishing proposal for his first book. I've written dozens of books, so I have experience doing this sort of thing. My friend found a New York publishing agent who saw promise in his basic concept, and together we created one of the most meticulous, well-conceived proposals I've ever done. Our original proposal generated interest but no takers. But we believed in the idea so much that we morphed the proposal, based on the initial feedback, and sent it to a new set of publishers. Still nothing. Four versions and many months later, the idea died a painful death. If I treated this failure as permanent and unchangeable, I'd embrace the *What a waste of time!* voice in my head. But if I look at this experience through a learning lens, I can point to all of the ways I've grown in both knowledge and relationship with my friend. He's a gold mine of insight, and because I had to understand the way he thinks in order to create these proposals, I feel like I've completed multiple master's-level classes.

- **Think creatively about the disappointment or blockage you're facing.** Treat the roadblock as a forced reroute that has the potential to take you somewhere you didn't know you needed to go. In the introduction to this book, I told the micro-version of my wife's journey toward health after an ominous diagnosis. Facing a lifelong battle with a chronic disease can kick-start a downward cycle of despair, especially if you've struggled to trust God your whole life. But along the way she's experienced the extraordinary intervention of Jesus in her story. Time after time, in all kinds of ways, she's seen financial, medical, and relational miracles—often just in the nick of time. It's as if Jesus has been smiling at her all along, with the *Watch what I can do!* attitude of a child.

- **Depersonalize your setbacks by defining them as something you did, not something you are.** The lies listed by the men on my retreat are all assaults on their identities, not merely their performances as men. When we translate our disappointments into guilty verdicts about our identities, we collude with the enemy of God in his mission to "steal and kill and destroy" us. Fight back against his identity-destroying strategies by asserting the authority of Jesus over the lies you're hearing, then simply repeat, again and again: *That's something I did, not something I am.*

- **List, on paper, three ways this failure is temporary, not permanent.** For example, about my book-proposal failure, I'd write: 1) Maybe the process has given me the knowledge base to face the specific challenges confronting me right now. 2) Maybe the work we completed on these multiple proposals can be used in a future, more successful book idea. 3) Because I was forced to work with an agent my friend discovered rather than my own longtime agent, maybe the imbalance of this challenging relationship strengthened my "perseverance muscles" in ways I could never replicate otherwise.

The idea is to take an active role in reframing our failures from permanent to temporary.

## THE WEED GROWING IN CONCRETE

On my way to work, I drive an interstate highway that snakes through downtown Denver. The road is bound by concrete walls on either side, and those walls are constructed in sections that leave tiny gaps where they're fitted together. During the summer, if the traffic is slow and I can risk a sideways glance, I'll almost certainly see weeds growing out of those gaps in the concrete (as I did just this morning). It's always hard to fathom how this is possible; I can't keep my grass alive when I'm killing it with kindness, but large, healthy weeds can find a way to grow in the concrete gaps of a sun-beaten wall.

These weeds are a study in grit. They'll grow and thrive no matter what obstacles they must overcome, no matter how hard it is to sink their roots into the pavement. They're determined to grow, no matter what. And in this context, "weed" may be our heroic calling as people who have been captured by the heart of Jesus and are determined to lean into the kingdom mission he's given us.

We're created by Jesus to grow—and so we grow, even if it means we must search for the gaps in the concrete wall and find our source of life there. **Hard = Good.**

# QUESTIONS FOR SMALL-GROUP
# DISCUSSION OR INDIVIDUAL CONTEMPLATION

1. In general, have you treated hardships as bad things or good things in your life? Explain.

2. If you think about the common experiences of "The Hero's Journey," how do they relate to your life?

3. When has a hard thing in your life had a profoundly good impact, and why?

4. Which of the 11 "resistance exercises" of spiritual grit was your favorite, and why?

5. What idea from the resistance exercises have you already tried, and what happened as a result?

1   Dan Bronzite, "The Hero's Journey—Mythic Structure of Joseph Campbell's Monomyth" (www.movieoutline.com).

2   Ibid.

3   Jenny Williams, "What Is Grit, Why Kids Need It, and How You Can Foster It" (www.afineparent.com).

4   Glennon Doyle Melton, "Good Grief," *O, The Oprah Magazine* (March 2017), 36-39.

5   Minda Zetlin, "How Emotional Judo Can Help You Take Control of Every Conflict" (www.inc.com//Business-books).

6   Mallory Simon, Sara Sidner, "What Happened When a Klansman Met a Black Man in Charlottesville," CNN.com (December 16, 2017).

7   From the author's transcription of an interview with Scott Strode, CEO of The Phoenix gym, on the Colorado Public Radio program "Colorado Matters," hosted by Ryan Warner. First aired September 14, 2017.

8   Angela L. Duckworth, Christopher Peterson, Michael D. Matthews, Dennis R. Kelly, "Grit: Perseverance and Passion for Long-Term Goals," *Personality Processes and Individual Differences*, 1099.

9   Matthew O'Neill, "Life on Parole," *Frontline* (July 18, 2017).

10   "The 12 Steps of Alcoholics Anonymous" (www.aa.org).

11   Ibid.

12   Annie Murphy Paul, "Can You Instill Mental Toughness?" *Time* magazine (April 19, 2012).

13   Daniel Burke, "How Faith Led Hillary Clinton 'Out of the Woods'" (CNN.com).

14   From a list of responses given at a men's retreat sponsored by Greenwood Community Church in the fall of 2012.

15   Jim Axelrod, "For the Record: Michael McDonald," CBS Sunday Morning (December 17, 2017).

# CHAPTER 4

# EMPHASIZING STRENGTH OF CHARACTER OVER ACCOMPLISHMENT

## THE JOURNEY INTO SPIRITUAL GRIT

Our achievements promise to give us the confidence we crave, but they rarely deliver on that promise long-term. Real confidence flows from strength of character, not a padded résumé. In this chapter you'll explore a wide menu of character-building experiments that Jesus can use to make you whole again, from the inside out.

*"To be yourself in a world that is constantly trying to make you something else is the greatest accomplishment."*

—Ralph Waldo Emerson

### Jesus Teaches About Serving Others

Then the mother of James and John, the sons of Zebedee, came to Jesus with her sons. She knelt respectfully to ask a favor. "What is your request?" he asked.

She replied, "In your Kingdom, please let my two sons sit in places of honor next to you, one on your right and the other on your left."

But Jesus answered by saying to them, "You don't know what you are asking! Are you able to drink from the bitter cup of suffering I am about to drink?"

"Oh yes," they replied, "we are able!"

Jesus told them, "You will indeed drink from my bitter cup. But I have no right to say who will sit on my right or my left. My Father has prepared those places for the ones he has chosen."

When the ten other disciples heard what James and John had asked, they were indignant. But Jesus called them together and said, "You know that the rulers in this world lord it over their people, and officials flaunt their authority over those under them. But among you it will be different. Whoever wants to be a leader among you must be your servant, and whoever wants to be first among you must become your slave. For even the Son of Man came not to be served but to serve others and to give his life as a ransom for many" (Matthew 20:20-28).

My daughter Lucy was 18 when she spent half of her last summer break before college as a staff counselor at Camp Barnabas in Missouri. It's a Christian camp for special-needs adults and children (many of whom are severely disabled), and Lucy served at the camp every summer during high school. When the last parents picked up the last camper, she was exhausted. I met her at a nearby airport to make the 13-hour drive back to Denver easier for her and to give her all the space she needed to tell about her experience. A few hours into the journey,

Lucy told me a story that typified the sort of challenges she faced every day at camp. Here it is, in her own words:

> There are moments at camp when you don't know what to do next, but you're in charge, and people are looking to you for leadership, so you have to start doing something. One week, I was helping a junior counselor with her camper. The three of us were standing on a porch near the dining hall when I saw that the camper had been unable to control her bladder and had created a big puddle of urine on the deck. Counselors' and campers' shoes were piled up all over the porch, and I knew I'd need to do something quickly before the urine spread to the pile. So I pushed the shoes out of the way, trying to figure out what to do next. The puddle was in a well-traveled place, the camper's clothes were soaked with urine, her cabin was far away, it was pouring rain, and we had just 10 minutes before the camper was supposed to be at dinner. This is the kind of predicament I faced many times every day: how to solve a complicated mini-crisis while under pressure.
>
> I had to start somewhere, so I asked a couple of other counselors who were walking by to stand around the pee-puddle to make sure no one stepped in it. Then I walked with the camper to the closest bathroom to make sure she had nothing left in her bladder. I saw another counselor in the bathroom and asked her to stay with the camper while I went to find cleaning supplies to take care of the mess. I ran in the rain to a nearby supply shed and then to the camp kitchen to get a bag, gloves, sanitizer, and paper towels. Then I ran back to the puddle, mopped it with paper towels, sanitized the area three times, put everything in a trash bag, and threw it away. I told the counselors who were guarding the spot that it was all clean and they could leave.
>
> I rushed back to the bathroom where the camper and the fill-in counselor were still hanging out, then walked the camper to her cabin as the storm got worse. Once there, I got the camper into the bathroom and gave her a fresh set of clothes. I put her soiled clothes in a laundry bag, then realized she'd brought only one pair of shoes and they were soaked in urine. What to do now? I wasn't sure this was the best plan, but the camper was hungry and we were going to be late for dinner, so I gave her clean socks, then sprayed her shoes with sanitizer several times. Then I told the girl's counselor to take gloves with her that evening so she could tie the camper's shoes if needed. (Later that night we gave the camper's shoes a more thorough cleaning.) Then we walked all the way back to the dining hall, arriving only five minutes late. I told other staffers we were late because we had to clean up an accident, but nothing more. No one asked any questions, and no one considered what I'd done as extraordinary in any way. This was simply a normal thing that happened at camp all the time.

I doubt the "pee incident" will appear on Lucy's Nobel Prize nomination; it's not the sort of achievement we typically celebrate. But it's clear that this kind of experience is helping Lucy develop strengths that will fuel her impact on the world for the rest of her life. Challenging responsibilities that require fast, creative problem-solving are a rich fertilizer for growing spiritual grit.

> *Challenging responsibilities that require fast, creative problem-solving are a rich fertilizer for growing spiritual grit.*

The leaders at Camp Barnabas like to say it's a "yes" camp. Special-needs people are accustomed to the "no's" that govern their lives, so the camp's mission is to plunge them into the kinds of camp activities that all able-minded and able-bodied kids experience. If a camper wants to try something, the answer is always yes. But the camp is also intent on creating a transformational culture, because it stresses strength of character over the pursuit of accomplishment.

A research team led by Harvard Business School professor Bill George interviewed 125 leaders to learn how they developed their strengths. In his final report, George made this observation: "Analyzing 3,000 pages of transcripts, our team was startled to see that these people did not identify any universal characteristics, traits, skills, or styles that led to their success. Rather, their leadership emerged from their life stories. Consciously and subconsciously, they were constantly testing themselves through real-world experiences and reframing their life stories to understand who they were at their core. In doing so, they discovered the purpose of their leadership and learned that being authentic made them more effective." [1]

The message of this research is simple and profound: We discover our core *essence* in the context of challenging circumstances that require spiritual grit to overcome. And the narrative we tell ourselves has tremendous power to shape our response to tough situations. Stretching experiences expand the boundaries of our character and give us a better story to tell about our purpose and impact in the world.

At the end of the summer, all Camp Barnabas staffers receive a plaque to honor their service. It features a laminated photo of the staffer helping a camper. Authentic strength of character is quietly celebrated as the highest value, and all achievements are subordinate to a determination to serve. Real transformation is the product of this kind of kingdom of God culture, for both camper and counselor. And that's because the challenges faced by counselors at the camp shape a powerful self-narrative for those who persevere.

# A QUESTION OF CORE

Spiritual grit is *not* rooted in our ideas; it's fed by the deeper well of what philosophers and theologians call our ontology, a formal way of describing the way we're wired. Our ontology is like the operating system of a computer—the difference between a Mac and a PC, for example. Some basic questions reveal what is true about us at our core:

- What words do people close to me use to describe my personal characteristics (courageous, humble, dependable, peacemaker)?

- What words describe my ongoing struggles in life (hopelessness, envy, addiction, inferiority) and why?

- In what ways do I trust my heart, and why do I doubt my heart (integrity vs. manipulation, humility vs. arrogance, selflessness vs. selfishness)?

- When do I feel free to offer my strengths in nearly effortless ways (listening well to friends, inspiring others to persevere, serving the least of these, making others laugh when they need it most)?

- When do I sense I'm having a positive effect on others, and what's happening inside me when I do (calm leadership in trying circumstances, engaging others to help them grow, surprising others with my commitment, faithfulness and loyalty when others fall away)?

Who we are—not what we accomplish, but *our core presence*—is our chief tool for influencing others with redemptive impact. It's not our ideas, strategies, training, connections, abilities, or resources. It's our strength of character. Edwin Friedman, in his masterwork on leadership, *A Failure of Nerve*, calls this dynamic *bringing our non-anxious presence* into every situation. [2] Whatever is at the orbital center of our souls will change and influence the dynamic of every social system we enter. Our words are not game-changers for people, but our catalytic presence is. Therefore, whatever is driving our catalytic presence is paramount.

> *Who we are—not what we accomplish,*
> *but our core presence—is our chief tool for*
> *influencing others with redemptive impact.*

I live in a house filled with females—a wife and two daughters, yes—but even our two cats, a Chinese dwarf hamster, and our dog are females. And so (and I'm sorry this sounds stereotypical), escalating emotions are the wallpaper of my life. Over the years, I've discovered—mostly through abysmal failure—that when I throw words at all that emotion, it's like throwing gas-soaked rags on an already roaring fire. But when, instead, I bring the strength of my calm presence to the situation, the fire dies down on its own. It's my non-anxious presence, not my words, that changes the combustible reaction of escalating emotion.

In the same way, it is our non-anxious presence, the result of inviting Jesus to strengthen our core from the inside out, that's our primary tool for living a missional life of impact. But neglected, abused, or broken tools can't do the work they were intended to do. Moreover, tools that suddenly start operating on their own can damage or destroy. For us to be of any benefit to others, we must recognize our utter dependence on the hand that wields us.

This is a lesson the Apostle Paul had to learn. The "Pharisee of Pharisees" tells of a fantastical vision—so vivid he's unsure if it actually happened or was a dream—when he is "caught up into Paradise" and overhears "inexpressible words." The experience is so transcendent that he emerges from it radiating a kind of glory. But then his story takes a dark turn...

> Because of the surpassing greatness of the revelations...there was given me a thorn in the flesh, a messenger of Satan to torment me—to keep me from exalting myself! Concerning this I implored the Lord three times that it might leave me. And He has said to me, "My grace is sufficient for you, for power is perfected in weakness." Most gladly, therefore, I will rather boast about my weaknesses, so that the power of Christ may dwell in me. Therefore I am well content with weaknesses, with insults, with distresses, with persecutions, with difficulties, for Christ's sake; for when I am weak, then I am strong (2 Corinthians 12:7–10, NASB).

Paul is invited into the counsel of the Holy; he sees and hears such great truths that the revelation is almost too much for him to handle. Then, overwhelmed by this beauty, he does what we all do: He begins to believe that the glory he's *tasted* is actually the glory ascribed to *him*. The tool forgets that a hand is wielding it: "Look what I've done," says the hammer, "*all by myself*." And so, because all of Paul's impact will ultimately come down to who he *is*, not what he *does*, God jams a thorn in his side—something so frustrating, painful, and irritating that Paul calls it "a messenger of Satan."

Often, after I've been reminded of the latest thorn in my side, I lament how pitifully my own strength performs under pressure, and I whisper a well-worn prayer: *Sorry, Lord. Sorry, sorry, sorry.* Not long ago, as I was breathing this prayer, I asked Jesus if he had anything to say to me, and then I waited. After a moment or two, the Scripture reference for Psalm 33:13-22 popped into my mind. So I turned there, and here's what I read:

> The Lord looks down from heaven and sees the whole human race.
> From his throne he observes all who live on the earth.
> He made their hearts, so he understands everything they do.
> The best-equipped army cannot save a king, nor is great strength enough to save a warrior.
> *Don't count on your warhorse to give you victory—for all its strength, it cannot save you* (emphasis added).
> But the Lord watches over those who fear him, those who rely on his unfailing love.
> He rescues them from death and keeps them alive in times of famine.
> We put our hope in the Lord. He is our help and our shield.
> In him our hearts rejoice, for we trust in his holy name.
> Let your unfailing love surround us, Lord, for our hope is in you alone.

Assume "warhorse" is just another way of describing my skills, abilities, and gifting, and that Jesus is telling me a hard truth through the conduit of the psalmist: These things are not to be counted on. Our abilities entice us. We're sorely tempted to depend on them to rise to the occasion rather than throw ourselves on the mercy of Jesus and beg for *his* strength, *his* courage, and *his* perseverance. How can we remind ourselves of our need for dependence on him unless we encounter circumstances that drive us to it?

That's the job of my thorn and your thorn, isn't it? It's what C.S. Lewis calls a severe mercy [3]—severe because it exposes our addiction to our own competence, mercy because it leverages us into a posture of desperate dependence. All of Jesus' best friends were desperate people who understood the currency of grace. When we are thirsty enough and desperate enough, he has a shot at convincing us to give with abandon *who we are,* not just what we have.

The point of all this—the point we so often miss because we know what "thorn" means in our own lives, and it's a scary and frustrating reality for us—is that the thorn's purpose is to expose our true weakness, leading us to drink from the reservoir of strength Jesus is offering us. We need strength of character to do what we have to do. But the strength we need is the strength Jesus has; it's from him and in him, and we won't drink from that water supply unless we know our own wells are dry. The thorn in our side pierces our well, draining it and leaving us empty. And we must be empty and acknowledge that emptiness before we will invite him to fill us, again and again.

# USING THE ROBERT FROST FILTER

Robert Frost, the iconic American poet, is best known for his poem "The Road Not Taken." Here's the "tweet-able" portion of the poem—the exclamation point at the end of it:

"Two roads diverged in a wood, and I—
I took the one less traveled by,
And that has made all the difference." [4]

Consider our search for identity—the hunger we all have to understand who we are and our purpose in life—using the "Robert Frost filter." In contemporary Western culture, the road *most* traveled leads us to an identity defined by our accomplishments. It's the reason our default question when we first meet someone is "What do you do?" rather than "What do you believe?" The road *less* traveled, by contrast, leads us to an identity defined by our core strength—the passion we've developed for something higher than ourselves that, in turn, gives us the determination to persevere.

If we take the most-traveled road, we will tie our identities to the elusive and hollow "immortality symbols" that our culture has force-fed us. In his book *Escape From Evil,* Ernest Becker writes, "The symbols of immortal power that money buys exist on the level of the visible, and so crowd out their invisible competitor...No wonder economic equality is beyond the imagination of modern, democratic man: the house, the car, the bank balance are his 'immortality symbols.'" [5] Accomplishment, with all it promises us, offers us the illusion of immortality. It might be more accurate to call it a bait and switch. We're told, again and again, that our accomplishments and resulting accumulations will give our lives transcendent meaning. But once we're actually holding these immortality symbols, expecting them to be solid and heavy, we discover they're made of papier-mâché. They don't transfer the weight of meaning and identity to us the way we were promised they would. Jesus targeted this dynamic when he said, "If the light you think you have is actually darkness, how deep that darkness is!" (Matthew 6:23).

> *Accomplishment, with all it promises us,*
> *offers us the illusion of immortality.*

We're surrounded by mirrors that distort who we really are. They insist on defining us, primarily, by the road *most* traveled—by our relative level of accomplishment when compared to others who are "getting it done." Years ago my neighbor John, father of six kids, decided to terrace his steep-sloping backyard over the course of the summer. So he drew up the plans for it, submitted them to the homeowners association, and used some kind of tripod-y thing to mark boundaries and levels. Then he shoveled away a mountain of rock, installed a new drainage system, cut and rolled all his sod, moved his sprinkler system, uprooted and replanted a tree, leveled his yard with a Bobcat, built all the forms for pouring a concrete patio and retaining walls, attached stone façades to the walls, and re-sodded.

Like a stowaway on a rocket ship, I watched all this happen. Every time I checked to see how John was doing, I found myself asking, "You're going to do what?" I felt so dwarfed by John's capabilities. I couldn't even keep our *trees* from dying of thirst, and here's this guy across the street engineering the landscaping equivalent of the Taj Mahal. That feeling—the gnawing accusation that we're not the sort of people who have what it takes, or at least *enough* of what it takes—is the vulnerable underbelly exposed by our addiction to accomplishment as a mirror of our identities.

If we follow the road less traveled, we'll discover our identities and purpose as Jesus develops our core strengths. This process is the antithesis of self-help. Author William Paul Young says, "We need Jesus to tell us who we really are…Self-help is an attempt to try to lift ourselves by our own bootstraps to some level of performance that is different than what we believe to be the truth of our being."[6] Self-help schemes promise us the capacity to meet our needs outside of a desperate dependence on Jesus. The original sin of Adam and Eve was, simply, that they thought they could be their own gods. The promise of self-help taps into this foundational temptation.

> *Self-help schemes promise us the capacity to meet our needs outside of a desperate dependence on Jesus.*

In Jesus' "inaugural address," when he announces the beginning of his public ministry and what his mission is all about, he quotes a prophecy from the book of Isaiah that I've already referenced: "He has sent me to proclaim release to the captives" (Luke 4:18, NASB). Jesus has come to set captives free; this is his primary occupation, then and now. And when we join the "family business" by committing ourselves to him, we inherit his job description. And there is no more brutal captivity than the captivity of a false identity. This is why Jesus, again, insists to Nicodemus, "You must be born again." We need a new identity that comes from a new birth.

We're called to discover our true identities outside of our accomplishments, renovating our ontology—our core operating system—by abiding in our relationship with Jesus.

# EVERYDAY STRENGTH TRAINING FOR THE SOUL

The encounter between Jesus, the brothers James and John, and their mother may be the most embarrassing story in the New Testament. It's a scene that would fit nicely in the reality-show world: A hovering Jewish mother tries to clear the path to achievement for her two sons and isn't afraid to promote their cause right in front of their resentful friends. This mother has the chutzpah to ask Jesus to elevate her sons to a position of honor on a par with his own. The right-hand seat next to a king is reserved for a person of "equal dignity and authority."[7] The left-hand seat is next best. In answering her, Jesus turns the tables on a pecking-order culture that prioritizes the appearance of honor over the substance of character: "You don't know what you are asking! Are you able to drink from the bitter cup of suffering I am about to drink?"

Those who sit in the seats of honor and authority in the kingdom of God are, indeed, served a special beverage reserved for its upper class— it's the "bitter cup of suffering." Not a great marketing slogan. And James and John, out of their minds and out of their element, answer, "Oh yes, we are able [to drink from that cup]!"

Jesus is characteristically blunt in his response: "You will indeed drink from my bitter cup. But I have no right to say who will sit on my right or my left. My Father has prepared those places for the ones he has chosen."

Jesus then exposes the gaping chasm between conventional values and kingdom-of-God values.

| CONVENTIONAL VALUES | KINGDOM-OF-GOD VALUES |
|---|---|
| Leaders lord it over their people, reminding them who is in power and who is not. | Leaders expect their service to others to cost them pleasure, not add to it. |
| Leaders use their authority in unnecessary ways just to keep people in their place. | Leaders focus on the needs of others, studying them to find ways to bless them, not to keep them down. |
| Leaders use their positions to get what they want, without regard for others. | Leaders use their positions to give more broadly and deeply than they could otherwise. |
| Leaders horde their power rather than give it away for the benefit of others. | Leaders don't need others to prop up their identities with manufactured honors. |

Jesus ends this encounter with an exclamation point: "For," he says, "even the Son of Man came not to be served but to serve others and to give his life as a ransom for many." The contrast between the pursuit of accomplishment (a conventional value) and the pursuit of service (a kingdom-of-God value) is clear: The first is governed by a desire to extract life from others; the second is governed by a desire to invest in others.

When we emphasize strength of character over accomplishment, we extend the kingdom of God because we're elevating service over honor. Character-strength, like the vast underwater foundation of an iceberg, gives our ontology its weight—and it's the focus of the Invisible Rabbi's reclamation project in our lives. He's inviting us to follow Jesus closely, because his presence will infect our presence with endurance, character, confidence, and hope. And when we respond to that invitation by actively cooperating with what he's trying to do in us...

**1. We build the strength of humility.** Contrary to what we may have been told in the church, Jesus doesn't want to be in control of our lives. He gives us the freedom to choose obedience; he doesn't force it. If he did, we'd be mere proxies for his will—like a pastor asking everyone in church to stand up, reach into the back pocket of the person in front of them, and decide what that person should give for the offering. Jesus wants mutuality in his relationship with us because he pursues us from a foundation of humility. He says, "I no longer call you slaves, because a master doesn't confide in his slaves. Now you are my friends, since I have told you everything the Father told me. You didn't choose me. I chose you" (John 15:15-16).

> *Contrary to what we may have been told in the church, Jesus doesn't want to be in control of our lives.*

Humility is his standard operating procedure, and it presses us forward as the Invisible Rabbi keeps us intimately attached to him. It allows us to pick up and put down our skills and expertise and strategies because they are mere tools, not intrinsic to our identities. That means...

- **We find great meaning and delight in acts of service that no one will ever trace back to us.** When we're in the presence of a truly humble person, we discover (if we're paying attention) that most of that person's profound acts of love happen below the surface.

  My nephew Tim was a Boettcher scholar—he received a prestigious full-ride scholarship that many thousands of top students apply for but only a handful win. At his wedding reception, soon after he'd graduated, I overheard one of his friends say that he was first drawn to Tim because of the way he served others; he hadn't learned Tim won the Boettcher until he'd known him for two years. Humility is focused on serving and isn't interested in false sources of identity.

- **We enter into social situations with a focus on what we can offer, not on what we hope to receive.** We look for what others need before we look for what we need.

  Maybe it's because small-talk is my Achilles' heel, but at social gatherings where I'm meeting a lot of new people, I often use service as an on-ramp to more substantial conversation. I notice when pitchers need to be refilled, messes need to be cleaned up, and dirty plates and cups need to be cleared, and I take care of whatever needs to be done. The subtle momentum of this carries over into my conversations, where I'm already primed to focus on the stories of others rather than my own.

- **We develop the mindset of an "apprecionado"**—a word my longtime friend and pastor Tom Melton created to describe a person who moves through life appreciating beauty with the focus and delight of an aficionado. It means we slow down to pay attention to excellence in all its forms, pausing to relish what we're experiencing, creating space in our lives for awe.

  I was speaking at a conference in Chicago and invited a friend who was traveling with me to take advantage of a break and head downtown to experience live jazz in an iconic venue. Sitting 15 feet from the bandstand, I didn't know if my friend would hear the extraordinary sounds coming out of the sax-player's horn as background music or if he'd be transfixed by their beauty. People who embrace the perspective of an apprecionado treat beauty with the humility of a child, slowing down to take in the joy of it, recognizing when something big and great is happening. And that's exactly what the smile on my friend's face told me was happening inside him.

- **We replace self-deprecation—often an expression of false humility—with self-detachment.** I don't mean we're not in touch with what's going on in our souls; I mean we don't try to pump life out of the well of *self*. We recognize our true source of life is in the heart of Jesus, so when others glimpse that beauty in us, we react with a relaxed sense of detachment. That means we can enjoy something about ourselves with the same enthusiasm others enjoy it without slipping into arrogance, because we know our strengths don't prove our worth. When I was first exploring my calling as a ministry leader, I savored every kind comment as if it were a juicy bite of steak and every critical comment as if it were moldy bread. Over the years, as

I've sunk my roots deeper into the shocking wonder of Jesus, I've received kind comments with greater appreciation and enthusiasm and then quickly forgotten them. I don't hold on to the words others use to express the impact I've had on their lives, but I don't negate them with self-deprecation, either.

- **We find little meaning or delight in "pecking order" forms of honor.** A primary way Jesus teaches is observational: He observes what's happening around him and uses that to make a point. For example, this shrewd bit of surgery:

> When Jesus noticed that all who had come to the dinner were trying to sit in the seats of honor near the head of the table, he gave them this advice: "When you are invited to a wedding feast, don't sit in the seat of honor. What if someone who is more distinguished than you has also been invited? The host will come and say, 'Give this person your seat.' Then you will be embarrassed, and you will have to take whatever seat is left at the foot of the table! Instead, take the lowest place at the foot of the table. Then when your host sees you, he will come and say, 'Friend, we have a better place for you!' Then you will be honored in front of all the other guests. For those who exalt themselves will be humbled, and those who humble themselves will be exalted" (Luke 14:7-11).

When we "go low" in the way Jesus intends here, he will "go high" with us. We don't crave pecking-order honors because we've already experienced their hollow payoff. We know that, like the woman at the well, we'll still be thirsty unless we drink the "living water" Jesus is offering us.

- **We serve people who have little or no ability to repay us.** Immediately following Jesus' go-low advice to the dinner guests who are competing for their place at a meal hosted by a respected religious leader, he adds an exclamation point:

> Then he turned to his host. "When you put on a luncheon or a banquet," he said, "don't invite your friends, brothers, relatives, and rich neighbors. For they will invite you back, and that will be your only reward. Instead, invite the poor, the crippled, the lame, and the blind. Then at the resurrection of the righteous, God will reward you for inviting those who could not repay you" (Luke 14:12-14).

In the economy of the kingdom of God, giving to those who can't repay us is the gold standard. This is one reason the Camp Barnabas culture is so life-changing for the young people who serve there. As they work long days to meet the needs of people who not only can't thank them but sometimes punish them, something deep and powerful is unlocked in them. They find a satisfaction in serving that has nothing to do with payback—it's the joy we experience when we feel the strength of Jesus flowing through us into others.

**2. We build the strength of the stretch.** It's a hard truth to swallow, but Jesus grades almost everything we do on a curve. The widow who drops her mite in the Temple collection box gives the most of anyone because it's all she has. She doesn't give a higher *amount*; she gives a higher *percentage*. This same dynamic is at work in Jesus' mustard-seed illustration: The smallest seed grows into the biggest tree. Here, he embraces the beauty of something that's fundamentally unfair. It's not *fair* that a widow's penny has more value than a rich man's fortune, but Jesus is all about the percentages. And that means he will assess what we have to give and determine the value of our giving based on how much of it we spend. There is strength in the stretch. Jesus says, "When someone has been given much, much will be required in return; and when someone has been entrusted with much, even more will be required" (Luke 12:48).

It's natural to grumble about our challenges and difficulties when life seems unfair. We measure fairness by a surface understanding of what others have given or endured and how our reality compares. But Jesus never determines fairness by comparing and contrasting my "hard facts" with yours. Instead, he considers what we've already been given, and if it's a lot, a lot more will be expected of us. When we're tempted to resent the unfairness of our hardships, it's good to remember what Jesus has already invested in us and that his expectations might now be elevated. It's not accurate to call him *demanding*; he's simply interested in promoting growth, not the passivity that leads to atrophy.

Growing things change because they're alive. Dead things stay the same. Jesus wants us to have "life, and have it abundantly" (John 10:10, NASB). And that means he's going to acknowledge our starting point, whatever it is, then stretch us. How can we better embrace this dynamic in his love for us?

- **Instead of approaching hardship with resentment, we approach it with an awareness of the resources he's already given us.** It's painful to be childless when you long to be a mom or dad—but what other "relational resources" are helping you cope with this hardship? It's painful when an injury prevents you from playing the sport you love—but have you considered how you might help others as a coach? It's painful to lose your home to a flood—but have you considered the grace you experienced in the overwhelming support of your neighbors and friends as you recover? Focus on what you have to offer, not what's been taken from you, as you move through your pain.

- **Instead of incessantly comparing ourselves to others—what they have and don't have—we embrace the story Jesus is telling in our lives.** On the shores of the Sea of Galilee, just before he ascends to his Father, Jesus skewers Peter's comparison mentality. Peter has just been told he'll eventually be martyred for his faith in Jesus. Then he spies his friend John walking behind them and asks Jesus what's going to happen to him. "If I want him to remain alive until I return, what is that to you? As for you, follow me" (John 21:22). The only comparison Jesus advocates is internal: We accept the challenges he's given us while embracing the resources he's given us to meet them.

- **Instead of focusing on what we *accomplish*, we pay more attention to what we *invest*.** Growth in our lives, we already know from Jesus, is mostly up to him (Paul said, in 1 Corinthians 3:6, "I planted the seed in your hearts, and Apollos watered it, but it was God who made it grow"). But the investment that leads to growth is mostly up to us. I've described my difficult journey as a high school football player with a widow's mite of talent. My performance was glaringly bad compared to others'. But early on I determined that the only thing I could do better than anyone was *try*. I knew I couldn't control the extent of my athletic ability, but I could control my level of investment in practice and effort on the field. That investment never *elevated* me to excellence, by conventional standards. But one of the stars on the team once asked if he could buy me lunch, then used that time to tell me how much I inspired him. Even now, 40 years later, that moment in a booth at a fast-food taco joint brings tears to my eyes.

> *Early on I determined that the only thing
> I could do better than anyone was try.*

**3. We build the strength of gratitude.** In light of all of the emerging research into grit, the U.S. military has made some changes to its basic training regimen that are designed to strengthen resilience in novice soldiers. One of those additions is counterintuitive: It's all about developing a habit of gratefulness. "Participants learn how to 'hunt for the good stuff'—to look for and appreciate the ways in which they are fortunate." [8]

We're driven to pursue accomplishment, in part, because we've failed to accurately value what we already have. A grateful mindset takes a regular inventory of the relationships, advantages, blessings, and provisions that we're already enjoying but may have taken for granted or overlooked. Gratefulness reinforces our foundation and reminds us that the challenges in front of us pale in comparison to the momentum behind us.

A grateful attitude toward the big things in life—health, provision, relationships—is like picking low-hanging fruit. It's important to recognize and remind ourselves of these basic blessings. But we will strengthen our spiritual grit if we expand our gratefulness to the small things in life, things like...

- a good joke

- a kind word or positive attitude from a cashier

- a burst of sunshine on a cloudy day

- a favorite song

- a friend who offers to pray for us, out of the blue

- the smell of the trees and bushes and flowers on a summer evening

- the smell of the air after a good rainstorm

- a friend at work who stops by to see how we are

- that first taste of our favorite home-cooked meal

- freshly laundered sheets

- a light that turns from red to green when we're running late

- a moment of unexpected peace and quiet at home

- a garment that actually looks better on us at home than in the store

- a letter of gratitude from a child we're sponsoring through Compassion or World Vision

- candlelight

- the feeling we have after we've worked up a good sweat

- the sight of a thunderstorm rolling in and the sound of the first raindrops on our windows

- a whiff of cologne or perfume that transports us for a moment

- a favorite holiday movie on a cold winter's night

- anything shipped in bubble wrap

- the Sunday comics section

- the sound of the wind rustling through leaves

Our simple response to these shafts of beauty radiating through our life? Just this: *Thank you, Jesus. Thank you, Jesus. Thank you, Jesus.* That's it, murmured under our breath or proclaimed to the heavens. In *The Sound of Music,* there's a reason Maria invites the frightened Von Trapp children to remember the things they're most grateful for when a violent thunderstorm scares them. Her song "A Few of My Favorite Things" is intended not only to calm their fears but also to strengthen their courage in the midst of that fear. That's what gratefulness does.

**4. We build the strength of generosity.** What if we were generous to every person we met? Generosity, like gratefulness, expands and strengthens the scope of our influence.

Leaders at the Denver Rescue Mission, an outreach to the broken and addicted in my hometown, say one of the most successful strategies for changing patterns of poverty and drug dependence is a generosity-building program they call work therapy. The idea is to give men and women in need of rehabilitation responsibilities that are crucial to the mission's daily operations. The most productive branch on the work-therapy tree is the mission's Harvest Farm, a working farm where 72 residents learn new skills and experience what it's like to make a tangible difference for others.

The mission's president and CEO, Brad Meuli, says, "I like work therapy because it gives those overcoming addiction something to help take their mind off of themselves and offers them a chance to start serving others. An addict is focused on himself, and feeding his addiction. But if he can build new habits of serving others, he feeds his addiction less, making it easier to work through." [9] On the surface, the work-therapy idea seems like a skills-training strategy, but the real engine of change is the leverage it brings to a self-focused life. When these recovering addicts learn to maintain farm equipment, tend crops, and care for farm animals, they're learning the power of generosity. Serving others first is the foundation for a generous mindset, and hard work in a challenging setting within a community of people who are part of something bigger than themselves reorients their self-focus to an others-focus. Meuli says: "[Work therapy] starts softening hearts toward others, helping our participants know that they are not alone in this world. It is the beginning of God doing his healing work in them." [10]

If we expand our definition of generosity to include *all* acts of others-centered giving, not just monetary ones, we significantly open up possibilities for generosity in everyday life.

- If you have a skill, any skill, find a way to donate that skill every now and then.

- Every day, give someone the gift of your touch, even if it's only a squeeze of the shoulder.

- If you have kids, offer to take kids from another family on an outing or adventure you're already planning.

- Carry a $5 bill in your pocket—just one every week—and look for an opportunity to use it on behalf of someone else.

- All of us have responsibilities and chores we hate to do; pay attention to what your family members typically resent having to do, and do it for them every once in a while.

- The next time you're tempted to have a garage sale, organize everything you would have sold and donate it to a charity instead.

- Sometimes we're asked to do something that's much harder than the asker realizes. Do it anyway.

- Tell people you often take for granted what specific character traits you most admire in them.

- Keep a vase of fresh-cut flowers on your desk, and give one away to someone at work every now and then.

- Some stores offer you a chance to donate to a charity during checkout. More times than not, say yes.

## WHOLLY WHOLE

Whichever path we choose at Robert Frost's fork in the road will form us. Do we want our identities wrapped around a quest for immortality symbols that will never satisfy our thirst for meaning, or a quest for character strength that results in wholeness, something so powerful that it can form and transform everyone in its sphere of influence? Jesus said we would do the things he did, and even greater things, as he makes us whole again. And we experience wholeness in the strength of character he's developing in us, not the empty promises of a lifelong pursuit of accomplishment.

# QUESTIONS FOR SMALL-GROUP
# DISCUSSION OR INDIVIDUAL CONTEMPLATION

1. If you had to choose one word to describe your ontology—the way you're wired—what would that one word be? Explain.

2. What has been a thorn in your side, and how has it been both a blessing and a curse?

3. How do you typically value your worth? What are the standards you use to make that valuation, and why?

4. What's one way you've lived with a focus on humility, and what's one way you haven't?

5. What's one way you've really stretched yourself in life, and what's happened as a result?

_____

_____

_____

_____

6. What's something small you're grateful for today?

_____

_____

_____

_____

7. Tell a story about the impact of another person's generosity on your life.

_____

_____

_____

_____

## ENDNOTES

1   Bill George, Peter Sims, Andrew N. McLean, and Diana Mayer, "Discovering Your Authentic Leadership" *Harvard Business Review* (February 2007).

2   Edwin Friedman, *A Failure of Nerve* (New York: Seabury Books, February 1, 2007).

3   Sheldon Vanauken, *A Severe Mercy* (HarperOne, May 26, 2009), 20.

4   Robert Frost, "The Road Not Taken," *Mountain Interval* (Forgotten Books, August 6, 2012), 9-10.

5   Ernest Becker, *Escape From Evil* (Free Press, March 1, 1985), 85.

6   William Paul Young, "Paying Ridiculous Attention to Jesus" podcast, Season 2, Episode 005.

7   "Why does Scripture emphasize the right hand of God?" (GotQuestions.org).

8   Annie Murphy Paul, "Can You Instill Mental Toughness?" *Time* magazine (April 19, 2012).

9   Denver Rescue Mission newsletter, Changing Lives (August 2017), 2.

10  Ibid.

# CHAPTER 5

# CHANGING OUR LANGUAGE, CHANGING OUR BEHAVIOR

## THE JOURNEY INTO SPIRITUAL GRIT

Our words matter. The story you're telling about yourself can either build up or tear down the hope you need to face your challenges with determination and passion. In this chapter you'll discover how to embrace and live out your true narrative— one that leads to confidence, not defeat.

*"The 'self-image' is the key to human personality and human behavior. Change the self-image and you change the personality and the behavior."*
—Maxwell Maltz

### Jesus Heals a Paralyzed Man

Jesus climbed into a boat and went back across the lake to his own town. Some people brought to him a paralyzed man on a mat. Seeing their faith, Jesus said to the paralyzed man, "Be encouraged, my child! Your sins are forgiven."

But some of the teachers of religious law said to themselves, "That's blasphemy! Does he think he's God?"

Jesus knew what they were thinking, so he asked them, "Why do you have such evil thoughts in your hearts? Is it easier to say 'Your sins are forgiven,' or 'Stand up and walk'? So I will prove to you that the Son of Man has the authority on earth to forgive sins." Then Jesus turned to the paralyzed man and said, "Stand up, pick up your mat, and go home!"

And the man jumped up and went home! Fear swept through the crowd as they saw this happen. And they praised God for giving humans such authority (Matthew 9:1-8).

In Edmund Berkeley's classic parable, a traveler meets three bricklayers working on a scaffold. He asks the first, "What are you doing?" And the man answers, without looking at the traveler: "I am earning a wage." To the second bricklayer, the man repeats his question: "What are you doing?" And the second glances at the traveler and shoots back, "I am building a wall." Then the traveler, persistent in his curiosity, asks the third bricklayer, "And what are *you* doing?" The third man stops what he's doing and turns to respond, "I am building a cathedral." [1]

All three give *accurate* answers, but only the third bricklayer responds by defining his narrative in its epic context. All three are telling a story about their own lives, but only the third bricklayer is telling a *true* story. I don't mean the first two are lying about what they're doing; they're simply not able or willing to see their stories for what they really are.

All of us, no matter who we are or what we do, are living inside an epic narrative. That's because we've been invited into the family of God as adopted sons or daughters. And when we respond to that invitation, our adoption differs from its conventional meaning in one significant way: "Born again of the Spirit" means we have the Trinity's spiritual DNA in us. Because our adoption involves a second birth, we are *blood* sons and daughters. "I have given them the glory [or spiritual DNA] you gave me," says Jesus to his Father on the eve of his crucifixion, "so they may be one as we are one. I am in them and you are in me" (John 17:22-23). As co-laborers in the family business of the Trinity, we are partners with Jesus in his mission to restore a trusting relationship between God and his creation, and there is no more epic occupation in the world.

> *All of us, no matter who we are or what we do, are living inside an epic narrative.*

The story *we think* we're living—the one we learn to describe to ourselves and others—will determine the breadth and depth of our influence in life. If we describe a small-story version of our lives, one that disregards our true calling as warriors who participate with Jesus in setting captives free, we will confine our impact to the surface facts of our existence. We tell ourselves we are only "earning a wage" or "building a wall." But if we intend to embrace the truth about our epic purpose, we'll need to change the way we describe our story. We'll know, when others ask, that our mission in life is building cathedrals, and we'll tell them so.

The Gospel of John begins with this truth: "The Word gave life to everything that was created, and his life brought light to everyone" (John 1:4). John is referencing the beginning of all things, when God *spoke* creation into being through his Word, Jesus. When God speaks, what comes out of his mouth is Jesus. Likewise, the Genesis account of Creation is driven by the power of the tongue: "God said, 'Let there be light' and there was light" and "God said, 'Let there be a space between the waters'…and that is what happened" and "God said, 'Let the waters beneath the sky flow together into one place'…and that is what happened" and "God said, 'Let the land sprout with vegetation'…and that is what happened." Again and again, God's *words* fashion reality. And because we are created in his image, our words also have creative power. They are the vanguard of our beliefs, and our beliefs form and shape our reality.

> *When God speaks, what comes out of his mouth is Jesus.*

If our words have the power to call forth reality in our lives, we must have greater respect for the story we're telling about ourselves and the story we're telling about others. We thwart the development of spiritual grit when our words keep us captive in a small story, not the epic story Jesus is trying to tell.

## FROM A FIXED MINDSET TO A GROWTH MINDSET

To change the way we talk about ourselves and our purpose in life, we'll need to morph our perspective from a "fixed mindset" to a "growth mindset." Psychological researcher Carol Dweck says a fixed mindset represents the belief that people who are good at something are *intrinsically* good at it—they're naturally gifted. A growth mindset comes closer to the truth: We get good at something because of hard work and determination. [2]

This shift in mindset means, simply, that whenever we experience success or witness another's success, we recognize the growth (not the intrinsic talent) that led to it. The iconic dancer Martha Graham once said, "Dancing appears glamorous, easy, delightful. But the path to the paradise of the achievement is not easier than any other. There is fatigue so great that the body cries, even in its sleep. There are times of complete frustration, there are daily small deaths." [3] Graham, the standard of excellence in the world of dance, is undermining the conventional narrative that people who achieve something great have an intrinsic advantage over the rest of us. Her talent is the fruit of growth, not genetics.

We enjoy the fruits of our *labors,* not the fruits of our *entitlements.* And we develop a sense of what we believe, and even what we will die for, from experiences that require perseverance in the face of weakness. Sarah Bourns, resident coordinator for a missionary prep program, explains what this looks like:

> I train and send around 100 students every summer on WorldServe cross-cultural internships, three to eight weeks in length. To prep them for these experiences, we spend five months in weekly team meetings, teaching times, and service-learning opportunities. One of our greatest tools, the one that students most refer to as helpful and challenging and meaningful, is our "30-Hour Famine" weekend (a ministry of World Vision). We put them in many difficult hands-on experiences while they're fasting from food and spending 30 straight hours in close proximity with their teammates. Peer leaders direct the experience, where a lot of the "junk" in a person or team is exposed in order to be dealt with.

We start them off on a grueling travel simulation, which usually
ends up in the rain and cold as they move from station to station—
visa control, immigration, taxi services, and so on. They're yelled
at in different languages, pick-pocketed, swarmed, and more "fun"
stuff like that. They sleep on a hard gym floor after they build
shelters using meager supplies. We wake them at dawn with a
loud call to prayer, ushering them into a mosque setting, then
testing them with other cultural simulations. They compete in an
"amazing race" experience all over campus, where they're repeatedly
challenged with faith questions, asked to share Bible stories, and
required to preach a sermon on the spot.

We break the fast with a crazy Indian market, where they have
to barter for their food and water, or with a "hunger banquet"
where everyone has different amounts of food based on the
countries they represent.

It's a pretty tough 30 hours! It's hard to see some of them
get frustrated or hungry or upset at each other, or even cry, but
I remind myself that the greater good is to build some grit into
them! *And* it works! Many students say that what they experience
on the weekend sets them up for what they know they will face
abroad or gives them a sober reminder that they're going to have
to keep fasting and praying to prepare themselves better. [4]

The intensity of this weekend experience exposes and solidifies
the convictions of these future missionaries. It changes the way they
describe themselves, and therefore the story they're telling about
themselves. When we persevere through challenges, we plant little seeds
in the fertile ground of our internal dialogue. We say things like this to
ourselves: *I'm the sort of person who can fast for 30 hours, endure hardships,
defend my faith under duress, and even persevere in the midst of assault.
I know this is true because I just did it.*

> *When we persevere through challenges, we
> plant little seeds in the fertile ground of our
> internal dialogue.*

Experiences that require spiritual grit are the building blocks for
deeply held beliefs about ourselves, as long as we hold to a growth
mindset about them. When we push the boundaries of our endurance
by persevering through a daunting experience, we recognize that our
ability to endure is fueled by growth, not intrinsic ability. And when
our internal dialogue shifts from a focus on our incapacities to our
capacities, conviction is the fruit. For example, on my wedding day,
I vowed to remain committed to my wife "in sickness and in health,"
but my *conviction* about my commitment to Bev is fueled by the

countless times I've faced and persevered through struggles in our marriage. It's my *experience* of perseverance, not my *rhetoric* about it in my wedding vows, that really matters. The story I'm telling about myself is *I'm the sort of person who stays committed in marriage, and I know this is true because I've done it.* Our internal strength narratives naturally produce conviction, which naturally produces a kind of gravitational pull on others, inviting them to persevere.

Five years ago I saw a poster advertising a 30-day fitness challenge at our health club. At the time, I was certainly "fitness challenged"—I was 45 pounds overweight. My wife has been committed to fitness for many years, but I preferred to let gravity have its way with me. The poster said the prize for the challenge winner was a free one-year family membership. And that made me stop and pay attention. I asked the desk staff how many people typically join the challenge, and they told me 40 or so usually start, but only 25 finish. *Wow,* I thought, *maybe I could actually win this thing.*

By the time I told my family what I was thinking, I'd already decided to do it. I picked out four classes a week at the club and asked my wife what I should do to change my diet. For 30 days I committed to this regimen, stuck with new habits, and lost 26 pounds. It wasn't enough to win the challenge; it wasn't even enough to place in the top three. But after a month of exercising with trainers I really liked and eating much healthier food I'd grown to love, I was hooked. In the end, I lost the 45 pounds and have kept them off. I feel so much better now and have reclaimed the energy I'd lost over the years.

Meanwhile, I was leading a national conference for youth pastors every year, and I started noticing something that disturbed me. So many of these heroic ministry people—persevering in one of the toughest jobs in the world—compensated for the stress of their work by eating way too much and exercising way too little. The elephant in youth ministry's living room is rampant obesity. Because of my own journey into a healthier lifestyle, facing and overcoming these scary giants in my life, I'd developed convictions I'd never had before. I could no longer just stand by and do nothing as the people I loved remained captive to a damaging lifestyle.

So I partnered with a good friend who's a fitness instructor to create a morning exercise option in a large, empty room at the conference, and we promoted the heck out of it. Fifty people showed up every day, and together we worshipped Jesus by doing something tough and sweaty to start our morning. We also changed the menu at the conference to offer some easy, healthier choices. In the end, the mustard seed of this conviction led to a change in our conference culture, inviting many into a different way of living that's still paying dividends.

# CHANGING OUR NARRATIVE ·

When Jesus returns to his hometown and encounters a paralyzed man lying on a mat, he sees an opportunity to expose the fixed mindset of the Pharisees and invite them to exchange it for a growth mindset. And simultaneously, he sees an opportunity to help the paralyzed man (and everyone who witnesses the miracle that's about to happen) reconsider his own narrative.

The man has obvious physical needs; that's why his determined friends bring him to the miracle-worker Jesus. But instead of addressing his surface captivity, Jesus first addresses his interior captivity. He is dead inside because of the killing impact of unforgiven sin. And so Jesus gives life to his dead soul by telling him "forgiven" is now his true identity. This infuriates and offends the teachers of religious law, who mutter an angry question: "Does he think he is God?" Jesus, studying how they're responding, calls out their assumptions: He labels their attitude "evil"—fundamentally contrary to the kingdom of God. And then he asks them to parse the difference between physical healing and spiritual healing. He decompartmentalizes the two, then (almost as an afterthought) vows to prove his authority over sin by physically healing the man.

Jesus doesn't say he will heal the man to prove his authority over sickness and death; he intends to prove his authority over *sin* by restoring the man's physical health. Interior and exterior brokenness are equally paralyzing. For both the paralyzed man and the assembled onlookers, Jesus is telling an epic story to people who are locked in a small story. He's inviting them into a new identity defined by grace, free from the false promise of self-redemption. And so, if the needy man finds only a release from the captivity of his paralysis, he remains a captive to sin. Jesus has not come to merely heal our physical brokenness; he has come to heal our broken, damaged hearts. He wants to give us a better story to tell…

> *Jesus is inviting us into a new identity*
> *defined by grace, free from the false promise*
> *of self-redemption.*

| THE SMALL STORY OF THE PARALYZED MAN | THE SMALL STORY OF THE RELIGIOUS TEACHERS | THE EPIC STORY JESUS IS TELLING |
|---|---|---|
| "My physical paralysis defines me. Healing it would fix my biggest problem." | "We know who you are, Jesus; we watched you grow up. So don't get too full of yourself." | "The problem of spiritual paralysis is actually a bigger deal than physical paralysis. I am Lord over sin, so I'm going to address that first." |
| "Meeting my surface needs would be the most encouraging thing that could happen to me." | "Maybe you have the gift of healing, given to you by God, but you are not God himself." | "The most powerful encouragement I can give you is freedom from the bondage of sin." |
| "You've forgiven my sins but have forgotten the most important thing: I can't move my body." | "Make sure you follow the rules and stay within the boundaries we've set for you, Jesus, because the rules are our source of life." | "I have ultimate authority over both the physical world and the spiritual world, and when I heal, I bring life to both worlds." |
| "Wait until my family sees that I can walk!" | "Wait until we get our hands on you, Jesus, because blasphemy deserves punishment by death." | "Wait until you see what I'm *really* up to: the redemption of all creation and the restoration of intimate trust between God and man." |

To shift our interior narrative so that it aligns more closely with the epic story Jesus is telling in our lives, we'll need to pay better attention to what sort of reality our words are constructing for us. The goal is to grow our spiritual grit, not wither it, with what we say about ourselves and others. Two micro-adjustments in our everyday habits will help us make the shift...

**1. From entitled respect to earned respect.** Instead of ascribing success, maturity, or achievement to your own or another's *innate* capabilities, focus on how grit plays a central role in every respected achievement. Notice the grit you see in yourself and in others; then honor what you discover.

Instead of saying, *Wow, that guitarist is really talented,* we say, *Wow, imagine how much practice it's taken for that guitarist to play that well.* Instead of *I'm not smart enough to win one of those scholarships,* we say, *I'm going to work so hard that it will be hard for them to give that scholarship to someone else.* Instead of *Look at all the advantages that person has had in life,* we say, *Look how that person has taken what he's been given and risked to multiply it.*

Over the years I've participated in many affirmation exercises at work, and people have sometimes graciously expressed their appreciation for my "wisdom." If I am wise, it's not innate. We gain wisdom through hardship and pain, when we're determined to walk through "the valley of the shadow of death" with Jesus, who takes ugly things and makes them beautiful. We pay the price for real wisdom; it is not given to us. Like the European White Truffle (the most expensive mushroom in the world), wisdom grows in dark places, and we have to dig for it.

The key to changing our mindset from entitled respect to earned respect is to describe the under-the-surface foundation for the good things we experience in others and ourselves. We see the massive underwater base of the iceberg and speak of it. And because words have creative force locked up in them, *it's crucial to say what we see.*

In the film *The Way, Way Back,* a single mom and her teenage son agree to spend the summer with the mom's boyfriend at his beach house on the East Coast. They travel to the coast in an old, wood-paneled station wagon with the boy, Duncan, sitting in the "way, way back" by himself. Once there, both the mom and Duncan try to integrate into the boyfriend's existing summer community of old friends. The boyfriend is divorced, and his older, rebellious teenage daughter is spending the summer with him at the beach house. The man is a subtly abusive and destructive presence in Duncan's life, who's lost and grieving the disintegration of his family.

The boy eventually finds community and redemption with a collection of oddball workers at a water park, where he stumbles into a job that he keeps secret from his mother. The manager of the water park, a free spirit named Owen who's getting a little long in the tooth, pursues Duncan with redemptive determination, slowly integrating him into a healing culture of friendships while giving him more and more responsibilities at the park. After Duncan discovers his mom's boyfriend is having an affair, his frustrations and heartbreaks finally boil over, and he escapes to the only safe place he knows—the water park. He finagles his way into spending the night there, and the next morning Owen spies him on a wooden bridge overlooking the park at daybreak.

At first, Owen tells Duncan that he should've gone home already, but the boy insists that the water park is the "only place I'm happy." When Owen questions how that can be true, Duncan begins to weep, then opens up about the abuse he's experiencing from his mom's boyfriend. He tells Owen that the boyfriend once asked him to "rate" himself on a scale from 1 to 10, and when Duncan struggled to answer, finally labeled him a 3. The boy cries out to Owen, "Who says that to somebody?"

OWEN: Someone who doesn't know you.

DUNCAN: I didn't even want to answer! I…shouldn't have to answer!

OWEN: Listen to me. That's about him, man. That's all about him. It's got nothing to do with you.

DUNCAN: How do you know?

OWEN: Because my father was the same way. *(Pause)* And that's why I hate patterns. And that's why you can't buy into that [stuff]. And that's why you gotta go your own way.

*Owen smiles.*

OWEN: And you, my friend, are going your own way. [5]

This is a sledgehammer scene in the film, because a man Duncan respects is paying close attention to him, admiring and delighting in the boy's *essence*, then speaking it out. It's a powerfully redemptive moment, and Duncan feeds off of it, ultimately changing his trajectory in life and calling out courage from his mother.

In a life persistently growing in spiritual grit, we're detectives looking for clues that will lead us to the source of the beauty we experience in others and in ourselves. And *when we see it, we say it.* And when others see it in us, we receive it; we don't deflect or minimize the "tastes of beauty" others find in us. Our focus is on:

- courage more than talent,

- hard work more than "luck,"

- what we (and others) have overcome more than how we've failed,

- appreciation for the "odds against" more than the "odds for,"

- people's details and nuances more than their obvious characteristics, and

- people's "overcoming narrative" more than how their stories compare to others'.

**2. From "I can't" to "I can."** At the risk of pointing out the obvious or sounding trite, "I can't" operates like a horde of termites chewing away at our grit. That's because our words drag our beliefs behind them, and our beliefs form our reality. Often we *do* feel overwhelmed by our challenges, so it seems inauthentic to put a positive spin on them. It's true: Spin doesn't build spiritual grit. Instead, we need a doable, authentic substitute for "I can't" that we can all adopt. Here it is:

Whenever you're tempted to say, "I can't," substitute *"I can, but it will be hard, and hard is doable."*

If you've already agreed with Jesus that Hard = Good, then this substitution is not a fake workaround; it's a commitment to the truth. But sometimes "I can, but it will be hard" rams into a hulking barrier called It's Not Fair. Changing what we say to "I can, but it will be hard, and hard is doable" prepares us to push through unfair circumstances and persevere anyway.

Christopher Paddock directs the Office of Student Conduct and Conflict Resolution at the University of Colorado. When students get into trouble at school, they end up in Christopher's office, usually because of a drug or alcohol charge. He loves his job because he finds great satisfaction in helping others overcome obstacles. The hardest challenge these suddenly needy young adults must face is the creeping insinuation that they won't be able to drag themselves out of the rut they've descended into. I asked Christopher to describe the most effective tool he uses in his work with troubled students:

> The most important thing is to have a sense of optimism for each student. The reason they meet with me is never positive, but it's vital that I reflect an "I can" attitude relative to their identity. Often, the student is a wonderful young person who's simply made a bad decision they regret, or because they've allowed themselves to move with the norms of a negative crowd instead of stand up for themselves. In every interaction, my goal is to communicate a central truth about their identity—that they are cherished, they are amazing, and they have the capacity to change the world. This "I can" reflection gives them permission to be vulnerable with me because they feel supported. And when you're locked in a challenging time, you're desperate for support and understanding. I don't judge students based on their actions; instead, I paint a picture of where their lives can go from here. [6]

People who live with an "I can" mentality bring out the grit in themselves and in others because their convictions are infectious. Consider the "I can" messages Jesus peppered his followers with over the course of three years. Here's a sampler, all from just the first 10 chapters of Matthew's gospel:

- "I will show you how to fish for people!" (4:19).

- "You are the salt of the earth" (5:13).

- "You are the light of the world" (5:14).

- "If someone slaps you on the right cheek, offer the other cheek also" (5:39).

- "You are to be perfect, even as your Father in heaven is perfect" (5:48).

- "Keep on asking, and you will receive what you ask for. Keep on seeking, and you will find. Keep on knocking, and the door will be opened to you" (7:7).

- "I tell you the truth, I haven't seen faith like this in all Israel!" (8:10).

- "Daughter, be encouraged! Your faith has made you well" (9:22).

- "Because of your faith, it will happen" (9:29).

- "Heal the sick, raise the dead, cure those with leprosy, and cast out demons" (10:8).

- "Look, I am sending you out as sheep among wolves. So be as shrewd as snakes and harmless as doves" (10:16).

- "When you are arrested, don't worry about how to respond or what to say. God will give you the right words at the right time" (10:19).

- "Don't be afraid of those who threaten you" (10:26).

- "Don't be afraid of those who want to kill your body; they cannot touch your soul" (10:28).

- "Not a single sparrow can fall to the ground without your Father knowing it. And the very hairs on your head are all numbered. So don't be afraid; you are more valuable to God than a whole flock of sparrows" (10:29-31).

- "Anyone who receives you receives me" (10:40).

And, of course, to the paralyzed man lying on a mat: "Be encouraged, my child! Your sins are forgiven" (9:2).

If you have "I can't" tendencies, start by making those two words a red flag in your life. Whenever you hear yourself speak or think some version of them, stop and replace them with *"I can, but it will be hard, and hard is doable."*

## EARNED, NOT GIVEN

When we change the way we talk about our stories, and the stories of others, we change our behavior. And a change in behavior will grow our spiritual grit. It's not possible to acquire the grit we need to persevere through setbacks, and to partner with Jesus in his epic purpose for our lives, unless we're *growing* in it. It's not given to us; it's earned through experience. And the spiritual grit we grow produces the nourishing fruit that others need to face their own challenges and pursue their own epic purposes.

# QUESTIONS FOR SMALL-GROUP DISCUSSION OR INDIVIDUAL CONTEMPLATION

1. In the bricklayer parable that opens this chapter, which one of the three bricklayers are you most like, and why?

2. How has someone in your life called out something good and beautiful about you, and what impact did that have?

3. What's one way that changing your interior narrative about yourself has increased your spiritual grit?

4. Do you tend to be an "I can't" person or an "I can" person, and why?

*ENDNOTES*

1   Edmund Berkeley, *Ride the East Wind: Parables of Yesterday and Today*, edited by Edmund C. Berkeley (New York: Quadrangle, 1973), 88.

2   Carol Dweck, *Mindset: The New Pyschology of Success* (New York: Ballantine Books, December 26, 2007).

3   Jens Giersdorf, Yutian Wong, Alexandra Carter and Janet O'Shea, *The Routledge Dance Studies Reader* (New York: Routledge, 1998), 96.

4   From an interview with Sarah Bourns, Envision Resident Coordinator for the Christian and Missionary Alliance Church.

5   Nat Faxon, Jim Rash, screenplay *The Way, Way Back* © 2011 Twentieth Century Fox film corporation.

6   From an interview with Christopher Paddock, director of the Office of Student Conduct and Conflict Resolution at the University of Colorado Boulder.

# CHAPTER 6

# FOLLOWING "WHY NOT?" INTO FREEDOM

Hardships and challenges can bully us into giving up and giving in—some brick walls seem insurmountable. But a life fueled by courageous endurance asks, "Why not?" when brick walls insist, "It's impossible." In this chapter you'll learn how to live with a determination to ask, "Why not?" in every situation.

*"You see things; and you say 'Why?' But I dream things that never were; and I say 'Why not?'"*
—George Bernard Shaw

### Jesus Walks on Water

Immediately after this, Jesus insisted that his disciples get back into the boat and cross to the other side of the lake, while he sent the people home. After sending them home, he went up into the hills by himself to pray. Night fell while he was there alone.

Meanwhile, the disciples were in trouble far away from land, for a strong wind had risen, and they were fighting heavy waves. About three o'clock in the morning Jesus came toward them, walking on the water. When the disciples saw him walking on the water, they were terrified. In their fear, they cried out, "It's a ghost!"

But Jesus spoke to them at once. "Don't be afraid," he said. "Take courage. I am here!"

Then Peter called to him, "Lord, if it's really you, tell me to come to you, walking on the water."

"Yes, come," Jesus said.

So Peter went over the side of the boat and walked on the water toward Jesus. But when he saw the strong wind and the waves, he was terrified and began to sink. "Save me, Lord!" he shouted.

Jesus immediately reached out and grabbed him. "You have so little faith," Jesus said. "Why did you doubt me?"

When they climbed back into the boat, the wind stopped. Then the disciples worshiped him. "You really are the Son of God!" they exclaimed (Matthew 14:22-33).

In 1981 David Marquet graduated at the top of his U.S. Naval Academy class. He left the academy and joined the submarine force, pursuing a dream he'd had since he was a boy to captain a ship in the Navy. At the academy he'd wrestled with the conventional leader-follower model of military leadership—a path that essentially confines creative, strategic thinking to the commanding officer, while subordinates are simply expected to follow orders. As a mid-level engineering officer on the nuclear-powered submarine *USS Will Rogers,* Marquet asked for and got permission from his commanding officer to experiment with a more empowering style of leadership he called intent-based. He gave broad guidance to the sailors under his command but let them figure out specific strategies themselves. His first experiments were disastrous, and he was forced to reembrace the leader-follower model.

Marquet was soon promoted to captain of the *USS Olympia*, a nuclear-powered attack submarine. After a year preparing to assume command of the ship, he was abruptly rerouted to the *USS Santa Fe* after its captain unexpectedly retired. At the time, the crew of the *Santa Fe* had a reputation as the worst-performing crew in the fleet. Morale was terrible, and performance was worse. Early on, Marquet's unfamiliarity with the sub led him to issue an order that was impossible for his men to follow, but his officers relayed the order down the chain of command anyway. When he discovered what had happened, Marquet decided it was time to experiment with intent-based leadership again. He began treating all crew members he'd determined were technically competent as leaders who could figure out the best way forward as long as they knew Marquet's broad (but clear) intentions. The atmosphere among crew members changed immediately and dramatically. Eventually, the *Santa Fe* earned the highest evaluation marks ever recorded in the Navy. And more of its crew were promoted to officer positions than any other sub in the fleet.

> *He began treating all crew members he'd determined were technically competent as leaders who could figure out the best way forward.*

Marquet's innovative solution to the *Santa Fe's* endemic performance problems was the fruit of a passion for asking, "Why not?" The U.S. Navy's chain-of-command expectations had been drilled into him, but he couldn't stop asking "Why not?"—even if, at first, it was a question he asked only himself. Still wary after the failure of his first intent-based leadership experiment, the daunting challenges he faced on the *Santa Fe* lured him back to his original convictions. His strong, reasoned belief in the value of giving others the freedom to lead, no matter their position in the pecking order, convinced him to "step out of the boat and onto the water." [1]

Marquet's story underlines an important truth about spiritual grit: Nothing fundamentally changes in our lives, or in our impact on the world, without asking, "Why not?" In a life that's always growing core strength, it's a vital question, repeated like a mantra.

> *Nothing fundamentally changes in our lives,*
> *or in our impact on the world, without*
> *asking, "Why not?"*

Because we're hard-wired to recoil from the *unknown* and naturally gravitate toward the *known*, we tend to edit out opportunities to grow and expand our spiritual grit. This editing process hides behind many pseudonyms, including *procrastination, shortcut, good enough, "That's not my strength," unreasonable, "I can't," unfair,* and pseudo-theological words like *mystery, unknowable,* and *the other.* Of course, "Why not?" scares us, so we find excuses to stay in our ruts, in the safety of the known. The antidote to the subtle ways we avoid the unknown in favor of the known is to respond to the Invisible Rabbi's nudges to explore where "Why not?" might take us.

## OVER THE GUNWALES

Commercial fishing is the most dangerous job in America. In the last decade, more than 150 professional fishermen died after falling overboard. [2] John Aldridge's name should have been on that list. Several years ago, in the middle of the night, Aldridge was on deck trying to fill his lobster boat's storage tanks before hauling in the evening catch. To open the storage hatch, he had to move a 125-pound cooler out of the way. He pulled on the cooler's handle so hard that it snapped, vaulting him off the back of the boat and into the dark, churning sea. The roar of the engines and the sea drowned out Aldridge's screams as the boat motored away on automatic pilot. He quickly assessed his chances: "Today's the day I'm gonna die." [3]

Aldridge wasn't wearing a life preserver, but he soon noticed that his big rubber fishing boots were remarkably buoyant. Instinctively, he removed both boots, emptied them of water, then stuck them under his arms with the openings face-down, creating air pockets that kept his torso above water. Fifteen feet away, two shark fins appeared on the moonlit surface of the sea. Aldridge knew that sharks sense fear in their prey, so he calmed himself by taking slow breaths and remaining still until the sharks swam away.

Four hours later his lifelong friend and business partner Anthony Sosinski woke up on the lobster boat and was shocked to discover he was alone. Meanwhile, the sun was coming up, and Aldridge was repeating the mantra he'd been saying to himself all night long: "You just gotta live 'til morning, gotta live 'til morning." Riding the top of a swell, he caught a glimpse of a fisherman's buoy on the horizon and knew if he could paddle to it he'd have a chance of rescue. A helicopter eventually appeared, flying low and directly over the buoy. Soon he was hauled up in a basket. Once on board, the pilot marveled that Aldridge had survived his ordeal: "Man, you are one tough dude. We don't find live people; we find bodies." [4]

Aldridge's story helps us understand how Peter, a professional fisherman, well-acquainted with the hazards of the sea during a fierce storm at night, feels when he almost drowns. The waves are frothing, driven by hurricane-force winds, when Peter and his friends see what looks like a ghost walking in between the swells near their boat. They are gripped with fear. But Jesus calls out, over the fury of the waves: "Don't be afraid. Take courage. I am here!"

And Peter, in a stunning moment of "Why not?" clarity, offers the ghost a bargain: "Lord, if it's really you, tell me to come to you, walking on the water." Jesus, likely with a big smile on his face, invites him over the gunwales. The only sane reason to step into a raging sea in the middle of the night, far away from shore, is because Jesus is doing the inviting.

When Jesus tells us to move through our fears, saying, "I am here," he's offering to be our "buoyant boots." We sink into what terrifies us, but we don't drown because he's holding us up. And like Peter, we need to know what it's like to step off the safety of the deck into the dark unknown. "Why not?" is the path into our deepest resolve, where we discover who we are and what God made us to do.

## LIVING WITH "WHY NOT?" MOMENTUM

A "Why not?" mentality works like this: When we face a difficult challenge or opportunity, we fight the pull toward a cowardly response simply by asking, "Why not?"

Here's how this might look in everyday life:

**1. We shift our attention from our capabilities to our courage.**
My wife loves to dance, and she's very good at it, but I feel weak and exposed whenever I try to keep up with her because it's not one of my known strengths. So I avoid the possibility of feeling embarrassed or ridiculous by defaulting to "I can't."

We were on vacation in a mountain town this summer, and I picked up a flyer that listed free family events, including country-western dance lessons that were being offered at the library. My first thought: *I hope Bev doesn't see this.* You already know what happened—she asked what I was looking at, read the flyer, and insisted we all head over to the library for an hour of dancing fun (or dancing purgatory, if you could read my thoughts).

My first impulse was to find a plausible reason to torpedo the whole thing, to resist an experience that most often makes me feel tense and self-conscious. But the antidote to the cycle of "I can't" that undermines spiritual grit is to simply ask, "Why not?" When I did that, I exposed the true impediment: I was ashamed of my lack of rhythm and coordination and didn't have the courage to serve my wife by dancing badly anyway. Then I was accountable to Jesus, because I recognized that my reaction was more about my courage than my capability. I asked him for strength and suppressed the negative self-talk that "I can't" bombards us with. I went to the dance lesson and stumbled my way across the floor with my wife and a long succession of elderly women (the instructor had us change partners every five minutes or so).

"Why not?" kept me walking on the water, smiling most of the time, because grit-growing experiences reintroduce us to our need for courage and our only true source of it.

**2. We stop using subtle excuses to maintain our distance from God.** When something in Scripture confounds us, seems to conflict with our understanding of God, or uses unfamiliar language or concepts, we often resolve the dissonance by telling ourselves that these truths are beyond us or that God is an unknowable mystery. Because "God's ways are not our ways," it's natural to react to his otherness by skipping over the hard stuff or ignoring the things that don't make sense.

- Somehow a virgin is "overshadowed" by the Spirit of God and conceives a son, who is both divine and human. *Yeah, that makes sense, until I really think about it...*

- Jesus tells us we'll do the stuff he does, and "even greater things." *What does that mean, and how is that even possible?*

- Jesus demands to know the name of an evil spirit harassing the Gerasene demoniac and then gives Legion permission to enter a herd of 2,000 pigs, who promptly drown themselves in a lake (Luke 8:26-33). *That sounds like something Penn and Teller might do, but if I saw Jesus actually do this, just being around him would freak me out.*

- Jesus distributes a few loaves of bread and a couple of fish to a massive crowd and ends up with 12 baskets of leftovers. *I think I know how that could happen. Just kidding.*

- Jesus tells Peter to throw a line in a lake, open the mouth of the first fish he catches, and use the large silver coin he finds there to pay a tax. *Well, I understand why Jesus did that. Or not.*

When we slow down to ask, "Why not?" whenever we encounter a difficult story in the Bible, we expose the true obstacle: We aren't willing to pay *ridiculous attention* to what we're reading, to discover the underlying truth that eludes us. In Jesus' parable of the sower (Matthew 13), the "rocky soil" translates to a growth environment compromised by push-back, difficulty, and even persecution. We don't fully understand his heart and his words and his intentions, Jesus is telling us, because we stop pursuing him when it's hard. But Jesus tells us his job description is to reveal the heart of his Father; when we come to know Jesus, we'll know God. It's not only possible to know the depths of God's heart, but Jesus is doing everything he can to make that possible. So we lean into confounding stories in the Bible because he's already told us that if we keep knocking (Matthew 7:7), he will open the door of understanding to us. Our persistence reconnects us to the Invisible Rabbi, who unlocks the heart of Jesus and invites us in.

**3. We seek and ingest feedback that requires courage to hear.**
I have a close friend who models "Why not?" with me all the time. Last week I told him about a challenge I was facing at work and my frustrations over the feedback I was getting. "People keep giving me advice about what I should do, but their responses don't recognize my reality and seem stronger than the situation warrants."

My friend stopped me mid-sentence and asked me a "Why not?" sort of question: "Have you considered the possibility that all of these people are responding to you this way because you're communicating emotions you don't have the courage to own?"

Wow. He nailed me right in the middle of my retreat from spiritual grit. He was calling me to step up and own my real emotions, recognizing that they'd been spurting out sideways all along, then move into my challenge with more integrity. The leverage of his "Why not?" moved me to lean into the reality of my own scary emotions by accepting their implications, instead of punishing the honest people in my life who were simply reflecting what they were experiencing in me.

When Richard Foster, a Quaker pastor and author of the spiritual classic *Celebration of Discipline,* was first contemplating writing his masterwork, he was blocked by fear and his own insecurities. So he felt prodded by the Invisible Rabbi to reach out to a man he considered a spiritual giant, a former missionary named Bill Cathers, and ask for prayer. When Cathers arrived at Foster's home, the first thing he did was solemnly confess all of his sins. Foster sat in silence, astonished by the man's behavior. *What is he doing?* he thought. *He's the spiritual sage.* When Cathers finally finished, Foster prayed a prayer of absolution over him. Then his guest fixed his steely eyes on Foster and said, "Now, do you still want me to pray for you?"

Foster writes, "He had seen into my heart! He knew that I had put him high on a pedestal as some spiritual guru, and he was pulling all that down into a crumpled heap. Sobered by his discernment, I replied simply, 'Yes, I do.'" [5]

If Cathers had not exposed Foster's false and destructive idolatry, he would have treated his prayers as a kind of incantation instead of a conversation with Jesus. Foster says the power of Cathers' prayer lingered with him his whole life.

All of us need at least a few people in our lives who have permission to prod us into "Why not?" clarity. Who have you invited to be that person?

**4. We refuse to be spectators in our own adventures.** When we lean into "Why not?" we live our life on the field, not on the sidelines. It's only on the field, where "Why not?" is lived out, that we're driven to trust the strength we see in Jesus. Jeremy Jones is a 33-year-old American Jesus-follower who planted a high-profile business in the heart of the Muslim world: a recreational climbing company called Climb Morocco. He knows a little something about grit. I asked Jeremy what fuels a "Why not?" attitude in those who hire his company to push them beyond their boundaries. He told me this story:

> I was taking a couple, a man and woman, rock climbing for the first time a number of years ago. It had been the woman's dream for many years to overcome her fear and make it to the top of a vertical cliff face. Her husband was really just along for the ride, there to support his wife. I put them on a somewhat challenging cliff face, and the difference between them was tangible. The wife physically struggled so much to make it to the top; she fell many times but persevered for almost an hour (with my encouragement) until she finally summited the cliff. Her hands were actually bleeding. The husband tried once, fell halfway up, and got discouraged. He was happy to come on down and watch the rest of the day. In my experience, desperation or an unwavering motivation are a necessity for grit. You are much more likely to push through difficult situations when you're driven by desperate resolve or by a hunger to fulfill a deeper passion. When you don't completely buy into the challenge, it's easy to think it's not worth it. The challenge seems bigger than it really is, and then you give up. [6]

The wife in Jeremy's story knew she was a main character in an adventure narrative, striving to overcome fear and failure as she lived out her courage in the spotlight. The husband, on the other hand, saw himself as a stagehand, a behind-the-scenes cheerleader in someone else's story. He was a spectator, not a player, so it was easier for him to give up when things got tough.

To persevere and grow our spiritual grit, we have to show up in our own adventures. Former Navy SEAL Brent Gleeson says, "When my SEAL Team was operating in Baghdad in 2003, none of us knew how well trained we were until that training was tested in battle. During our first gunfight, not one man hesitated. Our team members were doing their best to get into the fight, not out of it." [7]

Getting into the fight, not out of it, means we…

- *Assume an active, not a passive, stance.* We effect change by actively inserting ourselves into challenges, not by waiting for something good to happen to us. If we have a difficult medical problem, for example, we might seek out a specialist even when our general physician offers to treat us. We engage rather than defer.

- *Identify and face our fears instead of skirting them.* For example, it's easier to complain about the latest political news than it is to confront a spouse or a friend about a troubling behavior.

- *Say yes to challenges we know are beyond our capabilities, expertise, and courage.* For example, we sign up for that half-marathon because we know we'll be driven to depend on Jesus' strength, not our own.

- *Take responsibility for outcomes.* Rather than blaming outside factors such as our upbringing, opportunities, oppositions, and connections, we play the hand we've been dealt. If our anxious personalities are rooted in an abusive childhood, for example, we simply embrace the reality that everyday life is going to require more courage, and we remind ourselves to treat ourselves with kindness, refusing to compare our courage to another's.

- *Determine to be present wherever we are.* We focus on the people and situations before us and shove aside anything from the past or future that lures us away from the present moment. We don't allow past betrayals by friends to prevent us from trusting people now, for example.

- *Instead of repeatedly dipping a toe in the water, we plunge into the pool.* Always wanted to be a writer? Start a blog. Always wanted to play the piano? Take lessons for a month. Love musical theater and wish you could be part of a cast? Do what my middle-aged fitness instructor did: Show up for tryouts and accept a role in the chorus just to get your foot in the door.

- *Value growth over the status quo.* We're well aware that we're drawn to the safety and predictability of life as we know it. So experiment with life as you've never known it. Instead of giving money to a ministry, serve in that ministry. Instead of criticizing the decisions your neighbors make, volunteer to serve on the HOA. Instead of resigning yourself to a job that never asks you to risk, start a "side hustle" that demands your courage and creativity, and see where it leads.

**5. We stay on the horse when fear tries to buck us off.** Some horseback-riding instructors tell novice riders to perform an "emergency dismount" if the horse is spooked. Master horseman Rick Gore fumes, "The idiot that thought this up was not a horseman, and did not have a clue about understanding horses and the way they learn and think. This *suicide procedure* is a surefire way to teach a horse to run off, scare you, and learn how to get you off their back...If you get off a horse when a horse does something, you teach a horse when it repeats that behavior, you will get off of him." [8] The horse, says Gore, responds to fear-avoidance in a rider by avoiding fear itself—it will not allow a fearful rider to rest in the saddle. Fear in the horse is conquered only when the rider conquers his own fear and stays mounted.

"Why not?" will certainly surface our fears—that's actually the function of the question. Our answers can either catalog the dire possibilities or calibrate our risks before we leap. If we want to ride the horse, we'll have to reduce the number of times we bail out when things get rough.

This summer we took our entire small group to family night at a local concert hall for three hours of swing dancing. This venue features a mechanical bull—and for $5 you can ride it. I watched as people climbed onto the back of the beast and did their best to hang on. Some gave up and flung themselves off the bull as soon as it bucked hard enough to threaten their balance; others persevered even when they were hanging off the side. There is a parable waiting to be discovered here: When fear tries to buck you off, hang on sideways long enough to look that bull in the eye.

Jesus expected a lot from the people he interacted with, outing those who gravitated toward the easy path and away from what was hard. And he raised the bar on our capabilities. "I tell you the truth, anyone who believes in me will do the same works I have done, and even greater works, because I am going to be with the Father" (John 14:12). The definition of courage is not a diminishment of fear but our decision to move through fear. That makes courage dependent on our growing, trusting relationship with Jesus, not an *intrinsic* quality.

*The definition of courage is not a diminishment of fear but our decision to move through fear.*

# KINGDOM-OF-GOD MATH

Our "Why not?" is a crucial component in the organic "math equation" that produces spiritual grit…

Math is the study of how things work in the physical world. But MIT physics professor Max Tegmark believes math is also embedded in the *metaphysical* world: "There's something very mathematical about our Universe, and that the more carefully we look, the more math we seem to find. So what do we make of all these hints of mathematics in our physical world? Most of my physics colleagues take them to mean that nature is for some reason described by mathematics…and leave it at that. But I'm convinced that there's more to it…If you believe in an external reality independent of humans, then you must also believe that our physical reality is a mathematical structure. Everything in our world is purely mathematical—including you." [9]

There is a mathematical order to the universe, on a nanolevel, that reflects an order in the heart of God, who created all things—including us—out of himself. Math is therefore a kind of language that expresses not just our physical reality, but also our spiritual reality. Galileo writes: "[Natural science] is written in this grand book—I mean the universe—which stands continually open to our gaze, but it cannot be understood unless one first learns to comprehend the language in which it is written. It is written in the language of mathematics, and its characters are triangles, circles, and other geometric figures, without which it is humanly impossible to understand a single word of it; without these, one is wandering about in a dark labyrinth." [10] If God created the universe by speaking it into existence and the "grand book" of the universe is "written in the language of mathematics," then God speaks in math.

And so, when Peter sinks into the water soon after he steps onto it, and Jesus asks, "Why did you doubt me?" he is not merely expressing his disappointment in Peter's faith; he is correcting his math. The foundation of all life in the kingdom of God is expressed by a simple equation: $\triangle + (y \times JC) = \infty$.

1) The impossible (the Penrose Triangle, a symbol of the impossible),
2) is possible (represented by the Infinity Symbol),
3) when our "Why not?" (represented by y) is multiplied by Jesus Christ and added to the impossible.

We know this equation works, because Jesus drew it up for his disciples on his rabbinical chalkboard just after they were unable to cast a demonic presence out of a little boy: "Afterward the disciples asked Jesus privately, 'Why couldn't we cast out that demon?' 'You don't have enough faith,' Jesus told them. 'I tell you the truth, if you had faith even as small as a mustard seed, you could say to this mountain, "Move from here to there," and it would move. Nothing would be impossible'" (Matthew 17:19-20).

So when Jesus talks about the size of our faith, we know he isn't treating faith like some sort of magic spell or a spiritual commodity. Out on the waves in the middle of the night, he asks Peter, "Why did you doubt *me*?" (emphasis added). The size of our faith is fed by the variable we provide with our "Why not?"—which is driven by the depth of our trust in the heart of Jesus. We provide the "y" to this impossible equation, and he multiplies it to produce the possible. What we give isn't really very much—a mustard seed or a mite— but the equation must have our "y" if the impossible is going to be transformed into the possible. This impossible math will produce spiritual grit when we persistently pursue "Why not?" and then trust Jesus to meet us in our need.

# QUESTIONS FOR SMALL-GROUP
# DISCUSSION OR INDIVIDUAL CONTEMPLATION

1. In what way has asking "Why not?" led to something good in your life, and why?

2. What's one way Jesus has been like "buoyant boots" in your life, and how has that affected your ability to trust him?

3. What's one way you've shown courage in the face of your insufficient capabilities, and what resulted?

4. When has someone given you feedback that's been hard to swallow but ultimately good for you?

5. We build spiritual grit when we get into the fight, not out of it. Tell a story of how you've lived this truth in your life.

_____

_____

_____

_____

6. When have you "stayed on the horse" when you faced a fear, and what resulted?

_____

_____

_____

_____

## ENDNOTES

1     www.davidmarquet.com.

2     Centers for Disease Control, "Commercial Fishing Deaths—United States, 2000-2009" (July 16, 2010).

3     Jim Axelrod, CBS News "Lost at Sea: A Harrowing Story of Survival" (June 11, 2017).

4     Ibid.

5     Richard Foster, *Celebration of Discipline* (New York: HarperCollins, 1978, 1988, 1998), xvi-xvii.

6     Jeremy Jones, email interview, August 2017.

7     Brent Gleeson, "5 Common Fears of Leadership—And How to Conquer Them," Inc.com/Lead (January 28, 2015).

8     Rick Gore, "Discussing Horse and Rider Fear" (www.thinklikeahorse.org).

9     Max Tegmark, "Is the Universe Made of Math?" ScientificAmerican.com (January 10, 2014).

10     Quoted by Jeremy Butterfield, "Made of Maths?" www.plus.maths.org (May 20, 2014).

# CHAPTER 7

# EXPECTING MORE INSTEAD OF DOING FOR

## THE JOURNEY INTO SPIRITUAL GRIT

Lots of needy people came to Jesus hoping he'd help them, and he did—but not before asking them to invest their own courage and determination. Likewise, when we recognize our role in building others' strength, we'll ask them to do *more* before we do *for* them. In this chapter you'll learn about the dangers of overfunctioning for others and how to offer them a kind of love that strengthens, not weakens, their resolve.

*"Start by doing what's necessary; then do what's possible; and suddenly you are doing the impossible."*

—Francis of Assisi

### Jesus Heals a Man Born Blind

As Jesus was walking along, he saw a man who had been blind from birth. "Rabbi," his disciples asked him, "why was this man born blind? Was it because of his own sins or his parents' sins?"

"It was not because of his sins or his parents' sins," Jesus answered. "This happened so the power of God could be seen in him. We must quickly carry out the tasks assigned us by the one who sent us. The night is coming, and then no one can work. But while I am here in the world, I am the light of the world."

Then he spit on the ground, made mud with the saliva, and spread the mud over the blind man's eyes. He told him, "Go wash yourself in the pool of Siloam" (Siloam means "sent"). So the man went and washed and came back seeing!

His neighbors and others who knew him as a blind beggar asked each other, "Isn't this the man who used to sit and beg?" Some said he was, and others said, "No, he just looks like him!"

But the beggar kept saying, "Yes, I am the same one!"

They asked, "Who healed you? What happened?"

He told them, "The man they call Jesus made mud and spread it over my eyes and told me, 'Go to the pool of Siloam and wash yourself.' So I went and washed, and now I can see!" (John 9:1-11).

I'm a professional writer and editor, so my two teenage girls always want me to look over their school essays and assignments. I like to help, but I undermine their ability to grow their own grit if I do the work for them (even though that would take me a tenth of the time). So when one of them wants me to check something, I sit next to her and her open laptop. As I scan her work, I tell her when I see a mistake in a sentence, but I don't tell her what the mistake is. I force her to find it, and I ask questions if she needs help clarifying what the mistake is. If a sentence structure is faulty, I ask her to find a way to make it better. In essence, I ask her to do *more* instead of doing it *for* her.

My daughters don't like it, and I often dread it. But I do it anyway because I love them, and my desire to help them grow overshadows my desire to make their lives, and mine, easier.

This is a crucial habit to develop in our horizontal relationships with others and in our vertical relationship with Jesus. He grows our spiritual grit when he requires *more* before doing *for,* and we help strengthen the core of others when we do the same.

Here are some examples from the Gospels:

- When "doubting Thomas" questions the reality of Jesus' bodily resurrection, he asks Jesus to prove himself. Jesus could command Thomas to believe, doing the work of faith for him. Instead he asks his friend to do *more* before he will do *for*—to move toward him and touch his wounds (John 20:26-28).

- When the wine runs out during a wedding party in Cana, Mary asks Jesus to intervene because the wedding hosts are facing a colossal embarrassment. Instead of simply producing full vats of wine, Jesus asks the servers to fill some huge jars with water; then he asks them to dip into the jars and take the ladle to the host to sample. He requires a lot *more* before he does *for* (John 2:1-11).

- Before he gives the woman at the well the living water he has promised, he asks her to do more: to go and get her husband. Really, he's requiring her to be honest about her life before giving her the truth that will set her free (John 4:4-42).

- And Jesus could simply command the blind man's sight to return or touch his eyes to cure his blindness; instead he asks the man to submit to what seems like a humiliating series of random prerequisites: *Let me smear mud made from my spit on your face; then I want you to stumble through town until you find the Pool of Siloam; then wash off the mud, and you'll be able to see* (John 9:1-7).

Jesus insists on co-ownership in our reclamation project. Because we're no longer infants in our relationship with him, he won't do everything for us. If he did, we'd never grow. And growth is his focus.

# THE SOURCE OF OUR CHRONIC ANXIETY

Edwin Friedman, the pioneering systems-theory thinker, insists that it's our non-anxious presence, not our strategies or principles or rhetoric, that brings freedom to chronically anxious people and environments. Chronic anxiety, says Friedman, is a symptom of a common relational dysfunction called overfunctioning, when one person violates the boundaries of another by taking on that person's work for them. If I fix the mistakes in my daughters' essays myself, my daughters will get good grades, but they'll never grow in their ability to write, and they'll feel helpless and anxious when I'm not around to do the work for them. [1]

David Cox, professor of education at Arkansas State University, writes: "When someone is overfunctioning in a system, someone else is underfunctioning...What is unintentionally triggered is slipping into a vicious cycle of learned helplessness. The leader overfunctions and the followers compensate by downshifting to a learned helplessness form of existence. The leader typically responds by ratcheting up the overfunctioning, and the followers sink even lower into learned helplessness." [2]

Any behavior that produces helplessness in others is the polar opposite of setting captives free. Even so, in our desire to help and love others, we sometimes unwittingly make them captives to fear by overfunctioning for them. This cycle of helplessness is fueling an alarming rise in anxiety-related disorders in Western culture. Anxiety is now the most common mental-health challenge facing both adolescents and adults in the U.S. Thirty years ago researchers at the Higher Education Research Institute at U.C.L.A. decided to ask incoming college freshmen if they "felt overwhelmed by all [they] had to do" in the year prior to their enrollment. In 1985, one out of five (18 percent) said they did. By 2010, almost a third of incoming freshmen (29 percent) admitted they felt overwhelmed, and by 2016, the number had surged to 41 percent. [3]

> *Any behavior that produces*
> *helplessness in others is the polar*
> *opposite of setting captives free.*

Our overfunctioning parenting patterns have plunged our kids into chronic anxiety. This is exactly the culture-wide captivity that Edwin Friedman was trying to help others resist. Shortly before his death, he created a book of fables to describe, in story form, how destructive overfunctioning really is. In the first tale of this collection, a man who's waited his whole life for the chance to pursue his dream has a brief window of opportunity. He must leap at it because, writes Friedman, "If it were seen that he was not committed, the opportunity would not come again." And so the man leaves on his journey, hurrying toward his destination as his heart comes alive with the possibilities. But as he crosses a bridge through the middle of a town, he sees a man approaching from the other direction. The stranger has a large rope tied around his waist, and when he meets the man, he asks him to hold the other end of it. Taken off guard, the man agrees.

The stranger tells him to hold on tight and then jumps off the bridge. The man manages to brace himself against the bridge and hold on to the rope. He yells at the dangling stranger, "What are you trying to do?"

"Just hold tight...Remember, if you let go, I will be lost." The man can't haul up the stranger on his own, and his strength is fading. So he comes up with an ingenious plan to save the stranger and yells down his instructions. But when the dangling man won't exert any effort to save himself, the man responds: "I will not accept the position of choice for your life, only for my own; the position of choice for your own life I hereby give back to you...I mean, simply, it's up to you. You decide which way this ends. I will become the counterweight. You do the pulling and bring yourself up." When there is no change in the tension of the rope, the man yells down to the stranger, "I accept your choice." And the rope falls free. [4]

The temptation is for the man to overfunction for the stranger—to allow himself to take *all the responsibility* for a person who's depending on him. If the man in Friedman's story had given up his dream in order to save the life of the dangling stranger, he would have been responsible for the stranger's life—a domineering presence. This is exactly what God refuses to become in our lives. He wants relationship, not dominance. And that's why he offers us extraordinary compassion, but not empathy. Compassion is the emotional ability to care for others; empathy is "vicariously experiencing the feelings, thoughts, and experience of another." [5] The difference between the two is a chasm.

## THE PROBLEM WITH EMPATHY

In Jesus' parable of the prodigal son, probably the most well-known of all his stories, the father in the tale sees his reprobate son returning home after the son has squandered his inheritance and sullied the family name with wild living. What is the father feeling when he sees his son tramping toward home? "Filled with love and *compassion,* he ran to his son, embraced him, and kissed him" (Luke 15:20, emphasis added).

The father in this story (who represents God) is compassionate, for sure, but not empathetic. He loves his son, but he does not extend his tender love past his son's own boundaries by *inhabiting* his emotional space. Compassion waits for the son with an expectant hope; empathy scours the countryside to find him, then insists that he come home against his will because the man is unable to separate his identity from his son's.

To rescue us, God comes to live among us—but he doesn't *become* us. Jesus is fully God and fully *human,* not fully Rick, not fully you. Empathy attempts to stand in the shoes of others, to feel what they feel and see what they see. In contrast, compassion stands outside others, offering love and encouragement and support, but not overfunctioning for them. We don't do *for* others what love requires they *must* do for themselves.

On an episode of the BBC's *Life Story,* David Attenborough, the great British naturalist, narrates a gripping drama played out against the backdrop of a craggy, 400-foot cliff in Greenland. Two adult barnacle geese, a mother and father, wait at the bottom of the cliff, squawking for their five goslings to leap out of their nest far above them. Barnacle geese build their nests in these rocky perches, impossibly separated from their source of food on the ground, in order to protect their offspring from predators. But the goslings will die of hunger if they stay in the nest, so their parents must goad them into leaping off the cliff, using their tiny wings to break their fall as much as possible. Only three of the five survive this harrowing rite of passage. The parents quickly surround the surviving goslings to help them recover from the fall, but they don't otherwise intervene. And this is shocking to five British families watching this episode live. Empathetic horror and disbelief rule. A lone viewer seems to grasp the compassionate truth. *All* of the goslings would likely die if their nest weren't built on the top of a cliff, and their life-and-death journey to the ground is their best hope for their survival. [6]

Jesse Prinz, a philosopher and researcher at City University of New York, argues that empathy "influences people to care more about cute victims than ugly victims." And, he says, empathy fuels nepotism, subverts justice, and "leads us to react to shocking incidents…but not to longstanding conditions." [7] Friedman is even more suspicious of empathy—he sees it as "a focus on weakness or immaturity rather than on strength…and a way of avoiding issues of personal accountability." [8]

Jesus understands that some hurts and hardships are actually necessary for our healthy growth, so he does not let empathy stand in the way of a greater purpose. He wants us to be freed captives so we can enjoy an intimate, trusting relationship with him and join him in his mission. Empathy keeps our jail doors shut because it fuels an overfunctioning response to hardship. This is why, after Jesus shrewdly rescues the woman caught in adultery from execution, responding with ferocious compassion to her crisis, he bluntly tells her to "go and sin no more." He wants her to be free more than he wants her to feel comfortable with what she's done, now that she's been rescued from its consequences.

The issue is not whether we treat others' well-being as a priority—of course we do. The issue is whether we've taken the time to understand what well-being actually is, and whether the choices we make are helping or hurting true well-being. Friedman advocates personal responsibility *("You can do" instead of "I can do")* over empathy. He also urges "maturity over more data" *(not procrastinating a hard thing)* and "stamina over technique" *(hard work instead of quick fixes)*. A healthy person lives as Jesus lives in the kingdom of God—he is a come-alongside helper, not a usurper of control. He *will* hold on to the rope if we've fallen off the bridge, but he will *not* enable our state of helplessness if we refuse to climb back up.

## OFFER STRENGTH; DON'T UNDERMINE IT

Healthy cells in our bodies behave in a differentiated way, and so do healthy people. Author and pastor Jay Pathak emphasizes the role of differentiated relationships in building healthy community in a church. "It's helpful to understand what the opposite of differentiation is," he says. "An undifferentiated person says, 'I don't know how I feel without knowing what you feel and what you think.' It's like a cell that does not have an intact membrane and is dependent on other cells to figure out what it is. Cells that operate like that in your body we call cancer cells—they're not clear about their function, so they start either reproducing too fast or they steal life from other cells. Cancer kills people. In the same way, undifferentiated people hurt the people around them…If we say, 'I can't feel okay unless you feel okay, so help me to feel okay,' then we are not differentiated. Differentiation means I know what I think, I know what I feel, apart from you." [9]

Survival expert and television host Bear Grylls has built a career helping others experience greater freedom, and he does it by prodding them to differentiate themselves from their fears. The celebrities who spend a few days with Grylls never know what they're in for—it could be rappelling down 100-foot cliffs in the Snowdonia Mountains or exploring abandoned World War II munitions caves in the Italian

Dolomites. Because of his British Special Forces training, Grylls knows how to face dangerous challenges and overcome them. But it's his ability to remain closely connected to his clients while maintaining separation from their anxieties that sets them free to face their fears. He wants them to function for themselves because he's determined to build their core strength.

When Academy Award–winning actress Kate Winslet's feet lose contact with the concave part of a cliff she's descending, belayed from above by Grylls, she panics. He quickly rappels down to help Winslet traverse the cliff to a less dangerous perch. Once out of immediate danger, a shaken Winslet vents: "That was scary, actually. That *really* didn't feel great. There was an element of the unknown I wasn't too comfortable with." Grylls listens without diminishing her fears, then reaches for a thermos in his backpack and pours the actress a cup of tea: "The great thing about taking a fellow Brit on an adventure is that whenever there's a drama, a near-death moment—a cup of tea," he says with a smile. [10] Winslet laughs and accepts the cup, sipping it while suspended hundreds of feet up the side of a cliff.

Like Winslet, we all have an interior narrator whose running commentary focuses on our circumstantial fears, and that voice urges us to join ourselves to our anxieties. *"If I don't negate my own hurt and pain, my spouse may withdraw his love for me."* Or *"If I don't call my child's teacher to complain about her test grade, she may not get an A in the class, and that would reflect badly on my identity as a parent."* Our fear narration is frustratingly plausible, because the danger seems real to us. But there are always two dangers lurking behind every threat: the empirical danger (suspending yourself on the side of a 100-foot cliff is undeniably dangerous), and the internal danger fueled by our emotional processes ("I'm trusting my life to a thin bit of cord and a reality-show star").

The antidote to this cycle of anxiety is the kind of relaxed skepticism that characterizes Grylls' non-anxious approach to fear. He skewers the narratives that grip his paralyzed clients, separating truth from untruth with a joke. Grylls calls this "keeping cheerful when it's miserable," but its impact is much deeper than that. He's an expert guide for those who want to experience what freedom from captivity is really like. "To be honest," he says, "I don't feel like I am a survival expert…I think this a great arena for these [people] to… really challenge themselves, to really refine themselves." [11] And that refinement is fueled by spiritual grit—a determination to keep moving in the face of fear. "It's about being strengthened," explains Grylls. "It's about having a backbone run through you from the Person who made you. It's about being able to climb the biggest mountains in the world with the Person who made them." [12]

> *Refinement is fueled by spiritual grit—a determination to keep moving in the face of fear.*

Grylls uses circumstantial dangers to surface the emotional processes that keep his clients captive to fear. He's intent on exposing his clients' core beliefs about their identities (their ontology) by leading them into their anxieties, guiding them to face and then separate themselves from their internal fears by exposing them to external fears. To grow their spiritual grit, he stays relationally connected to them but doesn't overstep their boundaries by doing *for* them. Instead, he expects them to do *more* than they think they can do. And because Grylls refuses to overfunction for them, they learn to keep moving through their fears, even when their emotional processes try to jam on the brakes.

## REPLACING *FOR* WITH *MORE*

In October 2000, the *USS Cole* was attacked by suicide bombers while docked at a Yemeni port. In the chaotic aftermath of the attack that killed 17 sailors, the quick thinking and calm strength of the ship's commander, Kirk Lippold, was widely credited for saving the destroyer and the rest of its crew. Speaking to a group of students at Highland School in Virginia, Lippold later made his case for the importance of developing a differentiated core: "Leadership...boils down to one word, and that is *integrity*. If you have the integrity to do what's right regardless of the circumstances and the situation, you are a leader in your own right, because so many people today fail or waiver on that one key trait."[13]

Integrity means we maintain our personal borders and move with conviction, no matter what our circumstances are—just the way a healthy cell remains differentiated from aggressive invaders. A conviction is a belief that's decided *before* we enter into situations that test it. It's a determination to maintain separation from the anxiety that tries to bully us. And conviction-building is the work of Jesus in our everyday lives—he is our own personal Bear Grylls. He will ask us to do *more* before he does *for* us.

To partner with him in this work, we will move away from habits that ask him (and others) to *do for* us and double-down on our determination to *do more*. Here's how that might look:

**1. We move from ignorance about the forces at work in us to self-awareness.** We first have to pay attention to our behavior if we hope to understand it, moving from self-knowledge to self-awareness. For example, sometimes I get defensive when someone points out a mistake I've made—that observation comes from self-knowledge. But *why* do I get defensive? My answer to that question leads me to self-awareness.

Leadership consultant Dov Baron writes, "We have to develop self-knowledge before we can have self-awareness because 'We don't know what we don't know.' I've been asked many times: If a person could do one thing, and one thing only, to transform leadership, what would it be? In response I would say that that one thing wouldn't depend on the individual's level of intelligence; and it certainly would not involve extra charisma. My answer would be that those who lead in any capacity have massive self-knowledge." [14]

When entrepreneur Richard Branson saw an opportunity to fill a niche in the airline business that no one else was targeting, he built and launched Virgin Atlantic in 1984. Of course, he says, "Many people doubted us, assuming that we wouldn't know how to run an airline since we had no experience in the industry…I've found that knowing your business and yourself can also help you to know when to follow your instincts, so you can find the courage to move ahead and ignore the advice of naysayers." [15]

Having real influence in our relationships is dependent upon how well we understand our core operating system—our ontology. And the journey into self-awareness begins with the pursuit of self-knowledge. Self-knowledge drags our behavior into the spotlight, where we can study and consider *why* we do the things we do. This is why Jesus so often encourages self-knowledge, then prods people into self-awareness, before he releases them from their captivity. For example, pay attention to what Jesus does before he offers the woman at the well his "living water" (John 4):

"'Go and get your husband,' Jesus told her.

'I don't have a husband,' the woman replied.

Jesus said, 'You're right! You don't have a husband—for you have had five husbands, and you aren't even married to the man you're living with now. You certainly spoke the truth!'

'Sir,' the woman said, 'you must be a prophet'" (John 4:16-19).

From this point in the encounter, she leaves her façade by the well and reenters a daunting relational environment behind the walls of Sychar, her hometown, with a new power and presence. Because she is much more self-aware than before her encounter with Jesus ("Come and see a man who told me everything I ever did!"), she now has the spiritual grit she needs to move past her shame and offer life to the very people who've fueled it. Spiritual grit, the product of greater self-awareness, moves the woman from her place in the shadows into her role as the church's very first evangelist.

Likewise, we pay better attention to the things we do and say, and then move toward a deeper self-awareness, when we...

- **"Notice what we notice."** This phrase is one of my friend Tom Melton's favorite diagnostic filters for self-awareness. Simply, it means we pay attention to what captures our attention, then try to understand *why* our attention has been captured.

  For example, I love improvisational jazz—it plays all day long in our home, and I go out of my way to experience live performances (that's self-knowledge). But *why* do I love this particular style of music so much? Well, improvisational jazz is a form of relational courage. The players must listen to each other with fierce attention, then embrace risk after risk to create something unique and beautiful. Because I treasure intimacy in relationships—and courage, creativity, and beauty—I'm drawn to a form of music that exemplifies these things (that's self-awareness). I know this about myself because I slow down to notice what I notice. The result is that I have much stronger convictions about the music I listen to and its role in encouraging the growth of spiritual grit in me.

  I've mentioned that I love to watch the sport of cross-country running (self-knowledge). But *why,* exactly? I remember showing up for my oldest daughter's first meet with an attitude of grudging obligation; I was there only because it was important to my daughter. What I experienced was hundreds of teenagers pushing themselves beyond their capacities, facing their fears, and persevering when they felt alone and threatened. It's the inherent courage I witnessed in these insecure teenagers that drew me to this sport—and courage is a magnet for my heart (self-awareness). As a result, I'm more inclined to support and participate in fitness activities that require courage and grow grit.

- **Know our "emotional triggers" and regulate ourselves with that awareness.** When we recognize our emotions are stronger than situations warrant, we know something has touched one of our emotional triggers. For example, because of the formative influences of my childhood, I'm particularly sensitive to people and situations that make me feel invisible. When my needs seem ignored or my strengths taken for granted, I become irritable, angry, and defensive. But when I'm aware of those triggers, I respond more reasonably, more humbly, and more courageously—my spiritual grit allows me to stay connected in my relationships because I'm not at the mercy of my defense mechanisms.

- **Guard our personal boundaries when someone or something attempts to breach them.** Not long ago my daughter glanced at my open laptop and read a sensitive email I'd sent to a friend that included a mild concern about her. She later told my wife what she'd read. My wife, in turn, told me about their conversation and urged me to wait before bringing it up with my daughter. In that moment I was upset that my daughter had misconstrued my feelings about her, and I was angry that my boundaries had been violated. This situation touched on my emotional triggers, which hampered my ability to calmly, firmly express my determination to guard my boundaries. I had to loop back with my daughter when I was more on top of my emotions to help her understand my true feelings and make it clear that it was a violation of my boundaries to read a private note without my permission.

  Our default setting is to blame others. So self-awareness is a powerful way to take personal responsibility for our words and actions and respond with grit in difficult situations. It helps us to inventory our own role in a conflict before we turn our attention to others. Jesus said, "Why worry about a speck in your friend's eye when you have a log in your own?" (Matthew 7:3).

> *Self-awareness is a powerful way*
> *to take personal responsibility for*
> *our words and actions.*

**2. We move from watching others give to giving what we have.**
Resilience researcher Dennis Charney, dean of the Icahn School of Medicine at Mount Sinai in New York City, has spent his academic career studying people who suffer from post-traumatic stress disorder (PTSD). He's sought to understand why some trauma survivors never develop the disorder or are able to overcome it. Along the way he's discovered some surprising keys to growing grit, and one of them is *altruism* (sacrificial giving). "It's important to pay it forward," says Charney. "Helping others makes us feel competent, improves our problem-solving abilities, and gives us a larger sense of purpose. All of that translates to more resilience." [16] When we altruistically offer our strength to others, we build grit.

For example:

- People who are older than 55 who volunteer to help with two or more organizations have an astonishing 44 percent lower chance of dying than nonvolunteers. [17] Consider your strengths and what fuels your passions; then find at least one way to regularly volunteer with an activity or organization that fits you.

- Harvard psychologist Robert Brooks surveyed 1,500 adults, asking them to point to experiences when they were school-age children that permanently affected their motivation and self-esteem. A majority highlighted a time when a teacher or other adult asked them to help out with a significant responsibility. [18] How can you help another person realize a dream, and what sacrifices are you willing to make to do that?

- A study in the Journal of Child Development finds that volunteers who fulfill their commitments have parents who model helpfulness in their home. Kids who often don't fulfill their commitments have parents who don't model helpfulness. [19] Who do you know who has a track record of serving others with joy and courage? Find excuses to hang out with those people—let their operating systems infect you.

- Researchers studied human-rights activists in South America who face chronic civil conflict and unrest. The researchers discovered that victims of catastrophe who risked their own safety to rescue others improved their ability to persevere through disasters. [20] In the midst of a tough challenge or staggering trauma, look for little ways to give to others who are also hurting. The side effect of strengthening others' grit is that your own determination grows.

Jesus underscores a crucial truth about altruism that propels our movement from the sidelines to the playing field in our relationships: "I tell you the truth, when you did it to one of the least of these my brothers and sisters, you were doing it to me!" (Matthew 25:40).

**3. We move from offloading responsibility to shouldering responsibility.** When Geno Auriemma, record-setting coach of the University of Connecticut women's basketball team, showed up for a press conference before his team's Final Four playoff game in 2016, he turned his moment in the spotlight into an opportunity to make a point about grit. At the time, UConn hadn't lost a game in more than two years and was about to play for its fifth consecutive national title. Even so, Auriemma insisted that it was harder than ever to recruit enthusiastic kids for his team:

Because every kid watches TV, and they watch [professional athletes]…and what they see is people just being really cool. So they think that's how they're going to act. And they haven't even figured out which foot to use as a pivot foot, and they're going to act like they're really good players…So recruiting kids that are really upbeat, loving life, love the game, and have this tremendous appreciation for when their teammates do something well, that's really hard. So on our team we put a huge premium on body language, and if your body language is bad, you will never get in the game…[Some kids are] allowed to get away with just whatever, and they're always thinking about themselves. Me, me, me, me, me. 'I didn't score, so why should I be happy?' 'I'm not getting enough minutes; why should I be happy?' That's the world we live in today, unfortunately. Kids check the scoreboard sometimes because they're going to get yelled at by their parents if they don't score enough points. *(Shakes head)* Don't get me started. So…when I watch game film, I'm checking what's going on [over] on the bench. And if somebody's asleep over there, somebody doesn't care, somebody's not engaged in the game, they will never get in the game. Ever. And they know I'm not kidding. [21]

Auriemma's two-and-a-half-minute rant went viral on social media an entire year after it happened—during the 2017 NCAA Women's Basketball Tournament, when another coach posted it on his Facebook page. More than 40 million people have now viewed it. At its core is a message about expecting more from young people than their narcissistic, self-centered culture models for them. When Auriemma benched his star player the previous season, sports commentators assumed he was trying to "send her a message" in advance of an important game. But instead, the coach said the player "was acting like a 12-year-old," and he took her out of the game to remind her of her greater responsibility to the team. He wants players that have a passion for something higher than themselves and will respond well when they're asked to sacrifice for the sake of the team. He's attempting to build into kids something their culture has systematically extracted from them: personal responsibility and sacrifice.

In our everyday lives, we do what Auriemma does for his players when we:

- Insist our kids clean up after themselves—putting away clothes, washing their own dishes, and dealing with the messes they make.

- Assign kids regular family chores that must be completed before they can enjoy free time or receive an allowance.

- Expect young people to earn the money to pay for big-ticket items like cars, special trips, and upgrades to their bedrooms.

- Leave tough phone calls, tough complaints, and tough conversations to the person who is the primary owner of the problem.

- Use the "Three Musketeers filter" when we deal with tough stuff in our families: "One for all, and all for one." We expect everyone in the family to pull together and play a role in overcoming crises and meeting challenges such as medical setbacks, financial hits, and significant home projects.

- Listen without a fix-it-first mentality when someone shares a problem or challenge. We offer help only when it's requested or after we've asked permission to offer it.

- When the choice is between something hard-but-good and something easy-but-good, encourage the harder choice.

- Respond to an entitlement mentality by asking, "What part of that will you contribute?"

- Live by this loose rule: 1) Screw up one time, you get the grace of no present consequence, with a good-natured admonition to get it right the next time. 2) Screw up the same way a second time, you get the grace of a mild present consequence, with the hope that the strength required to persevere through it will help you get it right the next time. 3) Screw up the same way a third time, and you get the grace of a significant consequence, with the hope that it will awaken your sleeping spiritual grit so that there will be no "next time."

**4. We move from rescuing to encouraging.** Sheryl Sandberg is the first woman appointed to Facebook's board of directors—she works alongside Mark Zuckerberg as the company's chief operating officer. On a family vacation in Mexico with her husband, Survey Monkey CEO Dave Goldberg, Sandberg watched as he suffered a heart attack while they were exercising side-by-side on treadmills. He later died. In the face of knee-buckling grief and the prospect of carrying on as a single mother with two young children and a very demanding career, Sandberg dedicated herself to learning everything she could to help her shell-shocked kids recover and thrive.

In a profile for Inc.com, highlighting three of Sandberg's discoveries about persevering through hardship, writer Jessica Stillman says: "As a parent, your natural inclination is to rush ahead of your kids, clearing their path of obstacles and dangers, but following this impulse produces several problems. First, while this is a viable strategy for toddlers, it's pretty much impossible as your children grow older. And even if you could manage it, your kids won't learn the vital skills needed to navigate their own way through life if you're constantly fixing things for them. So what do you do instead of solving your kids' problems? You walk beside them while they navigate life's challenges on their own." [22]

After Moses died in the barren wasteland across the Jordan River from the Promised Land, his faithful assistant Joshua was tapped by God to lead his people into the land of Canaan and conquer it. Joshua was a sidekick suddenly thrust into a leading role. The pressure and fear must have been crushing. In response to the challenge, God didn't take the edge off of his mission. Instead, he offered Joshua the one thing he needed most: God's own presence. Speaking directly to Joshua on the eve of marching across the Jordan, God said:

> Moses my servant is dead. Therefore, the time has come for you to lead these people, the Israelites, across the Jordan River into the land I am giving them. I promise you what I promised Moses: "Wherever you set foot, you will be on land I have given you...No one will be able to stand against you as long as you live. *For I will be with you as I was with Moses. I will not fail you or abandon you...*This is my command—be strong and courageous! Do not be afraid or discouraged. *For the Lord your God is with you wherever you go* (Joshua 1:2-5, 9, emphasis added).

The courage to face our great challenges doesn't come from increased ability or decreased difficulty. Its source is the presence of God. In parenting language, Sandberg calls this dynamic "companioning"—offering support by "walking alongside them and listening." [23]

> *The courage to face our great challenges*
> *doesn't come from increased ability*
> *or decreased difficulty. Its source*
> *is the presence of God.*

Again, Jesus describes it this way: "I no longer call you slaves, because a master doesn't confide in his slaves. Now you are my friends, since I have told you everything the Father told me. You didn't choose me. I chose you" (John 15:15-16). Likewise, we focus less on our rescue plans for others and a great deal more on giving them the courage of our presence—our engaged, persistent, and determined presence.

A presence that communicates, *I'm with you, I believe in you, and it's going to be okay.*

A presence that communicates, *You didn't choose me. I chose you.*

**5. We move from refusing to pay the price for growth to spending what it takes.** Jesus has put a price tag on our growth, and it's often steeper than what we want to pay. For the rich young man the price of what he wants—eternal life—seems mind-boggling: "Sell all your possessions and give the money to the poor" (Matthew 19:21). Daunted by the price of that growth, the disillusioned man retreats into his rut. We know that Jesus loved this young man, and that's what motivated him to up the price of following him. Catch that again: *When Jesus asked the young man to pay a higher price to attain the growth he was pursuing, Jesus was loving him with all his heart.* Earlier, Jesus assured his disciples, "If any of you wants to be my follower, you must give up your own way, take up your cross, and follow me. If you try to hang on to your life, you will lose it. But if you give up your life for my sake, you will save it" (Matthew 16:24-25). Unlike a used car salesman who wheels-and-deals, altering the price as negotiations shift, Jesus is upfront about the price of discipleship. The higher the price, the deeper our commitment. And deep, intimate commitment is the best greenhouse for growth in our relationship with Jesus and with others.

Spending what it takes for the growth we crave might mean…

- **We carve out time—every day and every week—to nurture face-to-face relationships with our spouses, kids, or friends.** We know that "quality time is as good as quantity time" is a myth designed to assuage our guilt for the marginless way we live our lives. The truth is, depth in our relationships requires both quality *and* quantity time. That's the price of growth.

  Our circumstances will dictate how we live out this commitment. In our home, my wife and I take daily walks around our neighborhood, guard our evening meals together as a family, and reserve most Saturdays for family game night.

- **We raise our tolerance level for pain in our everyday lives.** Maybe that means getting up 10 minutes early to write a loving note to someone. Or maybe it means attending a new fitness class five times before allowing ourselves to quit. Or maybe it means broaching a tough subject with a spouse or best friend instead of hoping it will simply go away. Or maybe it means letting our kids experience the painful consequences of their choices. That's the price of growth.

- **We care as much about the future as we care about the present and the past.** Jesus loved people in the present, always with an eye to their future. He was interested in helping them overcome not only the hurdles right in front of them, but also all the hurdles down the line. For example, when we eat healthily now, it may feel like we're giving up something, but we're actually nurturing our future selves, who want to live full and active lives into old age. That's the price of growth.

- **We read a book or listen to a podcast that stretches our perspectives.** One of the young men in our small group has just given his life to Jesus, and a longtime regular in the group told him to listen to Timothy Keller's sermons online and read C.S. Lewis' *Mere Christianity* as an on-ramp into his new life. Keller is the founding pastor of New York City's Redeemer Presbyterian Church, and he's a great teacher, but he's also a demanding teacher. And Lewis' masterwork is profound, but it's not an easy read. Both suggestions will require this young man to think and grapple and chew. And that's just the challenge he needs. That's the price of growth.

- **We listen with curiosity to people whose views are in opposition to our own.** When I started listening to talk radio a couple of decades ago, I was intentionally exposing myself to political and cultural views that repelled me. I wanted to understand what I didn't understand. It was painful; I had to grit my teeth most days. But I increased my capacity to enter into life-giving conversations with a wider variety of people. That's the price of growth.

- **We slow down when we read, travel, talk, eat, and play.** We live in a culture that operates at a frenetic pace; in fact, according to an analysis of pedestrians in more than 30 cities around the world, our walking pace has sped up by 10 percent in just the last decade. University of Hertfordshire psychology professor Richard Wiseman, who analyzed the "pedestrian pace" data, says, "When you speed people up and they become stressed, they don't take care of themselves. They don't eat properly; they don't go to the gym; they start smoking." [24]

  God created us to savor life, not taste-test it. This is a "physician, heal thyself" truth for me. I keep up a demanding pace at work, home, and church, and I'm sometimes frustrated by people who move slowly through life. But I know that when "slow" isn't mixed into my "fast," I can't give others a dipper of water from the well of life within me. And I become my own worst enemy. So I get up before everyone else in the morning to enjoy slow before my fast begins. I take at least one solo retreat at a Trappist monastery in the Colorado mountains every year. For many years, I've spent one day a month in a silent retreat in a simple room at a convent an hour from home. When I meet with a friend, I set my end point for the get-together so I'm not anxious about the time; then I confine my focus to my friend and nothing else. In our family we take our time with evening meals, always lit by candlelight, with great music playing in the background, focusing on conversation. That's the price of growth.

Like everything else in life, we get what we pay for when it comes to growth. When we acknowledge that, we create a willingness to get past the sticker shock and make the investment. The only exception to this, on the face of it, is Jesus' free gift of grace on the cross, but even here, we must lay down our lives to pick up the life he's given us. That's the hidden cost of redemption.

**6. We move from receiving things to consume to producing things to consume.** In a consumer-driven culture, we're conditioned to receive, receive, receive. Our happiness, we're led to believe, is tied to how much we consume. But when a natural disaster hits, we discover that our true foundation for significance in life is not consuming, but producing.

During the aftermath of Hurricane Harvey in 2017, when scores of people in Houston and the surrounding area were still trapped in their homes and desperate for rescue, the "Cajun Navy" arrived on the scene like a water-born cavalry. The group is an ad hoc army of volunteers from the Louisiana coastland who own private boats and have dedicated themselves to assisting in search-and-rescue efforts. Formed during the aftermath of Hurricane Katrina, a storm that destroyed much of New Orleans, the Cajun Navy is credited with rescuing hundreds of needy people in Houston. Because of their experience piloting small boats in the shallow waters of the Louisiana swamps, these men and women had the expertise the Harvey survivors desperately needed.

Baton Rouge native Jordy Bloodsworth was only 12 years old when Katrina poured 14 feet of water down on southern Louisiana. His family lost everything when the water broke over the top of a levee and swamped their home. Twelve years later Bloodsworth watched as TV images showed Houston, the nation's fourth-largest city, filling up with water like a bathtub with the spigot left on. So he borrowed a friend's truck and hitched his 18-foot fishing boat to the back. "I was young during Katrina, and I know how it feels to lose everything," he says. "So being able to help others going through this situation that I have experienced, there's no way—*no way*—I could pass up helping." [25]

The profound impact of producing—adding rather than subtracting from the world—creates an indelible narrative of spiritual grit that supports and fuels future acts of courage. Many in the Cajun Navy have now made heroism their default setting in life, leaving behind families and jobs at a moment's notice over the last 12 years to help out during catastrophic rainstorms and hurricanes.

> *The profound impact of producing—adding rather than subtracting from the world— creates an indelible narrative of spiritual grit that supports and fuels future acts of courage.*

We elevate producing over consuming and invest ourselves in *more* rather than *for*, when…

- We create public or private art such as music, prose, poetry, painting, dance, film, illustration, stand-up comedy, and spoken-word performances.

- We build things instead of buy things.

- We gather money or petitions for a political candidate or campaign.

- We spend a day helping maintain a trail in a national park.

- We volunteer to lead tour groups at museums, art galleries, or historic homes.

- We tutor struggling students at a community center.

- We organize local efforts to bring justice and redemption to people who are marginalized or discriminated against.

- We lead a Bible study or book group designed to build a faith foundation in others.

- We read to kids in hospitals.

- We coach youth sports or academic teams.

- We plan a monthly support group for parents who want to build spiritual grit in their kids.

The idea is to reverse our learned tendency to approach life as consumers rather than producers. The first step is to simply recognize our own addictive consumer patterns and pause before we give in to them. In his passionate rebuttal of the "eye for an eye" standard of justice, Jesus offers a challenge that calls for heroic *producing*: "If you are sued in court and your shirt is taken from you, give your coat, too. If a soldier demands that you carry his gear for a mile, carry it two miles.

Give to those who ask, and don't turn away from those who want to borrow" (Matthew 5:40-42).

**7. We move from pursuing the heart of Jesus in a passive way to a slowed-down, active way.** It's impossible to comprehend the heart of *anyone,* including Jesus, when we're in a hurry. Hurry forces us into a thumbnail experience of others—we don't notice the nuances that characterize their hearts. And the nuances we discover in the things Jesus said and did are like open windows into his core. To discover that core, we actively slow way, way down when we read about things he said or did. I call this practice "wallowing in mud puddles." I define a mud puddle as any story about Jesus that we don't really understand so we simply jump over it. That's what adults do when they encounter a mud puddle—they jump over it. But when children come upon a mud puddle, they jump *into* it. Remember, Jesus told us we must become like little children if we hope to understand and live out the values of the kingdom of God.

But how do we slow down to consider the depths of Jesus' heart when *hurry* is the ocean we swim in? The Latin phrase *festina lente,* first introduced by the priest and theologian Erasmus in the Middle Ages, means to "hurry slowly." [26] When we approach Jesus in the spirit of *festina lente,* we uncover his nuances even when we're moving fast. For example, I use "reading filters" to unlock the heart of Jesus in any story about him. I choose a filter that helps me narrow my focus as I read; then I look for examples that pop out to me because of the filter I'm using.

Take a look at Matthew 15, for example. Let's say you've noticed something about Jesus in this chapter—that he really seems to hate rules and traditions that have nothing to do with the heart. So you create a filter based on that ("Jesus is opposed to rote traditions and rules"), and then, as an experiment, you scan Matthew 5, 6, and 7 in a *festina lente* sort of way, looking for examples of this truth about Jesus. What you discover will transform the way you see him, shedding your inherited understanding of him for something more like shocking wonder. The idea is to look for patterns and emphases that tie to some aspect of Jesus' heart or recurring themes in the Bible.

We look deeper than passive surface explanations can take us, and we never settle for cop-outs like this one: *"I don't really understand why Jesus did that, but that's Jesus for you."* We don't move past the confusing or difficult things about Jesus too quickly; in fact, we *seek* the mud-puddle moments in Jesus' life and ministry because they offer us the most insight into his heart.

# THE STAKES ARE HIGH

As I write this, parents in my local school district are reeling from two back-to-back suicides in the last 48 hours—first a high school junior, and last night an eighth-grader. It was Back to School night at my freshman daughter's high school yesterday, a chance for parents to follow their students' daily schedules and go to each class for a six-minute overview and meet-and-greet. In the hallways as we hurried from classroom to classroom, we saw little clumps of worried, anguished parents sharing the terrible news. A father from my neighborhood caught my eye and waved me over. He's a follower of Jesus, and he lost his own daughter to cancer when she was in elementary school. His face was contorted and angry. He spat out the question many were asking: "Why is this happening so often in *our* backyard?" I told him it's not just our backyard—suicide is the second-leading cause of death among adolescents in America, rapidly gaining on traffic accidents as the top killer. "You mean, in the whole country?" he asked. I nodded. And he turned and walked away, his shoulders slumped, slowly making his way down the hallway to his son's next class.

What I want to say, what I *need* to say but can't say in moments like these to parents ensnared by grief, is this truth: We live in the most affluent society in the history of the world, and one deadly (and counterintuitive) side effect of affluence is suicide. A 2012 study by the U.S. government found that the richer the neighborhood, the higher the risk of suicide. [27] Arizona State psychology professor Suniya Luthar studies resilience in teenagers, and her work reveals that affluent kids are among the most emotionally distressed in America. "These kids are incredibly anxious and perfectionistic," she says, but there's "contempt and scorn for the idea that kids who have it all might be hurting." [28]

If we have the means to make life easier for our kids, we will extract hardship from their path as often as it seems reasonable. It's just the way things work. And when we systematically make things easier for our kids, they don't develop the perseverance they need to keep moving through their inevitable seasons of disappointment, conflict, and depression. Spiritual grit is not merely a catalyst fueling our determined response to challenges, setbacks, and opportunities in our lives—*it's a core strength that can mean the difference between life and death.*

We can't always protect ourselves or our kids from danger, but we can partner with Jesus to grow spiritual grit in ourselves and in them. We can't neutralize every threat we face, any more than we can stop every mosquito from attacking us by hanging a bug light on our back porch. Bad stuff is going to happen to us, to our kids, and to our friends. But if we can't always diminish the impact or scope of our challenges, we *can* strengthen our response to them.

Jesus loves us, and *because* he loves us, he wants to grow our spiritual grit. He's inviting us to train with him, to discover the courage available to us when we attach ourselves more deeply to him in a lover's relationship characterized by dependence and passion. When we sink more deeply into his heart, we will find freedom from our captivity and the strength we need to face anything life throws at us.

The overarching truth Jesus tries to convey to his disciples on the eve of his horrific sacrifice on Golgotha is this: *You are my friends, and my Spirit is about to find a home in you—so I believe in your strength. I believe in you.* He tells them, "I am leaving you with a gift—peace of mind and heart. And the peace I give is a gift the world cannot give. So don't be troubled or afraid. Remember what I told you: I am going away, but I will come back to you again" (John 14:27–28). Later, he adds this exclamation point: "Here on earth you will have many trials and sorrows. But take heart, because I have overcome the world" (John 16:33).

And then Jesus tells them exactly what those trials and sorrows will look like. He wants them to know what they're about to face, with the expectation that they will "take heart," or respond with spiritual grit and determination. Their future will include persecution, shunning, murder, heartbreak, the physical destruction of their community, war, famines, earthquakes, arrest, persecution, hatred, religious deception, and sin.

And here, at the end of this sobering blast of reality, Jesus points to the necessity of spiritual grit: *"But everyone who endures to the end will be saved"* (Matthew 10:22). Endurance is his gift of "peace of mind and heart." It is the one variable that cannot be conquered by circumstance. And its only lasting source is Jesus. This is why the last declaration he makes to his Father before he walks out of Gethsemane and down Jerusalem's Via Dolorosa, dragging his own cross, is so important for us to remember today, in moments of great challenge and fear:

"I'm not asking you to take them out of the world, but to keep them safe from the evil one…Father, I want these whom you have given me to be with me where I am…I have revealed you to them, and I will continue to do so. Then your love for me will be in them, and I will be in them" (John 15:17, 24, 26).

# QUESTIONS FOR SMALL-GROUP
# DISCUSSION OR INDIVIDUAL CONTEMPLATION

1. In what ways are you tempted to do for, instead of expect more of others, and why?

_____

_____

_____

_____

2. Jesus often asked the people who asked him for help to do more before he would do for. How have you seen this pattern in your relationship with him?

_____

_____

_____

_____

3. When has someone in your life overfunctioned for you, and what impact did it have on you?

_____

_____

_____

_____

4. What's your reaction to Edwin Friedman's fable about the man and the stranger on the bridge?

_____

_____

_____

_____

5. It's a challenge to accept that empathy might be a less helpful response to others' needs than compassion is. In what ways do you agree with this, and in what ways do you disagree?

_____

_____

_____

_____

6. Who in your life has offered strength to you, and what impact has it had on you?

_____

_____

_____

_____

7. When have you paid the price for growth in your life, and what has been the outcome?

_____

_____

_____

_____

1   David Cox, essay for Arkansas State University, 2006.

2   Ibid.

3   Benoit Denizet-Lewis, "Why Are More American Teenagers Than Ever Suffering From Severe Anxiety?" *The New York Times Magazine* (October 11, 2017).

4   Edwin Friedman, *Friedman's Fables* (New York: The Guilford Press, 1990), 9-13.

5   From the Merriam-Webster definition of empathy.

6   Ella Davies, "Barnacle gosling's terrifying cliff tumble," BBC.com (October 17, 2014).

7   David Brooks, "The Limits of Empathy," *The New York Times* (September 29, 2011).

8   Edwin Friedman, *Leadership in the Age of the Quick Fix* (1999, 2007), 134.

9   Jay Pathak, "Paying Ridiculous Attention to Jesus" podcast, Season 2, Episode 29: "Jesus Was a Party Animal."

10   *Running Wild With Bear Grylls* (Season 2, Episode 3, July 27, 2015).

11   Daniel Xu, "Bear Grylls Recounts Experiences on New Celebrity Survival Show," www.outdoorhub.com (July 23, 2014).

12   Roxanne Wieman, "The Wild Faith of Bear Grylls," *Relevant* magazine (June 29, 2010).

13   Michael McKinney, "The Well-Differentiated Leader," www.leadershipnow.com (March 23, 2007).

14   Dov Baron, "Why Being a Self-Aware Leader Is Not Enough" (*Entrepreneur*.com, June 4, 2015).

15   Richard Branson, quoted in an interview in *Entrepreneur* magazine (June 3, 2013).

16   Virginia Sole-Smith, "Bounce Back!" *Real Simple* magazine (March 2017).

17  Stephen G. Post, "Altruism, Happiness, and Health: It's Good to Be Good," *International Journal of Behavioral Medicine* (2005, Vol. 12, No. 2), 69.

18  Virginia Sole-Smith, "Bounce Back!" *Real Simple* magazine (March 2017).

19  *Child Development* (Vol. 57, 1358-1369).

20  Pilar Hernández-Wolfe, "Altruism Born of Suffering: How Colombian Human Rights Activists Transform Pain Into Prosocial Action," *Journal of Humanistic Psychology* (September 1, 2010), 229–249.

21  From a recorded segment of the 2016 Women's NCAA Basketball Final Four news conference, transcribed by the author.

22  Jessica Stillman, "Sheryl Sandberg: If You Want to Raise Resilient Kids, Always Do These 3 Things" (Inc.com, May 8, 2017).

23  Ibid.

24  Fiona Macrae, "Pace of Life Speeds Up as Study Reveals We're Walking Faster Than Ever" (DailyMail.com, May 2, 2007).

25  Emily Wax-Thibodeaux, "'Cajun Navy' Races from Louisiana to Texas, Using Boats to Pay It Forward," *The Washington Post* (August 28, 2017).

26  Larry Davidson, Ph.D., "I Have Learned to Hurry Slowly" (*PsychologyToday*.com, May 7, 2010).

27  Mary C. Daly, Daniel J. Wilson, and Norman J. Johnson, "Relative Status and Well-Being: Evidence from U.S. Suicide Deaths" (Federal Reserve Bank of San Francisco, 2012).

28  "Why Are More American Teenagers Than Ever Suffering From Severe Anxiety?" *The New York Times Magazine* (October 17, 2017).

# EPILOGUE: SPIRITUAL GRIT AND THE PARABLE OF TWO SONS

In Jesus' parable of two sons (Matthew 21:28-32), a father asks both of his sons to work in the family vineyard. The older son at first refuses but later changes his mind and goes to work. The younger son agrees to work but never shows up. Jesus asks the leading priests and elders which son has obeyed the will of the father. "The first," they reply. Then Jesus points out that those who *do,* not those who *talk about doing,* are advancing the kingdom of God.

Likewise, spiritual grit is the fruit of doing, not talking about doing. And this kind of doing is the fruit of the heart, as the parable reveals. The older son's words contradict his heart and create dissonance in him. Under the pressure of this dissonance, he reengages his heart and does what is congruent with who he truly is. In the end, he follows his heart into doing what his father has asked him to do.

The elder son's grit is messy and tainted and even a little ugly— and Jesus tells this story for the sole purpose of celebrating this son's circuitous determination. He is, likewise, celebrating *our* circuitous determination right now. Whatever you're facing, wherever you are on the spiritual grit continuum, *Jesus is for you.* He wants you to rise to the occasion, and he's not worried or disappointed when, at first, you don't.

> *Whatever you're facing, wherever you are on the spiritual grit continuum, Jesus is for you.*

The only thing we can do is start from wherever we are right now. Jesus is inviting us to work in his family vineyard, so let's pull on our boots and gloves and walk through the gate...

# BONUS: THE SCHOOL OF INTENSIFIED LONGING

*"What shall we do, what shall we do with all this useless beauty? All this useless beauty."*

—Elvis Costello

When my daughter Emma was little, she made a serious push for us to buy a pony, which she insisted would not only thrive in our suburban backyard but also command all her caregiving attention. Later, she replaced her pony obsession with a giraffe obsession. The longings of childhood point to a fundamental craving: *Emma, like all of us, craved to be known and enjoyed and befriended by a loving someone who would never let her down.*

This craving is a symptom of what French philosopher and scientist Blaise Pascal once described as a *God-shaped hole in our souls.* He meant we're born with an insatiable thirst for true happiness that no pony (or its countless adult variations) can ever satisfy. And so, Pascal tells us, all that remains is an "empty print and trace" marking our soul. [1] We long for joy, hunt for it, but often doubt we'll ever find it…

When Madeline, the long-suffering heroine in Dickens' classic tale *Nicholas Nickleby*, is surprised when the best man she's ever known

(Nicholas) professes his love for her, she responds to his passionate declaration with caution and fear:

> I feel you know what it's like to be without happiness, but do you know what it's like to be afraid of it? To see the world as so conniving, you cannot take pleasure in the appearance of something good because you suspect it is only a painted drop behind which other troubles lie? That has been my life. Every good thing has been a trick. Until you. Yet I am afraid to take your hand. What if you cannot or will not save me? [2]

Are we more like Madeline in our relationship with God than we'd like to admit? Is Jesus' apparent goodness, and his invitation into intimate relationship, just another of life's shell games? Will the "greatest good thing" in the history of the world—the revelation that God has become man in order to restore our relationship with him and save our lives—turn out to be a terrible trick in the end? It seems impossible for us to trust Jesus with *all* our heart. Do we even have *all* our heart left to give? The only path into abandon, moving through our caution and fear, is to pay better attention to the heart of Jesus— ridiculous attention.

Once we experience the heart of Jesus, doing whatever it takes to grow in an intimate relationship with him happens naturally. This is the obvious point of the parables Jesus tells about a treasure hidden in a field and a pearl of great price in Matthew 13. It's perfectly reasonable to give up something of comparatively low value to acquire something of inestimable value. If we comprehend the value of the pearl and the treasure, we'll give up everything to get them. And so we take our first steps into a passion for something higher than ourselves by slowing down and paying ridiculous attention to the heart of Jesus so we can properly value the treasure that he is. As we do, we enter into The School of Intensified Longing, where our encounters with Jesus as he really is, not as we assume he is, entice us into the higher love David Brooks points to as our foundation for grit.

To magnify our longing for Jesus, here are nine perspectives on his heart:

# 1. THE HEART OF JESUS PURSUES THE "ONES," NOT THE "NINETY-NINES."

Every year I speak at a remote mountain gathering my friend Carl Medearis has been hosting for many years. It's called Simply Jesus (simplyjesusgathering.com). It's a temporary community of 500 Jesus-lovers from all over the world, held on the grounds of a sprawling ranch in western Colorado. Last year, at the end of one of the evening sessions, Carl invited everyone to hang out by the campfire. Then he added this enticement: Brad Corrigan would be playing his guitar and singing. Well, in that group of people, almost no one knew who Brad Corrigan was. They heard "campfire guitar guy." They didn't know that Brad is one of three members of one of the most popular independent rock-and-roll bands in history.

The band is called Dispatch—when they broke up several years ago, more than 100,000 people from all over the world showed up for their farewell concert at Boston's Hatch Shell outdoor concert venue. The band has since reunited and is on tour for much of the year. But Brad's home base is Denver, where I first met him more than a decade ago. You'd never guess he's a rock star. For much of the year he lives in Managua, Nicaragua, near a massive trash dump called La Chureca that is home to tens of thousands of the poor. Brad launched a ministry called Love, Light, and Melody (lovelightandmelody.org) as an outreach to the people who live and work in the dump. Humility defines him, and it's why he traveled a long way to attend the Simply Jesus gathering, for the sole purpose of playing his guitar at a late-night campfire.

I found my way to the fire pit, along with a couple dozen others. People were talking and warming themselves when Brad started to play and sing. It didn't seem to matter to him that most people treated his music as background for their conversations—after all, that's what we do at Starbucks. They kept talking, and Brad kept playing. I sat about 10 feet from him, staring at him and thinking: *There are hundreds of thousands of fans all over the world who would kill to be 10 feet away from Brad Corrigan at a campfire in the Colorado mountains, and they would be listening to him, not talking over his music. But the people around this campfire don't know who he is—he's just campfire guitar guy.*

Almost an hour into this extraordinary confluence of natural and man-made beauty, I knew it was time for me to head to bed. It was hard to leave because Brad was in the middle of an improvised worship song, singing into the starry heavens. I retreated from the fire and picked my way along the pitch-dark path to my car. I'd made it a short distance before Jesus stopped me in my tracks—it was as if he'd put his hand on my back and said: *I want you to pay attention to what happened here tonight. What Brad did reveals the depths of my heart, and I want you to drink it in.*

*Jesus, tell me more,* I responded.

And Jesus reminded me: *Rick, remember my parable of the lost sheep? The shepherd has a herd of 100 sheep, but he leaves 99 of them on the hillside so he can pursue the missing one. Rick, this parable reveals my heart. What*

*Brad did tonight is leave the 99 on the hill to go after the one. If only one person tonight listened and was blessed—if only one person was drawn to me because of the way Brad expressed his gift—then the sacrifice he made to be here is worth it. If you want my heart, that's the kind of heart you'll need to hunger for. That's the kind of heart you must live out in your everyday life. My heart is focused on the ones who know they need me, not the 99 others who are oblivious to their need.*

Jesus is always in pursuit of the *ones*. The crowds (the 99 on the hillside) seem to have greater potential. But this is "Jesus Economics"—he values the little, not the big. The *individual* is of inestimable value; each person a treasure. On that beautiful night in the Colorado mountains, 30 feet from a roaring campfire and a soaring worship song, Jesus pitched over the tables of the moneylenders camped out in my soul, upending my persistent belief that the many are more important than the few and that the gifts I have to give are wasted if few receive them. He reminded me of why he pays ridiculous attention to the widow's mite. To the mustard seed. To a bit of salt and a bit of leaven. He is after the overlooked and the isolated and the overshadowed. Because a little thing—*even a little you and me*—can change the world.

## 2. THE HEART OF JESUS IS PLAYFUL.

One day over lunch, I asked a pastor who'd planted a storefront church in a strip mall 10 years ago to tell me what that experience has been like. He described both victories and heartbreaks—and the hurdles he's had to overcome along the way. And then he said something that riveted me: "Christian people, or people who've grown up in the church, are a lot more critical than people who have no connection to the church. They're a lot more picky and demanding about little details, and whether or not you're 'getting it right,' as far as they're concerned." I nodded, not just because I knew what he was saying was true, but because I knew it's also true about *me*…People (you, too?) who have had a long relationship with the church don't often exude a playful, relaxed attitude toward Jesus or the brothers and sisters who are on this journey with us.

*We want to get it right, and we really want others to get it right, too.*

When we read aloud from the Bible, we always sound serious, and we assume everything Jesus said sounded serious when he said it. After all, there's serious business going on here, right? In contrast, when the great Christian thinker and theologian Dallas Willard was asked to offer the one word that best defines Jesus, he chose *relaxed*. [3]

After his disciples try to shoo away the parents who are bringing their babies to him, Jesus responds with vigor: "Let the children come to me. Don't stop them! For the Kingdom of God belongs to those who are like these children. I tell you the truth, anyone who doesn't receive the Kingdom of God like a child will never enter it" (Luke 18:16-17). Let that sink in...When we adult-erize Jesus, we miss the importance of play in the kingdom of God. The Swiss psychologist and child development pioneer Jean Piaget famously said, "Generally speaking there is continuity between a child's play and work." [4] In other words, *play is the work of childhood.* And Jesus pushes that observation even further: Play is a distinctive reality in the kingdom of God, because it belongs to children, and play is a child's default setting.

We distance ourselves from true intimacy with Jesus when we refuse to play like children in his presence. When we treat everything about him and around him with the intensity of a root canal, we miss his smile. At his core, Jesus not only values play but created everything that was ever created in a spirit of play—the goofy diversity we see all around us suggests this is true. This might be why, by the way, in the Genesis account of Creation, Yahweh asks Adam to name the animals he's fashioned—he doesn't like to play alone.

We find the playful heart of Jesus buried in the midst of stories that we've always treated as serious, if we consider them from another angle.

- In an awkward post-Resurrection encounter with Thomas, who doubts that the man who's suddenly appeared inside a locked room is actually Jesus, the (smiling?) Messiah invites his friend to touch the holes in his hands and the wound in his side—just what a mischievous middle school boy might do in that situation.

- Maybe you've heard of people protesting their tax bills by paying them in pennies. Well, they have nothing on Jesus, who offers a slapstick answer to the Temple tax collectors who demand to know if Jesus has paid his fair share: "We don't want to offend them, so go down to the lake and throw in a line. Open the mouth of the first fish you catch, and you will find a large silver coin. Take it and pay the tax for both of us" (Matthew 17:25-27).

- On a night when his disciples are fighting heavy waves crashing into their small boat, Jesus decides to walk past them on the water, sort of like your brother jumping out from behind a corner to yell, "Boo!" Jesus reassures them: "Don't be afraid. Take courage, I am here!" A sassy Peter calls back: "Lord, if it's really you, tell me to come to you, walking on the water." And Jesus (laughingly?) responds: "Yes, come" (Matthew 14:22-31). Could it be that he is playful, on purpose, when he knows his disciples are stressed?

The playful heart of Jesus invites us into a more relaxed relationship with him. In our Pursuing the Heart, Not the Recipes community, we experiment in our pursuit of Jesus. We explore open-ended mysteries with the eccentric passion of Sherlock Holmes. We take risks with Jesus. We try things that seem crazy, then explore the meaning of what we've discovered. We taste things and smell things and touch things. And we do all this because we're attempting to change the dynamic of our pursuit to match the playful core of Jesus' heart.

And, just as I've done with the three stories about Jesus above, we recast the things Jesus said by considering how his meaning would change if he actually said them with a smile on his face. When we read stories about him, we *assume* we know Jesus' tone and countenance, but most often we're not given those specifics in the text. Because it's Jesus, and we expect him to be hyperserious—we can't conceive that the creator of play might practice it himself. Imagine Jesus smiling during this interchange with the woman caught in adultery, after he has shrewdly rescued her from a certain death sentence: "Where are your accusers? Didn't even one of them condemn you?"

"No, Lord," she said.

And Jesus said, "Neither do I. Go and sin no more" (John 8:10-11).

Only a person who is deeply relaxed can play in the face of challenges and threats and pressures.

"Playing with Jesus" means we respond to his playful heart, living with a relaxed openness to possibility. He's already climbing on the monkey bars and invites us to join him.

## 3. THE HEART OF JESUS IS DETERMINED TO TRANSFORM UGLY THINGS INTO BEAUTIFUL THINGS.

The day after the July 2016 ambush of policemen in Dallas, when a black, former Army reservist targeted and killed five white officers and wounded seven others, I was sitting in church as our African-American worship pastor led a mostly white, suburban congregation through our normal litany of praise songs. But then he lowered his guitar and paused, looking out over the congregation, and launched into a raw account of the grief and horror and fear we all felt at that moment. He used this emotional and poetic reflection as an on-ramp into the last worship song of the morning: "The Battle Hymn of the Republic."

"This song," he explained, "was written more than 150 years ago during a time of great racial strife in the U.S.—the Civil War. The violence fueled by racial division during this time is still the worst in American history. And in the midst of this wrenching moment in our journey, Julia Ward Howe writes a song of conviction and hope that helps redirect the nation's focus." And then he led his worship band into the song, starting with the *rat-a-tat-tat* marching rhythm of the snare drum. This song is best known for its crescendo—the "Glory, glory hallelujah!" chorus. But a lyric in the first stanza of the song, a phrase that's always been something of a mystery to me, caught my attention: "He is trampling out the vintage where the grapes of wrath are stored."

All my life, I'd heard this lyric but never really understood its meaning. So I stopped to ask Jesus to unravel it for me. And then he tore back the veil: Howe, a ghost voice from our dark past, was capturing the transforming heart of Jesus in the face of the relentless advance of hatred. Our storehouse of wrath is overflowing in Western culture, but Jesus is determined to make vintage-quality wine out of these terrible "grapes."

Jesus will make beauty out of ugliness, no matter how much ugliness we throw at him, because it's the default setting of his heart. And he is, right now, stomping on whatever ugly grapes we offer up to him, preparing them for his latest vintage.

On that summer Sunday in 2016, I sampled the "vintage wine" Jesus was already producing. I tasted it in the tears of gratitude on the face of an African-American mom describing how white officers surrounded her during the Dallas shooting, forming a wall of protection as she lay wounded on the ground. [5] I tasted it in the sea of sticky notes plastered to the walls of an urban Denver African Methodist Episcopal church by white neighbors pledging their love and support for a black congregation. And I tasted it at the Potter's House Church in Dallas, when a news photographer captured a white man with a Marine haircut reaching across the gap between pews to hold hands with an African-American woman as the congregation prayed. [6]

Jesus, who works his redemption through the "shrewdness of a serpent" and the "innocence of a dove," is always looking for opportunities to bring hope out of hopelessness. It's like breathing to him, because hope defines his heart. The Gospel accounts of his three-year ministry are a relentless drumbeat of ugliness-into-beauty, including these examples from the first five chapters of Matthew:

- The story begins with an unwed mother giving birth to the Messiah in an ugly little stable. The baby is wrapped in a rough cloth (swaddled) and laid in a food trough for farm animals—the Beauty that created the world takes his first gasps of air in a nasty, smelly, dirty cave.

- His birth motivates a paranoid King Herod to wipe out all the young male Jews in the vicinity of Bethlehem. The slaughter of the innocents is one of the ugliest acts in human history, and it frames the invasion of Beauty into the world.

• Soon in his ministry, Jesus' miraculous ability to heal spreads his fame around the ancient world, attracting the mangled and diseased wherever he goes. And "whatever their sickness or disease, or if they were demon possessed or epileptic or paralyzed—he healed them all" (Matthew 4:24). Turning ugliness into beauty becomes his calling card.

• In his first, and still most famous, recorded teaching (the Beatitudes), Jesus insists that ugly things in our human experience open the door to beauty, including:

- the poor, who are blessed with the kingdom of heaven (meaning they're invited as beloved children into God's royal family) because they recognize their need for God;

- the mournful, who are blessed with the direct and overshadowing comfort of God;

- the humble, who are blessed with the inheritance of the earth;

- the wronged, who are blessed with justice;

- the persecuted, who are also blessed with the kingdom of heaven; and

- the mocked and slandered, who are blessed with a great reward.

The world is full of ugliness and always will be, but Jesus uses ugliness like clay. He takes what we offer him—what is repellent and destructive and heartbreaking—and refashions it into a work of art in us. Musician Michael Gungor captures this reality in the opening lines of his poetic song "Beautiful Things":

*All this pain..*

*I wonder if I'll ever find my way*

*I wonder if my life could really change, at all.*

*All this earth...*

*Could all that is lost ever be found?*

*Could a garden come out from this ground, at all?*

*You make beautiful things,*

*You make beautiful things out of the dust.*

*You make beautiful things.*

*You make beautiful things out of us.* [7]

# 4. THE HEART OF JESUS LONGS FOR AUTHENTICITY, NOT PERFORMANCE.

When iconic pop artist Andy Warhol famously proclaimed that everyone on earth would one day enjoy 15 minutes of fame, it sounded like celebrity hyperbole. He couldn't have foreseen not only how easily the future us would lay claim to our 15 minutes but also how effortless it would be for us to do it. In a digitally connected world, temporary fame is at our fingertips at every moment. Our reality shows traffic in unreality—*Survivor* creator Mark Burnett calls them "unscripted drama." But there's nothing plastic about the kinds of relationships Jesus values and grows—his heart is magnetically drawn to authenticity: "For everything that is hidden will eventually be brought into the open, and every secret will be brought to light" (Mark 4:22). Everything we hold in the dark must be dragged into the light, because artifice is repellent to him. The tortured protagonist Mr. Darcy in Jane Austen's masterwork *Pride and Prejudice* defines his complicated heart with a declaration that could well have come from Jesus' own lips: "Disguise of every sort is my abhorrence." [8]

Now more than any other time in history, the people of planet Earth have been formed by a performance culture. Our screens deliver a form of curated disguise to us that seems anything but abhorrent. Our entertainment sensibilities have also infiltrated the church, where we so often relate to others with the appearance of authenticity, while carefully avoiding the full price of it. The kind of authenticity that characterizes the heart of Jesus, and is relentlessly pursued by him as we get deeper into our journey with him, requires us to drag into the light things we've kept in the dark.

After coffee with my friend Casey Franklin, the pastor of a church plant that defines itself by its authentic relationships, he wrote me a brilliant note that expresses both the challenges and opportunities this presents. Here's a portion of it:

> People outside the church expect people who are inside the church to have it together. So when we talk to our neighbors or friends, we're a little insecure about letting people know what it's really like on "the inside." Do we "blow our witness" by letting other broken people know how broken we really are?
>
> Western culture, and especially our Western Christian culture, covertly pushes us into image-maintenance mode. It's especially hard for people to discover that leaders and pastors have struggles or issues or difficulties, because there's

an implied expectation of relative perfection. And when we struggle with doubt or weakness, we worry that it'd be devastating for others if it ever got out.

In our performance-based culture and perfection-obsessed society, we all put our best foot forward in relationships—this system is based on covering up our faults, weaknesses, and insecurities. We all play the game—knowing we don't have it all together but trying to make sure that everyone else thinks we do.

But what if we had the courage to embrace a kind of raw authenticity that was embedded within a redemptive reality? What if we valued knowing the scars, wounds, and struggles of others, because we had a sacred respect for how those things have shaped them into a force to be reckoned with? What if we all had an increasing freedom to be who we really are, tell it like it really is, and "out" our shortcomings and failures for what they really are? That would be a strange, messed-up, and liberated world. [9]

Our performance-driven society creates a hunger in us for things that are real because we are created in the image of God, and authenticity defines his heart. Not long ago I was sitting in the vast auditorium of a large church during the opening worship set. I felt a tension inside—a familiar discomfort with the way many churches frame worship. I saw band members positioned to spread out from one end of the stage to the other. No one was closer than 15 feet from the other, and the drummer was boxed in by Plexiglas. *They have valued performance over community,* I thought. *And Jesus values community over performance.*

The price of our performance standards is often authenticity, and that runs contrary to the heart of Jesus.

# 5. THE HEART OF JESUS DEFINES TRUE LOVE BY HOW WE TREAT OUR ENEMIES.

Jesus is an apple cart–upsetter. Just when you think you understand, for example, what love is really all about, he throws you for a loop. That's what happens when, early in his ministry, he redefines love for the crowds gathered to hear him teach: "You have heard the law that says, 'Love your neighbor and hate your enemy.' But I say, love your enemies! Pray for those who persecute you! In that way, you will be acting as true children of your Father in heaven" (Matthew 5:43-45). It is our response to our enemies—the people who hurt us and oppose us and drive us crazy—that defines the depth of our love. And that's because Jesus' own love is defined by how he treats his enemies. He doesn't say, "Be nice to your enemies, and smile when you're persecuted"—that's shallow and inauthentic. Jesus' love is bent on redemption, and that means it's soft when it needs to be and hard when it needs to be.

Jesus is free to love into redemption those who hate and oppose him because his love is not based on reciprocity. He longs for a mutually trusting, mutually passionate relationship with us, but he doesn't require that to give us the treasures of his heart.

During the first semester of her freshman year in high school, my daughter Lucy heard the sound of a shotgun blast and raced for cover. Not far away, a troubled boy had just killed one of Lucy's classmates. The killer had scribbled classroom numbers on his arm, a murderous "to-do list" of victims that included both teachers and students. Eventually, he took his own life in the school library as the police closed in. Lucy ended up darting into an open administrative office, hiding in a back room with a dozen of her classmates until a police SWAT team bashed into the office and ordered them to put their hands up, quickly marching them out of the school. She still experiences trauma from this experience.

In the wake of the shooting, the sheriff in charge of the investigation urged the public not to call attention to the killer by referring to him by name, but rather to refer to him only as "the murderer." But at the massive public memorial service for his daughter, the victim's father pointedly defied that request and named the teenage boy who took his beloved girl from him. Then, with a steady gaze at the thousands gathered to honor his daughter (including the sheriff), *he forgave him*. [10] It's possible to forgive human beings, but how can you forgive a monster? And that's the point: When we love others as Jesus loves them, even those who behave like monsters, we treat our enemies as broken people who are not beyond the reach of grace.

When we stay connected to Jesus, he gives us the freedom and courage to love our enemies the way he pursues the wicked tax collector Zacchaeus, the notorious woman who washes his feet with her tears, and the scandalous woman at the well outside the city walls of Sychar.

# 6. THE HEART OF JESUS HAS A SHARP EDGE.

If you remember your Harry Potter lore, *The Monster Book of Monsters* is not just a book about terrifying magical creatures—the book itself is a terrifying magical creature. Make a mistake opening the ornate latch on this oversized textbook and you get razor teeth, not pages. Author J.K. Rowling describes it as a "vicious guide to monstrous creatures." [11] She meant to imagine a book that can (literally) eat you alive. We have our own *Monster Book*, of course: "For the word of God is alive and powerful. It is sharper than the sharpest two-edged sword, cutting between soul and spirit, between joint and marrow. It exposes our innermost thoughts and desires" (Hebrews 4:12). This is some kind of untamed book, highlighting a Jesus described by C.S. Lewis as a lion who is good but not safe. [12]

The Bible describes a Savior with teeth, not the lamb-carrying, lullaby-singing, tousled-hair movie star we've most often been served. The nice Jesus who fits well in our safe and well-controlled lifestyle bears little resemblance to the Jesus described in our own *Monster Book*. Jesus told the crowds that most of them were headed for destruction and only a few were walking "the narrow way." He told them to honor the law but eviscerated the hypocritical rule-keepers who "tie up heavy burdens and lay them on men's shoulders." He told them they'd have to eat his flesh and drink his blood to have any part of him. He told them to turn the world upside down with the gospel.

The heart of Jesus has teeth.

That's because the purpose of the Incarnation—the Trinity's subversive plan to embed the Son among us, in enemy territory—is to "destroy the works of the devil" so that he can woo back his captive bride, his beloved. The whole of God's passion is focused on this mission, and to do it, our very nature must be reclaimed. And this is not going to happen without significant leverage, because the weight of our brokenness is heavy. It requires the *heavy love* of redemption to repair and restore our hearts. The brutality of the Cross hints at the brutality of the battle, the hard reality of a shattering blow delivered by the betrayal of Adam and Eve. Our redemption will require a kind of brutality as well.

This is why the Apostle Mark records Jesus saying: "If your hand or your foot gets in God's way, chop it off and throw it away. You're better off maimed or lame and alive than the proud owner of two hands and two feet, godless in a furnace of eternal fire. And if your eye distracts you from God, pull it out and throw it away. You're better off one-eyed and alive than exercising your twenty-twenty vision from inside the fire of hell" (Mark 9:43-48, MSG). It's not hard to understand the blunt intent of this declaration when we see it in light of a Lover's intent. Jesus is telling us to sacrifice the lesser for the greater. The greater, in this case, is Jesus himself. He wants to replace our love for lesser gods with a love for a Greater Reality. He wants intimacy with us because he's passionate about us. And like anyone who loves deeply, it grieves him when we prefer base lovers to his own great passion. He is, by his own account, a "jealous lover"—that means he wants us for his own. And that is the definition of Good News for a humanity that's otherwise cut off for eternity from our only source of life.

We can relax in the presence of Jesus, and open ourselves fully to him, because his heart has an edge to it. We feel safe walking through the valley of the shadow of death with him because he is "the lion of the tribe of Judah," not the poodle licking our leg.

# 7. THE HEART OF JESUS VALUES DEPENDENCE, NOT CONTROL.

Our knee-jerk response to the idea of dependence is most often to resist it. We generally hate weakness, and dependence is simply one common form of it. Put "dependence" on the back end of "drug" or "alcohol" or "emotional" or "financial" or "social" or "relational," and you've got an ugly problem. Nevertheless, Jesus relishes the beauty of our dependent attachment to him, the same way singer/songwriter Tom Waits relishes the longing we experience when a dependence we take for granted is gone:

*I never saw the sunshine 'til you turned out the light. I never saw my hometown until I stayed away too long.* [13]

It's *because* dependence requires vulnerability that Jesus makes it a primary theme of his teaching. His mission is to restore the sort of bare-hearted trust we were created to enjoy with him at the beginning of all things. And intimacy between two requires the vulnerability of each. This is why he warns us, again and again, to guard against living in the false security of our own strength—telling us we can do nothing apart from him (John 15:5). And when Jesus reveals to the Apostle Paul that his "power works best in weakness," he's describing the mechanics of a dependent relationship and its profound benefits—our weakness drives us toward a deeper attachment to him, which gives us access to his power.

A few weeks ago I was on my long drive home from work, speeding up on a stretch of road that leads to an interstate highway. Heading through one of the last traffic lights before I hit the open freeway, I slipped my sunglasses on and noticed something had fallen on one of the lenses. I glanced down to flick it away, and when I looked back up, the traffic in front of me had suddenly stopped. I slammed on my brakes, but it was too late—going 40 miles per hour, I plowed into the back of a pickup truck.

I was not injured because my beloved 2003 Volvo gave up its life for me. (The other driver was also uninjured.) In the wake of this trauma, I was saddled with the frustrating reality that everyone who's totaled a car must face: replacing that car. While I searched, I had to borrow my 18-year-old daughter's 1998 Honda Accord—the dictionary definition of a beater car (with an interior aroma infused by teenage-girl perfume and old gum).

My sudden dependence on my daughter's ugly-but-dependable car made me feel embarrassed and vulnerable, especially because my split-second decision cost me my own car. In that place of weakness, I was driven into the lap of Jesus, like a little child. My conversations with him were more frequent, passionate, and raw. My trust in him moved from the back burner to the front. In the midst of my vulnerability and need, I felt awake and alive to him. And this is exactly what he's after.

In Matthew 10, Jesus and his disciples have been traveling all over the region as he teaches in synagogues, heals people, and performs other miracles. Huge crowds, driven by hope and curiosity, gather around him. Compassion for them grows in him. So he decides it's time to spring a little surprise on the disciples. He calls them together and gives them authority to cast out demons and cure diseases. Then he tells them he's sending them out in pairs, apart from him. And their job description is daunting: "Announce to them that the Kingdom of Heaven is near. Heal the sick, raise the dead, cure those with leprosy, and cast out demons" (Matthew 10:7-8). Imagine listening to your boss hand over *that* assignment to you on a Monday morning.

But Jesus isn't finished with them. He gives them restrictions for their adventure that are guaranteed to make it exponentially harder: *Don't take any money, not even a little bit. Don't carry a traveler's bag or a walking stick or a change of clothes. Wherever you go, look for "worthy people"; then ask to stay with them. ("Don't worry, we'll probably stay just a week, until we're done casting out demons.")* He removes every source of comfort, help, and security, forcing them into the dependency that will give them the strength they really need, not the strength they think they need.

Simply, our dependence on our own strength works against the Jesus-dependence that gives us access to true strength and life. Jesus knows we can't muscle through all our challenges. To him, "Can you please help?" is the sweetest plea.

## 8. THE HEART OF JESUS LOVES STORY AND METAPHOR AND PARABLE.

Jesus is a master storyteller, and he uses every living thing to proclaim truth. Paul reveals, "For ever since the world was created, people have seen the earth and sky. Through everything God made, they can clearly see his invisible qualities—his eternal power and divine nature" (Romans 1:20). If we are to understand the depths of Jesus' heart—to appreciate his "invisible qualities"—we will pay better attention to the created world, listening to its parables speak to us about his "eternal power and divine nature." There is no recipe for the heart of Jesus, but there are stories that describe it.

If the native language in the kingdom of God is parable, its specific dialect is metaphor. And when Jesus uses a metaphor, it's always a perfect metaphor. Whether he's describing his followers as sheep among wolves or marking our relationship with him as grafted-in branches whose only source of life is the vine, or comparing our ability to grow in our relationship with him to four kinds of soil, Jesus' metaphors are so complete, so immersive, and so exact, that it's possible to drill deeper and deeper into them and still find continuing nourishment. And he has planted his perfect-metaphor stories by the trillions in the created world that surrounds us. Jesus tells the stories of his heart in the metaphors of living things. David sings this truth in Psalm 19:1-4:

> The heavens proclaim the glory of God.
> The skies display his craftsmanship.
> Day after day they continue to speak;
> night after night they make him known.
> They speak without a sound or word;
> their voice is never heard.
> Yet their message has gone throughout the earth,
> and their words to all the world.

This means the birds and the fish he created have a story to tell. But by far, the most prolific storytellers are insects—they make up 90 percent of all species living on Earth. When we slow down and pay attention to the invisible attributes of Jesus that he has embedded in these living parables, we look for surprising details that function like metaphors. For example, all insects have compound eyes, very different from our own human eyes. The insect eye is made up of ommatidia, many tiny visual units that function like pixels and form a sort of mosaic of sight. Dragonflies, for example, have more than 30,000 ommatidia in each eye. This gives them a 360-degree field of vision at all times. [14] Remind you of anything?

- David says, "The Lord looks down from heaven and sees the whole human race" (Psalm 33:13).

- The prophet Hanani warns Asa, the King of Judah, "The eyes of the Lord search the whole earth in order to strengthen those whose hearts are fully committed to him" (2 Chronicles 16:9).

- And the Apostle Peter, quoting the psalmist, warns the followers of Jesus: "The eyes of the Lord watch over those who do right, and his ears are open to their prayers" (1 Peter 3:12).

The dragonflies (and every other created thing) are telling the glory of God. And the story they're telling is about the heart of Jesus. The issue is *not* whether Jesus is speaking to us about his heart; the issue is whether we're paying attention to his parables. He loves story so much that everything he touches has the seed of a story planted in it. And every one of those seeds offers us a deeper understanding of the character, personality, and beauty of his heart.

When the rhythms of our lives morph from a kind of chosen deafness to a heart that's awake and alive to the truths Jesus is whispering—and sometimes shouting—in our surroundings, then our lives grow thick with meaning and brimming with adventure. Story and parable define Jesus' heart—and are invitations to an intimate conversation.

# 9. THE HEART OF JESUS IS EXTRAVAGANT.

Somewhere in Australia's Epping Forest, northern hairy-nosed wombats should be nervous. (If it were you or me, the fact that the word *hairy-nosed* is being used to describe us would be ample cause for dread.) Their anxiety is warranted because there are only 115 of them left in the world. This is distressing, but it's overshadowed by the number of *existing* species: The latest guess is that there are 8.74 million species in the world. [15] And almost half a million (400,000) are plants. [16]

Why are there more than 1,000 kinds of trees?

Almost a million (925,000) kinds of bugs?

More than 30,000 varieties of weeds?

And even *one* mosquito species would be five too many, but there are more than 3,000 species of them. Why? [17]

Annie Dillard writes: "Nature is, above all, profligate. Don't believe them when they tell you how economical and thrifty nature is, whose leaves return to the soil. Wouldn't it be cheaper to leave them on the tree in the first place? This deciduous business alone is a radical scheme, the brainchild of a deranged manic-depressive with limitless capital. Extravagance! Nature will try anything once. This is what the sign of the insects says. No form is too gruesome, no behavior too grotesque. If you're dealing with organic compounds, then let them combine. If it works, if it quickens, set it clacking in the grass; there's always room for one more; you ain't so handsome yourself. This is a spendthrift economy; though nothing is lost, all is spent." [18]

Creation, it's obvious, is extravagantly wasteful—impossibly stuffed full of so many varieties of things that if choices were pennies we'd all be trillionaires. And we'd be getting richer by the minute because thousands of new species are discovered every year, and researchers estimate it will still take hundreds of years for human beings, with all our clever little gadgets and insatiable curiosity, to discover all of them. Of the 8.74 million estimated species, only 1.7 million are known, with many more waiting to be encountered for the first time. We haven't even mentioned the number of stars in the "observable universe," recently pegged by one scientist as a number that begins with "1" and has 24 zeroes behind it. [19]

Wouldn't three or four zeroes be adequate?

On a Colorado backpacking trip to a tiny lake far above the tree line, I wandered up the hill from our campsite to lie down in the wide expanse of wildflowers that stretched to the horizon. The breeze bent the petals and stalks over and back again, like a drummer tapping the earth with his brushes to keep its rhythm. Lying there with the sun on my face amid the worship of this "cloud of witnesses," I was clobbered by this realization: *These flowers are here in this exact place all the time, whether or not there is anyone here to enjoy them. Their beauty seems wasted on this remote, rarely explored hillside. Yet Jesus seems unconcerned by the waste.* We see "useless beauty" all around us, as Elvis Costello reminds us.

In a tense encounter between Jesus and the Pharisees, Jesus accentuates the beauty of extravagance:

> One of the Pharisees asked him over for a meal. He went to the Pharisee's house and sat down at the dinner table. Just then a woman of the village, the town harlot, having learned that Jesus was a guest in the home of the Pharisee, came with a bottle of very expensive perfume and stood at his feet, weeping, raining tears on his feet. Letting down her hair, she dried his feet, kissed them, and anointed them with the perfume. When the Pharisee who had invited him saw this, he said to himself, "If this man was the prophet I thought he was, he would have known what kind of woman this is who is falling all over him."
>
> Jesus said to him, "Simon, I have something to tell you."
>
> "Oh? Tell me."
>
> "Two men were in debt to a banker. One owed five hundred silver pieces, the other fifty. Neither of them could pay up, and so the banker canceled both debts. Which of the two would be more grateful?"
>
> Simon answered, "I suppose the one who was forgiven the most."

"That's right," said Jesus. Then turning to the woman, but speaking to Simon, he said, "Do you see this woman? I came to your home; you provided no water for my feet, but she rained tears on my feet and dried them with her hair. You gave me no greeting, but from the time I arrived she hasn't quit kissing my feet. You provided nothing for freshening up, but she has soothed my feet with perfume. Impressive, isn't it? She was forgiven many, many sins, and so she is very, very grateful. If the forgiveness is minimal, the gratitude is minimal."

Then he spoke to her: "I forgive your sins."

That set the dinner guests talking behind his back: "Who does he think he is, forgiving sins!"

He ignored them and said to the woman, "Your faith has saved you. Go in peace" (Luke 7:36-50, MSG).

In response to her extravagant, even wasteful, act of grateful worship, Jesus responds with an extravagant and shocking act of mercy. Over-the-top behavior makes his eyes light up, because he is wildly exuberant in his expressions of love, creation, pursuit, kindness, and even judgment. The harlot, who is falling all over Jesus, is speaking his language. He gravitates to extravagant responses to people and situations because his heart is boiling with passion for his beloved. "Too much" is business-as-usual for Jesus.

# THE PATH TO THE HEART

I asked my longtime friend, author, and ministry leader Ned Erickson how he grew to love, and then be ruined by, the heart of Jesus. Here's a portion of the note he wrote to me in response:

It started with a crisis of sorts, not a normal one. I had been a Christian for nearly a decade, in ministry for three years, when I realized I didn't know jack squat about God. I knew the truth: If Jesus walked into the room that very minute, there was no way I would recognize him. I didn't know the first thing about him.

Brennan Manning says that the only way we can know anything for certain about God is by what we know about Jesus. Anything that is true about Jesus is true about God; anything untrue is untrue. It makes sense. It might sound elementary to you. But it was life-changing for me. Besides, it was easy enough to try.

So I started to get to know Jesus. I chose Mark. It's the shortest Gospel, and I began reading real slow. I paid attention to everything the man said, did, and didn't do. And before I knew it, everything had changed. He became real. He knocked me head over heels. I wanted to know more—to know him more—deeply, intimately. And slowly, like a ship coming out of the fog, I began to see him, smell him, feel him. I knew what his voice sounded like. And it only made me want more.

At the same time, it was like he started rubbing off on me. I started noticing things I never noticed before—leaves changing color, the sound of water hitting the sink. My ears listened differently. To people. I began hearing the questions they were asking underneath the questions they were asking. I watched television with new eyes. My judgmental spirit was gone. I cried at odd moments. I found myself liking the sensation I got when I helped other people. It was crazy.

And the craziest part: It was like all of a sudden I had found myself. It was like the more I got to know Jesus, the more he introduced me to the person he created: Me. The real me. The one that, if I am honest, I have always been afraid of. Because what if I don't like the real me? Or what if the real me does something stupid? Or what if the real me really isn't that cool? Or what if the real me gets hurt? But for the first time, with Jesus' encouragement, I was willing to give me a try.

And believe it or not, all of it has happened. I have never felt so much pain, been so broken, so weak, so pathetic, so vulnerable. It has been the hardest experience of my life. And it has been the best. Because now I know—now I know—that I am loved. Jesus loves me! Me! In all my mess, the way I am. Not only that, he likes me! If he had a free afternoon (and he does, countless ones), he would choose to spend it with me. And I would spend it with him. [20]

In The School of Intensified Longing, we cross an invisible line when we move more deliberately toward the heart of Jesus. We come to a place where it's impossible to see anything, hear anything, taste anything, smell anything, and experience anything that doesn't remind us of his heart. And in that place, he's not just camping out in our world, he *is* our world. This is truly when we're living in the momentum of a passion for something higher than ourselves, when we lower our bucket into a deeper well of spiritual grit.

1   Blaise Pascal, *Pensees* (New York: Penguin Books, 1966), 148.

2   From the author's transcription from *Nicholas Nickleby* (2002, United Artists), a film written and directed by Douglas McGrath, based on the novel by Charles Dickens.

3   From a private conversation with Bill Gaultiere, founder of the ministry Soul Shepherding, recorded in a blog piece titled "Dallas Willard's One Word for Jesus," posted on June 11, 2008 at soulshepherding.org.

4   Quoted by David Cohen, *The Development of Play*, 3rd edition (Routledge, London, 2007), 4.

5   Linda Massarella, "Dallas Mom: Hero Cop Died Protecting Me and My Sons," *New York Post* (July 10, 2016).

6   Mark Collette, "At Arlington Stadium, a Break from the Chaos," *Houston Chronicle* (July 10, 2016). Photo by Eric Gay, Associated Press.

7   Michael Gungor, "Beautiful Things" (Brash Music, February 16, 2010). Lyrics used with permission.

8   Jane Austen, *Pride and Prejudice* (Amazon Classics, 2017), 209.

9   Casey Franklin, pastor of the Inversion Community in Denver, Colorado. Used with permission.

10  "Dad of Girl Shot at Denver School: I Forgive Her Killer," *USA Today* (January 1, 2014).

11  Pottermore Wiki page (pottermore.wikia.com).

12  C.S. Lewis, *The Lion, the Witch, and the Wardrobe* (New York: HarperCollins, Reprint Edition, 2008), 80.

13  Tom Waits, "San Diego Serenade," *The Heart of Saturday Night* (Elektra/Asylum Records, 1974).

14  Adam Hadhazy, "20 Startling Facts About Insects," LiveScience.com (August 29, 2015).

15  Liz Osborn, "Number of Species Identified on Earth" (www.currentresults.com).

16  "Plant Species Numbers" (Botanic Gardens Conservation International website, www.bgci.org).

17  Osborn, www.currentresults.com.

18  Annie Dillard, *Pilgrim at Tinker Creek* (Harper Perennial Modern Classics, September 10, 2013), 66.

19  Elizabeth Howell, "How Many Stars Are in the Universe?" (Space.com, May 17, 2017).

20  Ned Erickson, author of *Falling Into Love* and *Clay,* founder of the Winston-Salem Fellows, from a note written to the author. Used with permission.

# APPENDIX:
# A SPIRITUAL GRIT
# SELF-ASSESSMENT

The gift of life should be delivered with a big sticker on the box: "Perseverance Required." We need spiritual grit to face life's challenges, disappointments, and opportunities. Even more, we need spiritual grit to live lives that are faithful to God and others.

All of us are on this journey, each of us at a unique point on the continuum. Discovering our progress toward spiritual grit is exactly what this self-assessment is for.

It's just 12 questions and takes less than two minutes to complete. You can take the assessment here and score it according to the instructions at the end. Or you can go to **GotSpiritualGrit.com** and take the digital version of the assessment, which will give you an automatic score.

Answer the following questions as honestly as you can—there are no "right answers." As you answer, think about how you compare to most people you know.

1. When things are going well, I tend to have positive feelings about God. When things are going badly, I tend to have negative feelings about God.

   ❏ Very much like me    ❏ Mostly like me    ❏ Somewhat like me
   ❏ Not much like me    ❏ Not like me at all

2. If I'm hoping or praying for something in my life and it doesn't happen, I sometimes wonder if God really cares about me.

   ❏ Very much like me    ❏ Mostly like me    ❏ Somewhat like me
   ❏ Not much like me    ❏ Not like me at all

3. I tend to gravitate to groups and experiences that challenge me to grow deeper in my relationship with God, even if they involve sacrifice.

   ❏ Very much like me    ❏ Mostly like me    ❏ Somewhat like me
   ❏ Not much like me    ❏ Not like me at all

4. I would describe my relationship with Jesus as "all-in"—it doesn't really matter much what happens to me because I know he loves me and I love him.

   ❏ Very much like me    ❏ Mostly like me    ❏ Somewhat like me
   ❏ Not much like me    ❏ Not like me at all

5. When I pray for something and feel God is silent, I get discouraged.

   ❏ Very much like me    ❏ Mostly like me    ❏ Somewhat like me
   ❏ Not much like me    ❏ Not like me at all

6. When I'm doubting myself, I tend to also doubt God.

   ❏ Very much like me    ❏ Mostly like me    ❏ Somewhat like me
   ❏ Not much like me    ❏ Not like me at all

**7. I would say I'm more committed to Jesus because of who he is, not so much because of how he comes through for me when I need him.**

❑ Very much like me    ❑ Mostly like me    ❑ Somewhat like me

❑ Not much like me    ❑ Not like me at all

**8. I think others who know me would say I live my life by Paul's words in Romans 8:38: "I am convinced that nothing can ever separate us from God's love. Neither death nor life, neither angels nor demons, neither our fears for today nor our worries about tomorrow—not even the powers of hell can separate us from God's love."**

❑ Very much like me    ❑ Mostly like me    ❑ Somewhat like me

❑ Not much like me    ❑ Not like me at all

**9. We naturally avoid hardship whenever we can. But I'm the sort of person who actually embraces hardship, depending on Jesus for my strength.**

❑ Very much like me    ❑ Mostly like me    ❑ Somewhat like me

❑ Not much like me    ❑ Not like me at all

**10. When facing a challenge, I tend to first rely on my own strengths before turning to Jesus for help.**

❑ Very much like me    ❑ Mostly like me    ❑ Somewhat like me

❑ Not much like me    ❑ Not like me at all

**11. In my everyday life, I see a direct connection between my passion for Jesus and my ability to persevere through challenges and hardships.**

❑ Very much like me    ❑ Mostly like me    ❑ Somewhat like me

❑ Not much like me    ❑ Not like me at all

**12. Paul said, "In my weakness, I am strong." But the truth is, when I'm feeling weak, I don't always feel like I find strength in my relationship with Jesus.**

❑ Very much like me    ❑ Mostly like me    ❑ Somewhat like me

❑ Not much like me    ❑ Not like me at all

# SCORING:

**For questions 3, 4, 7, 8, 9, and 11 assign the following points:**
5 = Very much like me
4 = Mostly like me
3 = Somewhat like me
2 = Not much like me
1 = Not like me at all

**For questions 1, 2, 5, 6, 10, and 12 assign the following points:**
1 = Very much like me
2 = Mostly like me
3 = Somewhat like me
4 = Not much like me
5 = Not like me at all

To calculate your spiritual grit, add up your total points to get your score out of a possible 60 points—for example, 43/60. Then divide your number (43, for example) by the total points possible (60) to get your percentage (in this case, 43/60 calculates to 72 percent.) Once you've calculated your percentage, here's a general guide to understand your results, with a description after each category that helps flesh out its meaning:

### 85-100 percent—Very High Level of Spiritual Grit

Your relationship with Jesus is deep, intimate, and all-consuming; like the Apostle Peter, your identity is hidden in the heart of Jesus. And like Peter, you would answer "Where else would I go?" if Jesus asked you if you were going to leave him. You embrace and move through hardship and seize opportunities with a determination to keep going no matter what. You might be disillusioned by people and circumstances, but you're rarely disillusioned by your relationship with Jesus. Your presence in any relational setting is a catalyst for disruption and growth.

### 70-85 percent—Moderately High Level of Spiritual Grit

Your relationship with Jesus matters a great deal to you, but you sometimes wrestle with doubts and distance yourself from Jesus when you feel on top of life. Like the disciple Thomas, you're committed to Jesus, but you sometimes require him to prove himself to you. In the midst of your challenges and hardships, you remember to depend on Jesus to help you through, but often not until after you've given it your best shot on your own. You see yourself as an honest person who tends to trust Jesus on the basis of results.

## 55-70 percent—Moderately Low Level of Spiritual Grit

Your relationship with Jesus is on-again, off-again. When things get tough or you're facing a great challenge, you're pulled back into a more dependent relationship with him. But most days your awareness of Jesus and your dependence on him tend to recede into the background of your life. Jesus is important to you, but like his follower Martha, you have a lot to do and a lot of hurdles to overcome, so you often find yourself simply plowing ahead, with or without him. Because of this, it's not unusual for you to feel tired and discouraged about the hills you have to climb in your life.

## 40-55 percent—Very Low Level of Spiritual Grit

Most of the time, your relationship with Jesus is compartmentalized. In fact, you're more comfortable referring to this part of your life as your expression of spirituality than as a relationship. There have been some seasons when you were more interested in God, but that's typically because of random circumstances in your life, not because you felt a desire to actively pursue a relationship with him. Like the crowds that followed Jesus early in his ministry, you tend to show up when something about him captures your interest, but you move on to other sources of strength and life after you lose interest. Because of this, most days you feel like you're fighting your battles and facing your challenges using your own resources, not depending on God to help.

# SPIRITUAL GRIT: 30 DAILY PROVOCATIONS FOR MICRO-JOURNALING

If you would like to kick-start your journey into a deeper experience of spiritual grit, focus on it for 30 days. These questions are designed to unlock quick responses. Don't try to craft an eloquent response, just let it spill out. A sentence or two is great—more than that is totally up to you.

**Day 1:** Perseverance implies that we're pushing through a series of challenges, big and small, to continue on a path we're determined to follow. What is a spiritual challenge you must push through today?

_____

_____

_____

_____

_____

_____

_____

**Day 2:** Every day has its own challenges. Consider your knee-jerk response to a challenge you faced today. What went through your head and heart?

_____

_____

_____

_____

_____

**Day 3:** What's the difference between a challenge that excites you and a challenge that makes you feel exposed, overwhelmed, or afraid?

_____

_____

_____

_____

_____

**Day 4:** Sure, we know Jesus loves us and that he's good, but that doesn't mean we don't experience hard things. When you're in the midst of something really hard, how do you experience Jesus' goodness? Or does he seem silent or withdrawn to you?

_____

_____

_____

_____

_____

**Day 5:** We go through seasons of life, some of them brief and some of them long, when it seems that everything that can go wrong, does. We even know people who seem permanently locked in that cycle. What do you think is going on in those seasons of your life, or with the people who always seem to be in that season?

_____

_____

_____

_____

_____

**Day 6:** In the Superman myth, Kryptonite has a consistent and predictable ability to sap the man of steel's physical strength. What is the spiritual equivalent in your life, something that always makes you feel weak?

_____

_____

_____

_____

_____

**Day 7:** What do you hate most about feeling weak?

_____

_____

_____

_____

_____

**Day 8:** Paul said, "In my weakness, I am strong." In what way have you recently experienced this truth?

_____

_____

_____

_____

_____

**Day 9:** What's a key indicator (or indicators) that you're attempting to face a threat or obstacle in your own strength instead of Jesus'?

_____

_____

_____

_____

_____

**Day 10:** It takes a lot of courage to persevere, even when we're depending on Jesus. Sometimes we feel the pressure to summon a courage we lack, so we do something (consciously or unconsciously) to sabotage ourselves. What's something you do to sabotage yourself?

_____

_____

_____

_____

_____

**Day 11:** Throughout history the people of God have complained about him. What's one recent complaint you've had about God, maybe something you'd never tell anyone?

_____

_____

_____

_____

_____

**Day 12:** What's one outside influence that's really helping you grow in your relationship with Jesus: a person, book, group, practice—whatever. Briefly explain why.

_____

_____

_____

_____

_____

**Day 13:** Think about the unfinished things in your life right now (books, chores, projects, commitments, and so on). What most often keeps you from finishing something you start, and why?

_____

_____

_____

_____

_____

**Day 14:** We all have a voice inside that says we should be doing something(s) better in our relationship with Jesus. What's one thing that nagging voice has been telling you lately?

_____

_____

_____

_____

_____

**Day 15:** Jesus tells us he wants to be the source of our strength when we feel weak and needy. How are you learning to depend on that strength?

_____

_____

_____

_____

_____

**Day 16:** When we have _not_ persevered through something big or small, we usually have a reason (or reasons) that we've learned to accept about ourselves. What's your typical reason?

_____

_____

_____

_____

_____

**Day 17:** I just heard a wildlife biologist describe how he studies musk oxen in the Alaskan wilderness. If a wildlife biologist studied you when you're faced with a scary challenge, what would he observe?

_____

_____

_____

_____

_____

**Day 18:** We're sometimes tempted to take shortcuts in life—we're not giving our best effort at something, and we know it. What's something like that in your life, and why do you give in to the temptation?

_____

_____

_____

_____

_____

**Day 19:** Looking back on your life, what's one experience you hated when you were going through it but now treasure because of what it produced in you?

_____

_____

_____

_____

_____

**Day 20:** What's one way you're seeing Jesus reshape the way you think because of a challenge or struggle you've faced with him?

_____

_____

_____

_____

_____

**Day 21:** How has your ability to persevere in the midst of challenges changed—either strengthened or weakened—in the last few years, and why?

_____

_____

_____

_____

_____

**Day 22:** Researchers have discovered that grit is fueled by a passion for something higher than oneself. Explain a key factor in growing your passion—not just your affinity—for Jesus.

_____

_____

_____

_____

_____

**Day 23:** We naturally avoid hardship whenever we can. How do you see yourself actually embracing hardship in your life, and why?

_____

_____

_____

_____

_____

**Day 24:** What's the difference between a passion that has persisted for a long time in your life and a passion that died?

_____

_____

_____

_____

**Day 25:** Think about your natural strengths. You can probably point to many ways they've helped you in life, but how have they actually hindered you at times?

_____

_____

_____

_____

_____

**Day 26:** Eugene Peterson (author of *The Message* paraphrase of the Bible) describes his life as "a long obedience in the same direction." [1] In your life, what is the relationship between passion and obedience?

_____

_____

_____

_____

**Day 27:** When you're struggling and your resolve is weak, people often say things that are meant to be encouraging. What has someone said or done that has increased your ability to persevere?

_____

_____

_____

_____

**Day 28:** Okay, here's a tough one...Our spiritual grit is truly lived out in the darkness, where no one but Jesus can see it. What's an example of your perseverance and spiritual grit that you think no one except Jesus has seen?

_____

_____

_____

_____

**Day 29:** Research into grit has clarified what it is and why it's important, but the leading researchers also admit they have no idea how to help people grow their grit. If you had a friend who wanted to develop more spiritual grit, what advice would you give?

_____

_____

_____

_____

_____

**Day 30:** Some people seem to have a natural ability to respond to challenges with grit and determination, while others really struggle, slipping easily into fatalism or a victim mentality. In your experience, what is it that either fuels or undermines spiritual grit?

_____

_____

_____

_____

_____

1  Eugene Peterson, *A Long Obedience In the Same Direction* (IVP Books, July 28, 2000).

# THE PROMISES OF JESUS

I will give you living water
(see John 4:10).

I will give you authority over
evil and the ability to heal
(see Luke 9:1).

I bring freedom to captives
(see Luke 4:18-19).

I brag about you to my Father
(see Matthew 10:32).

I bring sight to the blind
(see Luke 4:18-19).

If you will give your whole life to
me, you'll find the life you've always
hungered for (see Matthew 10:39).

I want to heal you
(see Matthew 8:3).

If you believe in me, I'll give you
eternal life (see John 6:40).

Your sins are forgiven
(see Matthew 9:2).

Your human efforts don't
accomplish much, but the truth of
my words and actions in your life
will (see John 6:63).

If you're poor and recognize your
need for me, I'll give you the riches
of my kingdom (see Matthew 5:3).

The truth will set you free
(see John 8:32).

If you're mourning, I will comfort
you (see Matthew 5:4).

My purpose in your life is to
give you a rich and satisfying life
(see John 10:10).

If you're humble, I will give to
you in a way that exceeds your
expectations (see Matthew 5:5).

I sacrifice my life for you, over and
over and will never back down from
fighting for you, no matter what the
threat (see John 10:11-13).

If you hunger for justice,
I will satisfy that hunger
(see Matthew 5:6).

I know you, and I've given
you the ability to know me
(see John 10:14-15).

If you're merciful to others,
you'll experience mercy yourself
(see Matthew 5:7).

The threat of evil will never prevail
in your life—not as long as I'm on
your side (see Matthew 16:18).

If your heart is pure, I'll show you
myself (see Matthew 5:8).

I'm entrusting you with a great deal
of authority and respect, and I'll
support and fuel your good impact
in the world (see Matthew 18:18).

If you work for peace, others will
see me in you (see Matthew 5:9).

I'll give you rest
(see Matthew 11:28-29).

If you have the courage to do what's
right and are punished for it, I'll
share all the riches of my life with
you (see Matthew 5:10).

Wherever I am I want you to be
with me (see John 17:24).

When people mock you or lie about you, I'll find creative ways to bless you (see Matthew 5:11-12).

My Spirit will guide you into all the truth you need to know and will show you the depths of my heart (see John 16:12-15).

Opening yourself to the truth about who I am will bring goodness and direction to every aspect of your life (see Matthew 6:22).

The love of God will be planted deep in you, and I'll always be with you (see John 17:26).

Notice that I care for the birds of the air and the flowers of the field. I will most certainly care for you, too! (see Matthew 6:25-30).

You belong to God (see John 17:9).

I already know all of your needs—including your basic needs like food and clothing and housing—and I intend to give you everything you need (see Matthew 6:31-32).

I will protect you (see John 17:12).

You have no need to worry about tomorrow—I am here helping you today (see Matthew 6:31-33).

I want to fill you with joy (see John 17:13).

If you give you will also receive; it's very hard to out-give me (see Luke 6:38).

I want you to experience close, intimate, committed community in your life (see John 17:23).

If you will allow me to fully train you, you will become like me (see Luke 6:40).

If you hear and understand the truths I'm trying to bring to you, your life will be like an overflowing harvest of blessings (see Matthew 13:23).

Because you're intimately connected to me, you can ask my Father for anything (see John 16:25-27).

You'll gain a great treasure—the goodness and truth embedded in my heart—when you understand how valuable that treasure is and give up everything to get it (see Matthew 13:44-46).

I have overcome all the trials and sorrows of the world, and you can find peace in my heart (see John 16:33).

If you stay connected to me, accessing my strength and power, nothing will be impossible for you (see Matthew 17:20).

You'll do the things I've done, and even greater things (see John 14:12).